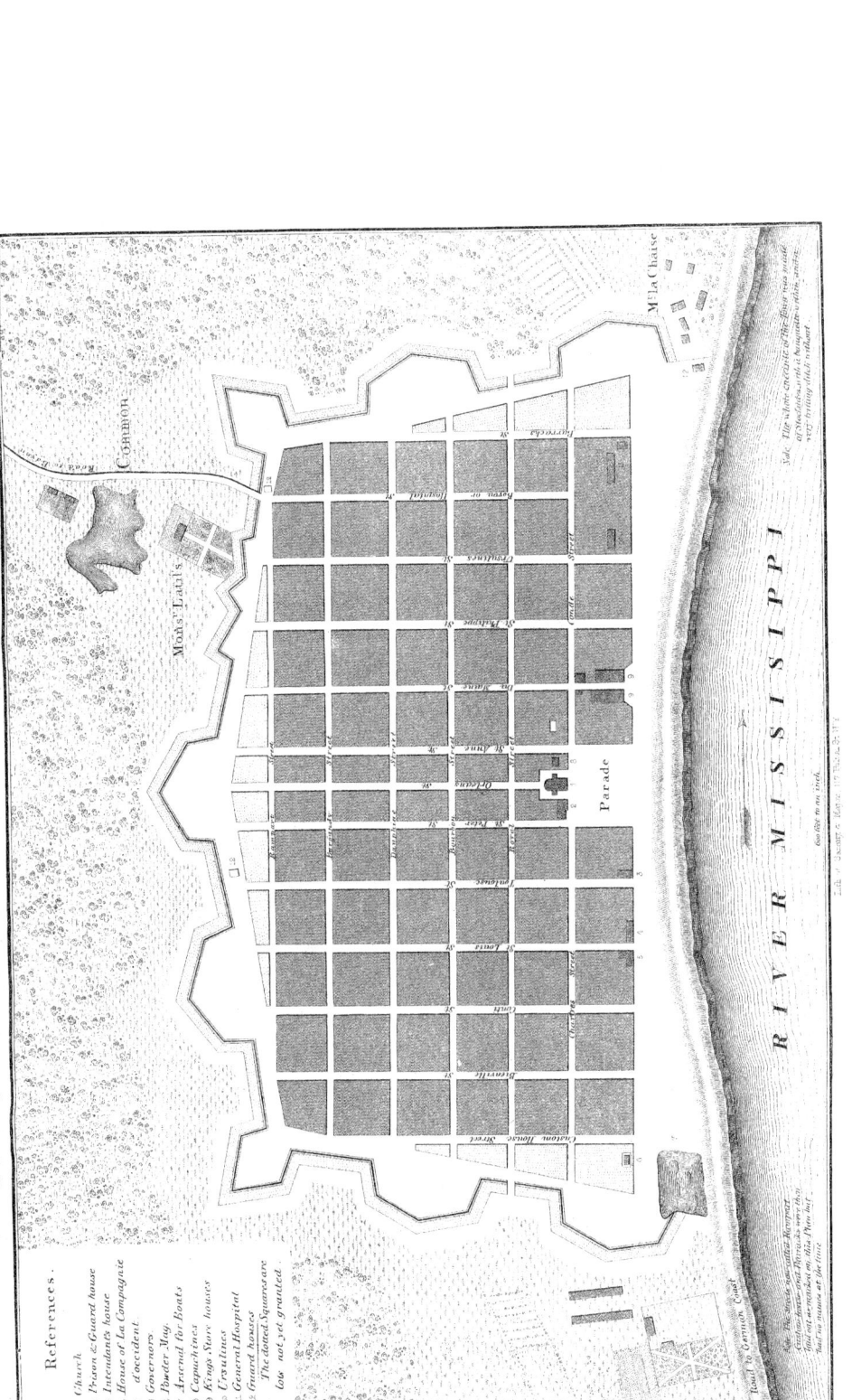

LOUISIANA:

ITS HISTORY

AS A FRENCH COLONY.

THIRD SERIES OF LECTURES.

BY

CHARLES GAYARRE.

DEBILE PRINCIPIUM MELIORA FORTUNA SEQUETUR.

NEW YORK:
JOHN WILEY, 167 BROADWAY.

1852.

ENTERED, according to Act of Congress, in the year 1852,

BY CHARLES GAYARRE,

In the Clerk's Office of the United States' District Court for the District of Louisiana

R. CRAIGHEAD, PRINTER AND STEREOTYPER.
53 *Vesey street*, *N. Y.*

CONTENTS.

FIRST LECTURE.

	PAGE
Anecdotes of De Vaudreuil	17
The Chickasaws sue for Peace	20
Effects of Paper Currency in the Colony	21
Trading Monopoly granted to Déruisseau	23
Lead Mines discovered in Illinois	24
Indian Difficulties	25
Proposed Expedition against the Chickasaws	27
Census of Louisiana in 1745	28
Dispute between Lenormant and Vaudreuil	29
Obstructions at the mouth of the Mississippi	30
Proposed Fortifications on the Mississippi	31
Means of Defence of the Colony	34
Terrible Hurricane in Louisiana	35
Lenormant's Remarks on Paper Money	36
Extent of the New Orleans District	38
Civil War among the Choctaws	39
Outrages committed by the Choctaws	40
Red Shoe killed	41
Renewal of Hostilities	42
Tixerant discomfited by Choctaw Hunters	43
The Indians attack the German Coast Planters	44
Baby, the Dancing Master, repulses the Indians	45
Death of Baby—Close of the year 1748	46
Views of the Government on Commerce	47

CONTENTS.

	PAGE
Ascendency of the French	49
Tranquillity re-established	50
Paper Money	51
Increase of the Military Forces	52
Paper Money counterfeited	53
Pierre Boucher	54
Lettres de Cachet	55
Distribution of the Troops	56
Complaints against Vaudreuil	57
Complaints against Rouvillière	58
Condition of the Colony	62
Introduction of the Sugar-Cane	63
Expedition against the Chickasaws	64
State of Agriculture	65
The Marquis of Vaudreuil	66

SECOND LECTURE.

Kerlerec's Opinion of the Indians	69
Kerlerec Endeavours to Conciliate the Indians	70
Changes among the Officers	71
State of the Colony	72
Character of the Troops	73
Tribute to the Indians	74
Tragic Occurrence	75
Fears of Invasion	77
Gain of the Mississippi on the Gulf	78
Fears of British Invasion	79
Religious Warfare	80
Intrigues of the English	82
Discontent of the Indians	83
Attack on Fort Duquesne	84
Rochemore	85
Introduction of the Sugar Cane	87
Recall of Rochemore	88
Help solicited from Spain	89
Departure of Rochemore	91
Cession of Louisiana to Spain	92
Treaty of Peace signed at Paris	93
Indignation of the Indians	95
Dissensions in the Colony	96
Description of Louisiana, by Redon de Rassac	97

CONTENTS.

	PAGE
Disputes between the French and English	98
Opposition of the Indians to the English	99
Expulsion of the Jesuits from Louisiana	100
Complaints against the English	101
Major Loftus ascends the Mississippi	102
Loftus attacked by the Indians	103
Loftus returns to New Orleans	104
Condition of Louisiana	105
Memorial of Kerlerec	108
Anxiety of the French Government	109
Letter of Louis XV. to D'Abbadie	111
Reflections on the Fate of Louisiana	113

THIRD LECTURE.

Arrival of the Acadians	116
Expulsion of the Acadians	117
Fate of the Acadians	118
Dispersion of the Acadians	120
Hatred of the Acadians to the English	122
Settlement of Acadians in Louisiana	123
The Mississippi a common thoroughfare	124
English Fortifications	125
Description of Baton Rouge	126
Protest against the Cession	128
Presentation of the Petition	129
Result of the Mission	130
Ulloa appointed Governor of Louisiana	131
Arrival of Ulloa	132
Treatment of the Superior Council	133
Character of Charles III.	134
Military Career of Charles III.	135
Administration of Charles III.	138
His Death	141
Career of Antonio de Ulloa	142
Early Career of Antonio de Ulloa	145
Character of Antonio de Ulloa	150
Don Estevan Gayarre	152
Don Martin Navarro	155

FOURTH LECTURE.

	PAGE
Ulloa's Instructions	158
Excitement Concerning the Paper Currency	159
Difficulty with the French Troops	161
Wretched Condition of Louisiana	163
Hostility of the Inhabitants to Ulloa	164
Character of the Inhabitants	165
Embarrassments of the Government	166
Commercial Decree	167
Anecdote	168
Commercial Regulations	169
Remonstrances of the Merchants	170
Doubts as to the Act of Cession	171
Seclusion of Ulloa	173
Proposition of Ulloa	174
Sojourn of Ulloa at the Balize	175
Marriage of Ulloa	177
Letter of the Marquis of Grimaldi	178
Return of Jean Milhet	180
Ulloa's Tastes, Habits, and Disposition	181
Unpopularity of his Wife	183
Conversational Powers of Ulloa	184
Letter of Aubry	185
Conspiracy against the Spaniards	186
General Insurrection	189
Petition for the Expulsion of Ulloa	192
Proceedings before the Council	193
Decree of the Council	202
Opinion of Foucault	203
Protest of Aubry	204
Reflections on Lafrénière's Address	205
Quotations from Lafrénière's Address	207
Character of Ulloa as Governor	208

FIFTH LECTURE.

Delegates appointed by the Insurgents	210
Embarkation of Ulloa	211
Manifesto of the Colonists	212

CONTENTS.

	PAGE
Appointment of a Committee of Inquiry	217
Depositions of the Witnesses	218
The Council's Letter to the Duke of Praslin	219
Representations to the King	220
Foucault's Letter to the Duke of Praslin	223
Aubry's Letter to the Duke of Praslin	224
Position of the Revolutionists	227
Letters of Ulloa on the Revolution	228
Petition of the Colonists	237
Foucault's Despatches	241
Aubry's Despatches	245
Council of Ministers in Spain	247
Grimaldi's Letter to Fuentes	262
Symptoms of Reaction	268

SIXTH LECTURE.

Letter of Aubry	270
Aubry and the Council	271
New Delegates sent to France	272
Foucault's Treachery	273
Departure of the Frigate	276
Increase of the Reaction	278
Scheme of a Republic	279
Anxieties of the Public Mind	280
Reaction in Favor of the Spanish Officers	281
Arrival of O'Reilly	282
The Career of O'Reilly	283
Message from O'Reilly to Aubry	287
Aubry's Speech to the People	288
Deputation from the City	289
Address of Lafrénière	290
O'Reilly's Reply	291
Close of the Interview	292
Landing of the Spaniards	293
Landing of the Troops	294
Reception of O'Reilly	295
The Closing Ceremonies	296
Aubry's Despatches	297
Letter from O'Reilly to Aubry	298
Aubry's Answer	300
Arrest of the Insurgent Leaders	301

viii   CONTENTS.

	PAGE
Death of Villeré	303
O'Reilly's Proclamation	305
Arrest of Foucault	306
Ceremony of Swearing Allegiance	307
Proceedings with respect to Foucault	308
Letter from Aubry	309
Foucault sent to France	310
Release of Braud	311

SEVENTH LECTURE.

A State Trial	313
Presentment of the Attorney-General	318
Remarks on the Plea of the Accused	331
Quotation from Vattel	332
The Judgment	334
Appeals to O'Reilly	337
His Inflexibility	338
The Negro Jeannot	339
Execution of the Prisoners	340
Death of Aubry	341
Comments on the Execution	342
Despatch of O'Reilly to Grimaldi	344
Feelings and Ideas of the Time	345
Charge of Duplicity against O'Reilly	347
Anecdote of Cardinal Richelieu	348
Maisons d'Acadiens	350
Polished Manners of the Colonists	351
Census of the Inhabitants	352
Concluding Remarks	353
APPENDIX	359

PREFACE

TO THE THIRD SERIES

OF

LECTURES ON LOUISIANA.

THIS is the third and last series of the Historical Lectures on Louisiana, embracing a period which extends from its discovery to 1769, when it was finally transferred by the French to the Spaniards, in virtue of the Fontainebleau treaty signed in November, 1762. This work is, as far as I could make it so, a detailed and accurate history of Louisiana, as a French colony. The preface to the first series of Lectures, which was criticised by some as unworthy of the serious nature of the subject which I had undertaken to investigate, accounts for the defects apparent in the whole production, if tested according to the rules of regular and classical composition, and shows that they proceed, in part, from the very fact of its accidental creation. As I already said in that Preface, I looked upon the first four Lectures, as *nugæ seriæ*, to which I attached no more importance, than a child does, to the soap bubbles which he puffs through the tube of the tiny reed, picked up by him for the amusement of the passing hour. But struck with the interest which I had excited, I examined, with more sober thoughts, the flowery field in which I had sported, almost with the buoyancy of a school boy. Checking the freaks of my imagination, that boon companion with whom I had been gambolling, I took to the plough, broke the ground, and turned myself to a more serious and useful occupation. This is, I think, clearly

PREFACE.

observable in the second series of Lectures. In the third and last series, which I now venture to lay before the public, a change of tone and manner, corresponding with the authenticity and growing importance of the events which I had to record, will be still more perceptible.

Should the continuation of life and the enjoyment of leisure permit me to gratify my wishes, I purpose to write the history of the Spanish domination in Louisiana, from 1769 to 1803, when was effected the almost simultaneous cession of that province, by Spain to France, and by France to the United States of America. Embracing an entirely distinct period of history, it will be a different work from the preceding, as much perhaps in point of style and the other elements of composition, as with regard to the characteristic features of the new Lords of the land.

Whatever may be the defects of this work (and they are numerous), their exposure cannot give me pain by defeating me in the pursuit of what I never aimed at—literary reputation. But notwithstanding their existence, I may be permitted to congratulate myself upon having thrown some light and interest on a subject, so far very little known—the history of the land of my birth. I rest satisfied with having been an humble pioneer, and with having erected in the wilderness the modest wooden structure, which, I hope, will soon give way to more stately edifices, showing the elegant proportions of a more classical architecture.

I beg leave, in conclusion, to refer those who think that the history of Louisiana which I have submitted to the public, is indebted to my imagination for many of its romantic incidents, and who may be willing to test the accuracy of my historical statements, to works, not of recent date, the authorship of which is attributed to: Bossu, Perrin du Lac, Charlevoix, Pittman, Dumont, Le Page du Pratz, Hennepin, Lahontan, Baudry des Lozières, Laharpe, and Laval; and I also refer to voluminous manuscripts copied from the archives of France

PREFACE.

and Spain, and which have become the property of the State. These are my vouchers, and I have nothing to fear from their examination, however minute and critical it may be, with regard to the detection of any intentional errors on my part, conscious as I am, that, in the composition of this work, I have been animated with the same feelings which must glow in the breast of a devoted son, who attempts truthfully and scrupulously to reproduce and to perpetuate, with the painter's art, the perishing features of a cherished mother.

BATON ROUGE, *July 15th*, 1851.

LOUISIANA:

ITS

HISTORY AS A FRENCH COLONY.

FIRST LECTURE.

ADMINISTRATION OF THE MARQUIS OF VAUDREUIL AS GOVERNOR OF LOUISIANA—ANECDOTES ILLUSTRATING HIS CHARACTER—THE CHICKASAWS SUE FOR PEACE—VAUDREUIL'S ANSWER—ORDINANCE CONCERNING LEVEES—EFFECTS OF THE PAPER CURRENCY IN THE COLONY—MONOPOLY OF TRADE GRANTED TO DÉRUISSEAU—DISCOVERIES OF MINES OF LEAD, COPPER, AND IRON—NEGOTIATIONS WITH THE INDIANS—DEPREDATIONS COMMITTED BY THE CHICKASAWS—POPULATION OF NEW ORLEANS IN 1745, SITUATION OF THE COLONY—MISUNDERSTANDINGS BETWEEN COMMISSARY LENORMANT AND GOVERNOR VAUDREUIL—OUTRAGE COMMITTED BY RED SHOE—REPORTS ON THE MOUTHS AND SAND-BARS OF THE MISSISSIPPI—MEANS OF DEFENCE ADOPTED TO PROTECT LOUISIANA AGAINST INVASION—TERRIBLE HURRICANE—FINANCES OF THE COLONY—PAPER MONEY AND STOCK-JOBBING—CIVIL WAR AMONG THE CHOCTAWS—A PARTY OF THEM ATTACK THE GERMAN COAST—GREAT ALARM—ASSASSINATION OF RED SHOE—INCREASE OF THE INDIAN DISTURBANCES—DARING OF THE CHOCTAWS—COWARDICE OF TIXERANT—HEROISM OF TWO NEGROES—DESPERATE RESISTANCE OF BABY, THE DANCING MASTER, WHEN ATTACKED BY THE CHOCTAWS—COMMERCE OF THE COLONY—ENCOURAGEMENT GIVEN TO AGRICULTURE—YIELD OF THE WAX TREE—THE CREOLES DECLARED FITTEST MEN TO WAGE WAR AGAINST THE INDIANS—CRUSHING BLOW GIVEN BY GRAND-PRÉ TO THE CHOCTAWS—HIS TREATY OF PEACE WITH THAT NATION—LARGE FORCES SENT TO LOUISIANA—COUNTERFEITING OF THE PAPER MONEY OF THE COLONY BY A COLORED MAN—HIS PUNISHMENT—GRAND-PRÉ MADE A KNIGHT OF ST. LOUIS—ORIGIN OF THE GRAND-PRÉ FAMILY IN LOUISIANA—QUARRELS BETWEEN VAUDREUIL AND THE COMMISSARY MICHEL DE LA ROUVILLIERE, THE SUCCESSOR OF LENORMANT—SUGAR CANES SENT TO THE JESUITS OF LOUISIANA—ARRIVAL OF SIXTY GIRLS—MANNER IN WHICH THEY WERE SETTLED IN THE COLONY—FRUITLESS EXPEDITION OF VAUDREUIL AGAINST THE CHICKASAWS—ANECDOTE OF THE COLAPISSA FATHER—DEATH OF LA ROUVILLIERE—HE IS SUCCEEDED BY D'AUBERVILLE—VAUDREUIL SENT TO CANADA—KERLEREC, GOVERNOR OF LOUISIANA IN FEBRUARY, 1753.

THE appointment of the Marquis of Vaudreuil as Governor of Louisiana, in the place of Bienville, produced a favorable impression on the colonists, and gave rise to flattering hopes. It was known that the Marquis was the son of a distinguished officer who had been Governor-general of Canada, and that he belonged to an influential family at the French court. His nomination was received as a token that the government intended to make serious efforts to put the colony on a more respectable footing, and it was presumed that the Marquis would not have accepted the post of a petty governor in so insignificant a colony, if he had not received promises that the province over which he had been called to rule, would soon be destined, under the powerful patronage of the mother country, to acquire more importance than it had so far possessed. His arrival in the colony was therefore hailed with joy, as the harbinger of better days. That joy rested also on the knowledge of the hereditary reputation of all the Vaudreuils for kindness and liberality. With respect to these qualifications, the present Governor of Louisiana was no unworthy representative of his ancestors. A few anecdotes related of him will fully illustrate his character.

It happened that one of his servants acted with insolence towards an officer of the garrison in New Orleans, who had come to pay his respects to the governor on one of his reception days. The marchioness having been informed of the fact, brought it to the knowledge of her husband, and insisted on the culprit's being dismissed. De Vaudreuil acquiesced in a demand which he thought just, and consented to part with that servant, although a favorite one. He sent for his privy purse, and after having paid the wages due to the servant, he added a bounty of three hundred livres. His wife expostulated with him on this strange piece of liberality, and observed that it was offering a reward to impertinence. Unmoved, and without returning an answer, the Marquis threw again three hundred livres to the lacquey, and seeing the flush of anger rising on his wife's brow : " Madam," said he, with great composure, " I do not reward him for his insolence, but for his faithful past services, and if you show too much displeasure to the poor devil, I will give him the whole purse, to indemnify him for his having incurred the mortification which you now inflict upon him."

Once, an officer of the garrison wrote against him to the minister of marine. The minister transmitted the letter to De Vaudreuil. One day, the same officer was addressing some gross flattery to the Marquis, who stood it for a while, but the dose becoming too nauseating, " What conduct is this ? " exclaimed the Marquis, " how dare you thus give the lie to your own written assertions ? Is it possible that you should so soon have forgotten a certain letter which you have written against me ? " " A letter against you, general, and from me ? " " Yes, sir." " I swear that nothing can be more false." " Beware, sir ; do not force me to look for that letter, for if you compel me to take that trouble, I will immediately have your commission taken away from you." The officer did not reply, and never, from that moment, did the Marquis open his lips on the subject, or show by any act that he remembered the circumstance.

It also happened, that a menial in his household had lost or mislaid a valuable piece of plate. The Marquis was at table when the offence was discovered, and the guilty one, trembling with emotion, and overwhelmed with shame at his being accused of so much negligence, and perhaps of theft, was brought up to his presence. The Marquis, at first, looked at him with some severity of countenance, but his face soon resumed its usual benevolent expression, and turning to his butler, he said : " Get a bottle of my best wine, and give it to this poor fellow to cure him of his fright." This is enough; no more can be wanted to give the measure of De Vaudreuil's heart.

Bienville, when he departed from the colony, had left it at war with the Chickasaws. These Indians, on their being informed that a new governor had arrived, sent to him four of their chiefs, with a Frenchman, their prisoner, named Carignan, to sue for peace. Vaudreuil answered that he would not treat with them, except it were in concert with his allies, the Choctaws, to whom they should make ample amends for all the injuries they had inflicted upon them at the instigation of the English, and except they should drive away from their villages the English traders, who, he said, were the authors of all their misfortunes. The Chickasaws took time to consider these conditions.

The necessity of providing against the ever threatening overflows of the Mississippi had struck De Vaudreuil, and jointly with Salmon, the king's commissary, he published, on the 18th of October, an ordinance which commanded the planters to have their levees made, or in a safe condition, by the 1st of January, 1744, under the penalty of forfeiting their lands to the crown. Evidently, this penalty was sufficiently stringent to secure the execution of the ordinance. Thus closed the year 1743, during which the expenses of the administration of the colony amounted to 348,528 livres.

In the beginning of 1744, the Chickasaws informed De Vaudreuil that they would accept his conditions, and dismiss the English traders from their villages, if the French could supply them with all the goods, merchandise, and ammunition, of which they stood in need. This, De Vaudreuil could not do, nor could he promise to do, without exposing himself to a breach of faith; and with no small degree of concern did he learn that the Chickasaws were negotiating with the Choctaws, to conclude a treaty of peace with them, without including the French. On this state of things, he wrote to his government : "I will do my best to defeat these negotiations, which, if successful, would be ruinous to the colony. We must not forget that we are in a state of the utmost destitution, that our warehouses are empty, and that, between us, who can only make *fair promises*, and the English, who can *give*, the Indians cannot hesitate in their choice. Many of them have already carried their furs to the English, and this example will be contagious. All that I can do is, to insinuate to the Choctaws that the Chickasaws are not in good faith in their proposals for peace, and that probably their only object is to lull their enemies into unguarded security, and to strike an unexpected blow upon them, or perhaps that they seek, under cover of their pretended negotiations for peace, to keep the Choctaws in a state of inaction, and in the mean time quietly to get in their harvests." The Marquis concluded his despatch by endeavoring to impress upon the government his conviction of the necessity of forwarding to him, as soon as possible, an ample supply of goods and merchandise.

Vaudreuil had found the colony in a deplorable financial condition. It will be recollected that the government had, in 1735, contrary to the advice of Bienville and Salmon, called in the depreciated paper money of the India Company, and had replaced it by pasteboard notes (*billets de cartes*), which, it was said, offered an infinitely better security than the preceding one, because the king's paper was not to be weighed in the same scale with the Company's paper. But hardly had nine years elapsed, when this royal paper was as much depreciated as its more modest predecessor. The depreciation was such, that it was necessary to give three hundred livres in paper for what might have been got for one hundred livres in coin. On the 27th of April, the council of state declared that it considered this condition of things as prejudicial to the finances of the government, to the welfare of the colony, and the progress of commerce, and that it had resolved to put an end to such disorders. It, therefore, determined to call in all pasteboard notes, and to pay one hundred livres for every two hundred and fifty livres worth of paper. Such was the rate established, and the mode of payment was not in specie, but consisted in giving drafts on the treasury in France. On these drafts the holders had again to lose a discount. It was also decreed, that all the pasteboard notes which should not be brought in within two months after the promulgation of this edict, should become null and void. In support of the justice of this high-handed and arbitrary measure, it was stated that the government did not feel under the obligation to take up those notes at par, because they had been given to meet expenses and claims which had been raised in proportion to the actual or expected depreciation of the currency in which these were to be paid. Such was the impotent apology offered by the government for its shameless breach of faith, and the poor, helpless colonists had to be satisfied with it. They had found out, too late, that the *King's paper*, although it went by a more lofty name, was as much of a worthless rag as the *Company's paper*.

Unfortunately, the Marquis of Vaudreuil marked the beginning of his administration by following the old nefarious custom of granting monopolies. On the 8th of August, he conceded to a man named Déruisseau, the exclusive right of trading in all the country watered by the Missouri, and the streams falling into that river. This privilege was for a term a little exceeding five years, beginning on the 1st of January, 1745, to terminate on the 20th of May, 1750. To this grant several conditions were annexed, among which were these:—Déruisseau bound himself to finish the fort established on the Missouri territory, to keep in it a sufficient stock of merchandise to satisfy the wants of the Indians, to maintain, at his own expense, the several Indian tribes of that district in a state of amity among themselves and with the French, to supply the garrison of the fort with the necessary means of subsistence, to pay to its commander an annual bounty of one hundred pistoles, and to transport to the fort, without charge, all the provisions and effects of that commander. It was stipulated by the governor, that he reserved to himself the right to modify, change, or alter any of the conditions of the grant, according to circumstances, and in the way which the prosperity of the country might require.

In rendering an account of what he had done, De Vaudreuil said, in a despatch of the 6th of December, that one of his reasons for granting to Déruisseau the monopoly of trade in the Illinois district, was to deprive the colonists in that region of all means of carrying on any kind of commerce with the Indians, and thus to force them into the cultivation of the soil. He added: "It would be proper to prohibit the introduction of negroes into that part of the country, in order to correct the indolent habits of the colonists, and to oblige them to work themselves. Moreover, negroes would be more productive in the lower part of the colony. It would not be expedient to allow negroes to be taken up to the Illinois, except when the white inhabitants should be weaned from their life of wandering and plunder, and when, having assumed sedentary habits, they should at least be occupied in causing their negroes to cultivate their lands. I send samples from the mines of lead and copper which we continue to discover at the Illinois. To work these mines, it would be necessary to send convicts."

The discovery and working of mines had always been the favorite object which the French government had kept in view, and De Vaudreuil encouraged the same delusion. It is difficult to imagine how the working of those mines could have been carried on with success in those days. The colony could not subsist on its own resources, and provisions had to be sent from the mother country. So scarce were those provisions, that, if all the despatches of the governors are to be taken to the letter as true, the inhabitants, since the very first day of the settlement of the colony, had always been on the eve of starvation. De Vaudreuil himself, in a letter of the 28th of October, 1744, wrote : " If flour had not arrived by the Elephant, the troops would have revolted on account of the want of food." In such circumstances, how could several hundreds of workmen have been supported in the mines of Arkansas or of Illinois ? How difficult would it not have been to furnish them with all the necessaries for their mining operations ? What returns would have indemnified the government for its enormous

INDIAN DIFFICULTIES.   25

outlays? It is astonishing that these considerations should not have precluded the very conception of any project of the kind. It will be recollected that, shortly after the arrival of the Marquis of Vaudreuil in the colony, the Chickasaws had made proposals for peace, but the Marquis had answered that he would not treat with them separately from his allies, the Choctaws; and when the Choctaws showed themselves favorably disposed towards the Chickasaws, he, under some pretext or other, postponed the consideration of the peace negotiations which had been opened by the Chickasaws, and succeeded at last in reviving the old hatred of these two tribes, and in renewing their acts of hostility, which had been temporarily suspended. Red Shoe, whose intrigues and tamperings with the English had so long been a source of uneasiness to the French, had even been gained over by the diplomacy of the Marquis. The fact is that the policy of the French was to keep the Indian tribes at war with each other, in order to waste away their strength and power. The Indians were not so simple as not to be fully aware of the game that was played upon them. But, by the contact of the civilization of a superior race, they had been inspired with wants which they could not shake off, and had by this means been put under the complete dependency of these two European nations, the French and the English, on which they had now to rely for the gratification of their newly acquired tastes and vices. The nature of the Indian was not such as to enable him to resist the tempting baits constantly thrown in his way by the two great rivals who, with mutual jealousy, were ever struggling for mastery over his tribes; and those ignorant children of the forest were, almost without interruption, driven into some acts leading rapidly to their destruction. Divided among themselves, they were to meet the fate which had befallen, under such circumstances, other far more powerful and more enlightened nations, and they certainly were entirely destitute of the necessary means to oppose an efficient obstacle to the wave of foreign invasion which was gradually gaining ground upon them. They were doomed!

On the 2d of January, 1745, the Marquis of Vaudreuil announced to his government the discovery of an iron mine in the Mobile district, and other mines in Illinois; but these discoveries did not lead to any practical results, and prove only one thing—that the experience of forty-five years had not convinced the French of the inutility of these fruitless and expensive researches.

During the whole of the year 1745, the Chickasaws proved very troublesome, and committed depredations which carried desolation and alarm throughout the colony. Red Shoe, with his accustomed versatility, had again become the ally of the English, and had even seduced his old rival, Alibamon Mengo, the hitherto constant friend of the French. But, although the French had thus lost the favor of the Cæsar and of the Pompey of the Choctaws, they still retained numerous friends among them, and the French and English factions, as they were called, became so excited that they nearly resorted to blows. On the 28th of October, the Marquis of Vaudreuil wrote to his government: "The Chickasaws, in spite of our efforts to rouse the hostility of all the other Indian nations against them, cannot be destroyed, except it be through another French expedition. Delay increases the difficulties, because these people become every day more familiar with the art of war, and they are gradually enlisting the sympathies of the Cherokees, who are powerful auxiliaries. All expeditions of this nature have been so unsuccessful, that I well conceive the reluctance of the government to renew the attempt. But the roads being now better known, we can accomplish more, and at less expense. Two hundred recruits, in addition to the regulars and militia we already have here, would be all that is wanted. To avoid exposing our men, we would, in attacking the strongholds of the Chickasaws, have recourse to trenching and mining. In having them partially attacked and harassed, we have to spend much in presents to our Indian auxiliaries. It would be better to make short work of it, and to bring this matter to a conclusion." The Marquis closed his despatch by complaining of being entirely destitute of provisions, merchandise, and ammunition, and informed his government that the Choctaws were tired of their war against the Chickasaws.

De Loubois, who was one of the oldest and most influential officers in the colony, advocated the same course which the Marquis of Vaudreuil was recommending, and, in a despatch of the 6th of November, strenuously insisted on the importance of forcing the Chickasaws to drive away the English, who, he said, had *avowed territorial pretensions extending to the left bank of the Mississippi*. For this reason, he agreed with De Vaudreuil in the conclusion, that another expedition against the Chickasaws was necessary.

In a document presented to the French government in 1744, the white population of New Orleans was put down at eight hundred souls, not including two hundred soldiers and the women and children. The black population did not exceed three hundred. A few of the houses were of brick, and the greater portion

CENSUS OF LOUISIANA IN 1745.

were wooden buildings, or were bricked up between posts.

"There are," said the author of this census, "twenty-five inhabitants whose property may be worth from one hundred thousand to three hundred thousand livres. Almost all the colonists are married. The most considerable of them is Mr. Dubreuil, who owns five hundred negroes, several plantations, brick kilns, and silk manufactories."

"At the German Coast, there are one hundred white inhabitants and two hundred negroes. Occupations: gardening and grazing."

"Pointe Coupée, two hundred whites, four hundred negroes. Occupation: the cultivation of tobacco and the raising of provisions."

"Natchitoches, sixty whites and two hundred blacks. Productions: cattle, rice, corn, tobacco."

GENERAL TABLEAU.

	White inhabitants (male).	Blacks of both sexes.
At the Balize,	troops only, no settlers,	30
New Orleans,	800	300
German Coast,	100	200
Pointe Coupée,	200	400
Natchitoches,	60	200
Natchez,	8	15
Arkansas,	12	10
Illinois,	300	600
Missouri,	200	10
Petit Ougas,	40	5
Pascagoulas,	10	60
Mobile,	150	200
	1700	2020
Women and children about	1500	
	3200	
Troops,	800	
	4000	

DISPUTE BETWEEN LENORMANT AND VAUDREUIL. 29

The old and the new Biloxi, the Pass Christian, and the Bay of St. Louis, where the first French settlements had been made, seem to have been entirely forgotten in this table, and yet they must certainly have retained some of the early settlers or their descendants. Taking into consideration omissions of this kind, and putting down the colonial population at 3500, it shows a remarkable decrease since 1731, when Louisiana was retroceded to the king by the India Company, at which time its population was estimated at 5000. This was a very discouraging proof of an absolute failure, so far, in the work of colonization, and yet the annual expenses of administration had been gradually increased, and now exceeded 500,000 livres.

Salmon, who had been for many years the King's commissary in the colony, had been succeeded by Lenormant, who had hardly entered upon the duties of his office, when he began to quarrel with the Marquis of Vaudreuil. The governor, in a despatch of the 6th of January, 1746, informed his government that the commissary retained for his private use, all the merchandise which he ought to have delivered as presents to the Indians, and that he had them retailed by his clerk to the inhabitants. By which operation, the Marquis pretended that Lenormant realized enormous profits. On the 9th of March, De Vaudreuil reiterated his complaints against Lenormant, whom he accused of starving the troops and of failing to supply the different settlements in the colony with the necessary provisions, and the Indians with the merchandise that they had a right to expect. "By his fault," said he, "I am placed in a very difficult position, being destitute of the means of paying for scalps and of remunerating our Indian friends and allies."

On the 22d of March, De Vaudreuil arrived at Mobile, where twelve hundred Choctaws had long been waiting for him, and for the usual distribution of presents by which the French used to secure their services. The celebrated Red Shoe had remained at home, and during the absence of the chiefs most favorable to the French, was intriguing to bring about a peace between the Choctaws and Chickasaws. But the chiefs who had gone to Mobile, arrived in time to defeat his machinations. In his anger at being thus foiled, he killed a French officer named the Chevalier de Verbois, and two French traders, who then happened to be among the Choctaws, and whose goods he plundered. On being informed of this outrage, De Vaudreuil immediately sent an officer to demand satisfaction, and obtained the promise that it would be granted.

Towards the end of the year 1745, the engineer Devergès had presented to the French government a memorial on the mouths of the Mississippi. "The bars," said he, "which are to be found at the mouths of the river, are so many serious obstructions. The pass which is the deepest, and which has been the only practicable one since 1722, when it was examined and became thoroughly known, is that of the Balize, where ships drawing from thirteen to fifteen feet water, have been able to run through with more or less facility, in proportion to the depth of the water on the bar; and it has ever since been observed that it has varied from eleven feet to fourteen feet and a half, so that it was but seldom that vessels drawing from thirteen to fifteen feet water could pass without stranding, and without making use of the warp, even after having been lightened of half their cargoes. This pass measures in width from thirty to forty fathoms, and the current is very rapid."

On the 24th of November, 1746, the Marquis of Vaudreuil wrote to his government: " On being apprised of the declaration of war, I visited the mouths of the Mississippi. From the mobility of the passes, and from the want of solidity in the land bordering on those passes, it is nearly impossible to think of erecting fortifications there. It is only necessary to preserve the fort which already exists at the Balize, less on account of its being effective as a means of defence, than because it serves as a place of depot for our commerce with the Spaniards. Besides, it is useful to maintain a post there, from which we can keep watch over the sea coast, and get timely information as to what may be going on in the gulf."

France being at war, it became necessary to provide for the defence of Louisiana. The spot which, on the Mississippi, seemed the most eligible for the construction of fortifications, was the *Plaquemine Turn*, then considered as being thirty-three miles from the Balize. It was the first solid ground to be met with on coming from sea, and on that account had been selected by the Commissary Lenormant. "This reason appeared to me," said De Vaudreuil, in one of his despatches, " to be a good one, and I agreed to it, because fortifications erected at that spot would have protected that considerable portion of the country lying between New Orleans and Plaquemine Turn. But on reflection, I observed (and the same observation struck with equal force both the engineer and the portmaster), that the situation of that Turn presented no obstacles to ships, which being once under weigh, could run up beyond it by the help of the same wind which had enabled them to come through the pass.

It would be impossible to stop them with the ten eighteen-pounders, which are the only pieces of artillery we can set up on each side of the river, because, availing themselves of a fresh breeze, the ships would have but one discharge to stand, and would be out of the reach of our guns before they could be fired at a second time. To command that passage, it would be necessary to have at least three batteries of twenty heavy guns on each side of the river, close to each other, and this would cost immense sums."

De Vaudreuil also stated, that the distance from that spot to New Orleans was another objection, because if fortifications were constructed there, they would require a permanent garrison, which, in time of need, would not receive with sufficient promptitude the assistance it might want from New Orleans.

" Besides," continues De Vaudreuil, " it has struck me that the only spot on the river which we could use to advantage, with our twenty eighteen-pounders, is the *English Turn*, which is fifteen miles distant from New Orleans, and is a natural fortification against ships, that are stopped there by the same east and south-west winds which had been so favorable to come up so far. Ships cannot turn round that point without the south-west wind, which but seldom blows from July to January, the very time when the conquest of the country is to be undertaken with better chances of success, because the river is low. But supposing that the ships of the enemy should be favored with a south-west wind, they would hardly get round the Turn and ascend four miles and a half, when this very wind would become unfavorable, and they would be obliged to wait for an easterly wind to move on. Moreover, it must be observed that there are between the plantations established at the Turn, large wooded tracts of land, thick with intertwined briers, brambles, and canes, forming impenetrable jungles which terminate in swamps, cut up with deep water courses and leading to quagmires. Through such a country, protected by good intrenchments and defended by some troops, it would be the height of temerity to penetrate.

"Another advantage would be, the great facility to concentrate there all our forces. These were my reasons for not hesitating in giving the preference to that spot. Therefore I have determined to establish on each side of the river, at those points where ships must come to catch the southwest winds, a fort made up of mud and fascines, with epaulments, the shelving sides of which are to be fenced and secured with hurdles, according to the plans and drawings of Devergès. For the construction of these fortifications, I have ordered, jointly with Mr. Lenormant, the inhabitants of New Orleans and of the neighboring country to send in the fifth of their negroes during six weeks. I hope that, in ten days, there will be a battery of ten eighteen-pounders in each fort. It would be proper to send sixteen twenty-four-pounders with their balls, and fourteen eighteen-pounders, to fill up all the embrasures which overlook the river. The intrenchments on the land side would be sufficiently fortified with the four ten-pounders we have at New Orleans. With this additional supply, the colony would be susceptible of defence."

It will be recollected that Bienville had been of opinion that fortifications could be erected at the Balize; and that he had, in 1741, contracted with Dubreuil for the partial construction of fortifications, for which he had agreed to pay 297,382 livres. The engineer, Devergès, had also decided in favor of the possibility of erecting effective fortifications at the Balize, and had estimated their cost at 532,408 livres. The Marquis of Vaudreuil entertained, as it is seen, a different view of the question, and preferred the English Turn; but modern engineers have pronounced themselves in favor of the site chosen by Lenormant, the Plaquemine Turn, where now stand the fortifications called Forts Jackson and St. Philip.

On the 26th of November, the Marquis wrote to the French government: "I received, in September last, the letter of the 6th of May, in which I was informed that three ships of the line and one frigate had left England, in the month of April, under the command of Admiral Knowles, who was to stop at Antigua and then at Jamaica. It is supposed that this armament is destined to operate against Louisiana. I have also been informed that General Oglethorpe was to return shortly to Georgia with additional troops, and that, perhaps, Admiral Knowles would combine with him in Florida. I gave information of it to the Governors of Pensacola, St. Marc, and St. Augustin.

"I am prepared for any event that may occur. I have the strong will to be equal to the emergency, whatever it may be, but I am sadly deficient in means to back this will. I have nothing wherewith to defend the East Pass, where a new channel has formed itself in the parts nearest to the Balize. This channel is from fifteen to sixteen feet deep on the bar at low water, and measures in length two hundred fathoms, through the battures which advance most into the sea, in the shape of a horse-shoe. This channel is divided into three outlets, or mouths. Two of these outlets are from ten to twenty-five fathoms in width each, and the third from thirty to forty, and they are separated from each other by battures and mounds of loam, or unctuous, slimy, and adhesive earth emerging from the sea. The largest of these outlets is on the right as you come in. We have labored to fortify this new pass with the help of the planters, who would have cooperated with more efficiency and readiness, if Mr. Lenormant had treated them differently. But he has even refused to supply them with the necessary tools, with provisions for the subsistence of their negroes, and with means of transportation. Latterly he went so far as to undertake to force them to complete the fortifications, to the injury of their crops. It was an unjust pretension, which was beginning to irritate the planters. I thought it proper, therefore, not to allow him to push the thing farther."

" With regard to the forces of the colony, I can dispose of four hundred white men, five or six hundred Indians belonging to the small nations, and from two to three hundred negroes who are to be relied upon. But we are wanting in arms and ammunition."

This was Louisiana in 1746. We have had its substitute under our eye in 1846. What a transformation! What a tale of wonder! It beggars comment!

Miserable as it was, the colony's situation was made still worse by a hurricane, as terrible as those which had committed such damage in 1740. A portion of the crops was destroyed, and the lower part of Louisiana would have been exposed to famine, if assistance had not promptly come from the Illinois district, which annually supplied New Orleans with a great quantity of flour. The boats from Illinois used to arrive at that town towards the end of December, and to depart in January. In those days, it is certain that hurricanes were more frequent than in ours. Nor is it to be wondered at, since it is well known that the physical laws which rule a wilderness are greatly modified, in proportion as it is gradually converted into the abode of civilization. It seems that, as a reward for the patient and persevering labor of man nature disrobes herself of her primitive rudeness, and that the elements, ceasing their old struggles, are soothed into gentleness.

Lenormant, whose province it was, in his capacity of intendant commissary, to preside over the finances of the colony, made on them a report, in which he said: " As soon as the paper money began to lose its value, there was an eager demand for dollars, which were bought at higher, or lower prices, in proportion to the wants of purchasers, and the cupidity or speculating avidity of sellers. Hence the origin of all the jobbing which took place in the colony, in relation to bills of exchange and dollars. It increased considerably during the years 1741, 1742, and 1743, but it would be difficult to convey an accurate idea of the ferment which sprung up in the colony on that occasion, of the number of transactions incidental thereto, and of the skill with which several individuals availed themselves of these circumstances, to the detriment of the interests of the king and the welfare of the colony."

"With regard to the question, whether it would be proper to venture on another emission of paper money, I think that it would be attended with considerable difficulties, in as much as the quantity of paper to be emitted cannot be known in advance, no more than the expenses of the colony, to which it is to be proportioned."

"Every thing is to be feared from the avidity of the inhabitants of this colony, and from their disposition to stock-jobbing. Their industry, of which a better use might have been made, has, at all times, taken this bad direction; for, although jobbing on the paper currency of the colony, on dollars and bills of exchange, began only in 1737, jobbing on the merchandise in the king's warehouses, and on every thing which was susceptible of it, has always been a favorite occupation in the colony. It may be said that it is the only pursuit to which the inhabitants have steadily adhered, much to the prejudice of the nobler one of improving the lands, and in utter disregard of other resources, which, if attended to, would put the colony in a flourishing condition."

"I admit that another emission of paper money, will afford relief to the treasury of the marine department at home; but a relief, which would only be temporary, and would not exceed the duration of one year, would not counterbalance the risks which are inseparable from the introduction and existence of this kind of currency in the country."

Thus, a century ago, Lenormant wrote, in anticipation, the history of the deleterious effects of a system, which we lately saw stretched to its fullest extent, until its apparently strong texture snapped under the hands by which it had been woven. But the hotchpotch of corruption, of financial gambling, of frantic stock-jobbing and of thieving speculation, the mushroom wealth of the few amidst the sudden ruin of the many, and the mass of lasting depravation and misery, which appalled our sight, from the year 1835 to 1843, throw into the shade all the foregone calamities which paper money, ill devised and more foolishly applied, had entailed upon the colony since its foundation. The historical records of the world teem with the similarity of causes and effects through the long avenue of ages, on which the eye of study looks back with distinct vision, but it may be more than doubted whether, from the observation of past events and its deductions, any practical lesson has ever been derived for the benefit of mankind.

On the 11th of May, in the year 1747, the Marquis of Vaudreuil, to put an end to the doubts which had arisen as to the precise extent of the New Orleans district, decreed that it began at the mouth of the Mississippi, including both banks up to the German Settlement exclusively, above New Orleans, and that it embraced also Bayou St. John, and that part of the country, back of the town, which was originally called Chantilly, from the princely seat of the Condés in France; but which, in our days, is known under the appellation of Gentilly, into which Chantilly has been gradually corrupted.

The fear of being attacked by the English still haunted the Marquis of Vaudreuil, and in a despatch of the 15th of May, he communicated to his government the precautionary measures of defence which he had taken. There being but seven or eight feet water over the Balize bar, which was rapidly filling up, he removed the guns from the fort which defended this mouth of the Mississippi, and withdrew two thirds of the garrison, leaving but one eight-pounder and two four-pounders, with a detachment of fifteen soldiers and one pilot, to fire signal guns when necessary, for the benefit of the French ships. The officer who had the command of this detachment was instructed to be on the look-out, and to abandon his post and run up to New Orleans with his men, whenever he should descry together several ships of the enemy. De Vaudreuil considered that the East Pass was the one through which the English were likely to come, as it was seventeen feet deep, and the French ship, *the Camel*, had lately got over the bar with the greatest facility.

"I send," wrote De Vaudreuil, "two plans and estimates for two forts, one of which is to be at the Plaquemine Turn, a situation which Lenormant still continues to extol. In addition to the reasons which I have already given against selecting that spot, I must say that the ground is only two feet and a half above the lowest water mark, and is covered with one foot water, when the river overflows. Moreover, it is probable that the ground is not sufficiently solid to bear up the works of fortification, and such is the opinion of the engineer, Devergès, whose knowledge is matured by long experience. At the English Turn, the ground is raised nine or ten feet above the lowest water mark, and can bear up the weight of any kind of work. It is urgent to determine, as soon as possible, on the choice of the site which is to be fortified."

Thus, the French government had the unpleasant prospect of additional expenses, to a large amount, to be incurred for the protection of Louisiana, when the current expenses of the colony, for 1747, had already, before the expiration of the year, exceeded those of the preceding ones, and had risen to 500,445 livres.

When the year 1748 dawned upon the colony, the apprehension of British invasion had not abated, and the insecurity of the colonists was made greater, by the feeling of enmity against the French, which had been gradually instilled into a considerable portion of the Choctaw nation. It will be recollected that, in 1746, Red Shoe had murdered the Chevalier de Verbois, and several traders, for which deed no satisfaction had as yet been given, in spite of the repeated demands and exertions of the Marquis of Vaudreuil. At the beginning of 1748, the animosity between the French and the English party among the Choctaws ran so high, that it broke into a civil war. The Choctaws of the English party were in the minority, and were therefore called *rebels*. They divided into small bands to make excursions against the French, and they proved exceedingly troublesome. One of these bands attacked the German Settlement, above New Orleans, on the left bank of the river, killed a white man, wounded his wife, and made his daughter prisoner. They also carried away three black men and two black women. This attack spread such consternation, that most of the planters abandoned their houses, and came down to New Orleans with their negroes. To send them back, it was necessary to use threats, and to give them, as a guarantee of protection, a strong detachment of troops to escort them to their deserted homes. But, when after a short stay, the detachment returned to New Orleans, rumors of danger began to be so rife again, that most of the planters, on the German Coast, who were on the left side of the river, crossed over to the right side, where they had to go through the laborious operation of clearing the ground of its timber and wild cane, whilst they had abandoned, through exaggerated apprehensions, well cultivated lands, comfortable dwellings, and a considerable number of cattle; but their fear of the Indians had overcome all other considerations. Such was the alarm which prevailed, at that time, even in the very vicinity of New Orleans!

The Choctaw who, at the head of a small band, had attacked the German Settlement, was, on his return to his village, killed by his own brother and chief, who belonged to the French party; and a brother of Red Shoe, who had been sent to Carolina to claim assistance from the English, was assailed at the Kaouitas and lost eight men. On the 14th of July, the Choctaws of the French party surprised a village of the English party and killed thirteen men, among whom were some distinguished chiefs. The Choctaws friendly to the English, being determined to have their revenge, attacked in their turn, on the 16th of August, a village of the opposite faction. The fight was more obstinate than is generally the case in Indian warfare, and the losses were heavy on both sides, but the allies of the English were obliged to give way, and were hotly pursued a distance of nine miles. It was estimated that they left on the ground eighty men killed, and that their wounded, of whom several died subsequently, amounted at least to the same number. Several other battles, in which the French party always had the advantage, speedily followed; and the Choctaws, being made cooler and wiser by such copious and repeated bleedings, began to discover that they were annihilating their own nation for the ultimate benefit of the English and of the French, who were goading them on with mutual emulation and satisfaction. Their wise men held several councils, and it was at last determined to make away with Red Shoe, who was the chief obstacle to the restoration of peace. In consequence of this determination, this celebrated warrior was killed, as he was returning to his village with a convoy of English merchandise. This blow might have proved effective, if the goods and their English owners had also been destroyed with Red Shoe; but such was not the case, and the English, availing themselves of the means they had on hand to bribe the Indians, gathered a goodly number of partisans, at the head of whom they placed a brother of Red Shoe, and succeeded in thus keeping up the civil war. The French establishments were again attacked, and some persons were killed. The English took advantage of the renewal of hostilities, to give more extension to their commerce. But Grand-Pré, who commanded at Tombecbee, having been informed that five English traders were preparing to depart from some of the Chickasaw villages, with sixty horses loaded with furs, posted himself in ambuscade with thirteen friendly Indians, and attacked the English, whom he defeated completely. One of them was killed, but the rest escaped, leaving all the horses of the convoy, with their rich loads, in the hands of Grand-Pré.

Whilst the French were obtaining these advantages on the Choctaw territory, they were exposed to great danger among the Illinois, who had been gained over by the English, and who had resolved to rise upon the French. Fortunately, the conspiracy was discovered in time; and the Chevalier de Berthel, who commanded in that district, acted with an energy which put a stop to the intended hostilities of the Indians. The Marquis of Vaudreuil, in transmitting to his government an account of all these disturbances among the Indians, said that they were to be attributed to the contempt which the red nations had conceived for the French, from seeing the smallness of their forces at their different settlements, and to the belief which had been impressed upon them by the English, that the King of France had no more ships to transport his warriors to Louisiana.

From this cause, or from another, the audacity of the Indians was daily on the increase. Some Frenchmen, who had gone in pursuit of game in the vicinity of New Orleans, were killed by some of those red marauders, and the Mobile settlement was thrown into such a state of alarm, that the Marquis of Vaudreuil thought it requisite, to quiet those apprehensions by his presence, and paid a visit to that place.

Whilst at Mobile, he caused every house to be fortified with palisades, and stationed all the neighboring small nations on the avenues to the town, to guard it against surprise. It was during the absence of Vaudreuil, that the sportsmen of whom I have spoken were murdered near New Orleans. Noyan, whom Vaudreuil had left in command during his absence, sent fifty men, one half of the line and the other half of the militia, to scour the country in search of the marauders. This detachment, commanded by Tixerant, met a party of Choctaw hunters, whom the French took to be the enemy they were looking after, and two men were sent to reconnoitre. But they were discovered by three Choctaws who were on the watch, and who uttered their customary shrieks, to give warning to the rest of their party. The two Frenchmen took immediately to their heels, and having joined their countrymen, communicated to them the panic with which they had been seized. The whole detachment retreated in haste, and did not think themselves safe, until they had put a bayou between them and what they supposed to be the enemy. Not satisfied with this natural protection, they set to work to fortify themselves. When the Indians saw the French retreat in a manner which resembled a flight, they, in the excitement of the moment, fired a few shots, which killed one soldier and wounded two. But the French and the Indians having come to a parley, the chief of the Indians apologized for what had taken place, and affirmed that the shots had been fired, not by his men, but by some runaway negroes whom he offered to deliver up to the French. Thus ended this affray; but the Marquis of Vaudreuil, having heard of it, was highly incensed at the want of firmness exhibited by the French. He complained bitterly to his government of the conduct of Tixerant, their commander, whom he called a drunkard; and this officer was ignominiously dismissed from the army.

At no time, since its foundation, had the colony been more harassed by the incursions of the Indians. Those attacks followed close on the heels of each other, and left little breathing time to the colonists. Thus, a short time after the happening of the events which I have related, a party of Indians made their appearance on the plantation of a man, called Cheval, at the German Coast, seized the arms of a number of Frenchmen and blacks who were working in the fields, and who, finding themselves destitute of all means of defence, fled to their boats and crossed the Mississippi, with the exception of two white men, named Bouchereau and Rousseau, who remained with two negroes, and who had the hardihood to attempt to drive the Indians out of a house which they were plundering. The two Frenchmen were soon killed, and the Indians sallied out to scalp them, but the two negroes fought so stoutly for the protection of the bodies of their masters, that they killed two Indians and drove the rest back into the house. The negroes clung to the battle-field, near the corpses, which, with touching fidelity, they were loath to abandon, until one of them was killed by a shot from the house, and the other had received several flesh wounds. It was only then that this brave man thought of retreat, and slowly moving towards the river, he plunged into the turbid stream. In spite of the loss of blood, he had swum more than half way across the Mississippi, when he was picked up by a boat.

The Indians, having no further resistance to overcome, issued out of their stronghold, and were going from one plantation to another in search of plunder, when they met a well known dancing master of New Orleans, named Baby. He was hyperbolically tall, thin, and sallow; his sunken cheeks almost kissed each other under the arch of his curved nose, and his small twinkling grey eyes, under their shaggy and bushy brows, looked out with a melancholy expression, and squinted right and left, in an opposite direction to each other, as if they were both, each on its own account, anxiously in search of the lost substance belonging to the body of which they formed a part. The eccentricities of Baby's mind, as well as those of his physical organization, had made him famous in the colony, and the doleful mien with which he used to give his lessons, had gained him the appellation of the *Don Quixote of dancing*. Baby, when spied by the Indians, was mounted on a small creole donkey, as lean and uncouth as himself, and on which he held himself up, as majestically erect as if he stood ready to dance the court minuet; his head was protected against the rays of the sun by a grey beaver as large as an umbrella; the heels of his long legs, armed with seven inch Mexican rowels, were almost sweeping the ground, so that it seemed as if both man and beast were walking together, and it was doubtful which one carried the other, if carrying there was. The Indians, who are not prone to laughter, were, however, moved to it by this strange apparition, and resolved to take alive the quadruped and the biped. With eager competition and with deafening shouts they rushed upon poor Baby, under the impression that he would be an easy prey, but they were soon undeceived. Baby had no other weapon than a hunting knife, but his long arm brandished it with so fearful a rapidity and action, his long and muscular legs gave such kicks, his elongated dagger-like spurs made such gashes, and his crane-like throat emitted such a variety of unearthly sounds, that the Indians shrank back in astonishment and affright, and Baby had time to take refuge, with his faithful donkey, in a house in which a young man, named Guillaume, had barricaded himself, with ten or twelve black boys and girls whom he had gathered together, and who had been forgotten, when the white and black population had fled across the river. The house was strongly built, and Guillaume and Baby, although they had but one gun and little ammunition, defended themselves with such effect against the attacks of the Indians, that they drove them away, after having wounded one of them dangerously. But Baby received in the neck a mortal wound, of which he died, the next day, in the Charity Hospital of New Orleans, whither he had been transported.

De Vaudreuil, on being informed of this attack, sent immediately several detachments of regulars, militia, and friendly Indians, in all the directions which the retreating enemy was likely to take. The French met the Choctaws on the Bayou St. John, where a sharp encounter took place. All the booty, ammunition, provisions, boats, and prisoners of the Indians fell into the possession of the French; and two only of these marauders, who dashed into the swamps and were lost sight of, could make their escape. " This is," writes the Marquis of Vaudreuil, with some degree of contempt, " what has caused so much alarm! If the inhabitants of the German Settlement and those of New Orleans were to be believed, that troop of Indians was composed of two hundred of the most intrepid of the Choctaw warriors. But I have always thought that there were, at most, no more than from twelve to fifteen vagabonds, who, knowing the timidity of the Germans, had come to steal some of their negroes with the intention of selling them to the English."

The Marquis went on saying that a black woman, who had been made prisoner by these Indians, informed him that they were thirteen in number, as he had always presumed; and he complained of the want of energy showed by the Chevalier D'Arensbourg, who commanded at the German Coast, and who, with a force of one hundred and twenty to one hundred and thirty men whom he had under his orders, could not act in time to check the depredations of a handful of Indians, or intercept their flight. Thus closed the year 1748. It proved a very unquiet and onerous one to the colony, the expenses of which amounted to 539,265 livres.

On the 2d of January, 1749, Maurepas, who was then at the head of the government in France, framed some instructions relative to the commerce of the colony, and addressed them to the Marquis of Vaudreuil, and to Michel de la Rouvilliere, who had succeeded Lenormant as Intendant Commissary. "I recommend you," wrote the minister, "to prevent, with great care, the carrying on between Louisiana and the English colonies of any contraband trade, which may enable the colonists, to the detriment of the King's interests, to sell their indigo to the English, and to receive in return other merchandise, negroes, or money. Let it be your special duty to prevent this, and it requires the more care and attention on your part, from the fact that English smugglers have for some time past found their way into the colony. I have even been informed that ships have been fitted out in Louisiana for Carolina. Should there be no end put to this state of things, the taste for this fraudulent trade would strike deep roots in the colony. The will of the King is, that you should strictly prohibit all trading between Louisiana and the English. You must not, under any pretext, receive in the colony any of their ships, and those that attempt to penetrate into any of her ports must be confiscated. In a word, you must neither tolerate, nor allow to go on without punishment, any kind of trading with the English, and his majesty would admit of no excuse on your part. This applies also to trading with the Dutch."

It is evident that this system was not calculated to relieve the distresses and the necessities of the colony, nor to promote its commercial prosperity. In our days, and on the exuberantly fertile soil of Louisiana, teeming with every sort of produce, in her noble city of New Orleans, that Cybele of the western waters, rising in pride with her shining crescent of ships, if not with her tiara of towers, *commerce is king*, but a king who began with being the veriest of slaves. May, for the benefit of all nations, the shattered fetters for ever remain at the feet of the enfranchised sovereign, and may the trident of Neptune be for ever the sceptre of peace, extended throughout the world over the elements of discord!

If the government acted with short-sighted illiberality with regard to commerce, it seemed disposed to show more favor to the agricultural interest; and in order to give more extension to the production of wax from the Candleberry tree (*Cyrea myrifica*), it authorized the Marquis of Vaudreuil to purchase the whole crop of this kind of wax, for the account of the king, at the rate of ten to twelve livres a pound.

During the year 1749, no change happened for the better in the affairs of the colony, which continued to suffer greatly from the hostilities of the Indians. The

Marquis of Vaudreuil, in a despatch of the 22d of September, speaks of incessant attacks made by the several Indian nations throughout the extensive territory of the colony, and describes the general alarm which existed from Natchez to New Orleans. "To destroy entirely the Indians," said he, " there could be nothing so effective as a force composed of the creoles of the country. They alone are able to scour the woods, and to make war after the fashion of these barbarians. But unfortunately there is not a sufficient number of them."

The year 1750 brought some relief to the colony. The struggle which had continued so long among the Indians, between the partisans of the French and those of the English, seemed to be drawing to a close, and the ascendency of the French had prevailed. Of the thirty-two Choctaw villages then occupied by that nation, only two remained in the possession of the English party, and even in these two villages some of the warriors were wavering, and disposed to abandon their chiefs to make peace on their own account. The English party, however, showed a great deal of energy, and in the beginning of June, in a desperate fight in which they engaged, they lost one hundred and thirty scalps. This was a crushing blow; and one still more effectual was struck, in September, by Grand-Pré, who, at the head of a party of the Choctaws attached to the French, entirely subdued the English party, and forced them to sue for peace, which was granted to them on the following conditions:—
1st. That capital punishment should be inflicted on any Choctaw, be he a chief or a common warrior, who should kill a Frenchman; and that, if the friends or kinsmen of that chief or warrior should oppose the infliction of the penalty, then that the whole nation

should take up arms, and make these men share the fate of the culprit they had attempted to protect. 2d. That death should be the penalty incurred by any Choctaw, be he a chief or a common warrior, who should introduce an Englishman into his village; and that revenge for his death should never be sought by any one of the nation; and further, that the Englishman thus introduced be put to death. 3d. That the whole Choctaw nation should continue to make war upon the Chickasaws, and should never cease to strike at that *perfidious race* (so called in the language of the treaty) as long as there should be any portion of it remaining. 4th. That in the villages of the *rebels* (as were designated the Choctaws of the English party), all the forts should be destroyed as speedily as possible, and that, on both sides, the prisoners and the slaves taken during the war should be restored. This was called the "*Grand-Pré Treaty*," and was intended as a curb and a bridle sufficiently strong to manage the Choctaws for the future.

Thus tranquillity was at last re-established in the colony. A detachment of troops was stationed at the German Coast, and another at the Tunicas, where, at the request of that nation, a fort was built by the French. Those Indians had long since prayed for the construction of a fort, to protect their women and children when their warriors were gone on war expeditions. With regard to the Chickasaws, they also, exhausted by their prolonged struggle against the French and Choctaws, had sued for peace; and in token of their desire to bury the hatchet of war, and as the interpreter of their sentiments, they had sent to the Marquis of Vaudreuil a French woman and some children, whom they had, in the course of the preceding year, made prisoners at the Arkansas. The

Marquis answered that he would take their petition into consideration, but that if they wished to obtain peace, it was necessary that they should behave better than they had done so far. The truth is that the French wanted no peace with the Chickasaws, who had been their implacable enemies since the foundation of the colony, and that they had resolved on their entire destruction. With them, for the accomplishment of this purpose, it was merely a question of time. On this subject, De Vaudreuil wrote to his government : " With regard to the Chickasaws, we must wait patiently and postpone all action, until we are able to undertake another expedition against them. From the unsuccessful expeditions which took place from 1736 to 1740, the Indians have drawn the inference that we are not able to destroy or to subdue the red men. Until we have returned full retaliation for the failure of our past operations, and until the impression produced by that failure be entirely wiped off, we shall always be in an extremely critical situation."

It will be remembered that, in 1747, the Intendant Commissary, Lenormant, had opposed a new emission of paper money; but his successor, Michel de la Rouvillière, pursued a very different course. The expenses of the colony had greatly increased; its scanty resources had diminished; and with almost a total absence of help from the mother country, it was very difficult for De Vaudreuil and Michel de la Rouvillière to carry on the colonial government. To relieve their necessities, and perhaps also to gratify the wishes of many, who looked with delight at the prospect ever offered to the greedy, by the manufacturing and throwing into the market of a quantity of paper money, these two high functionaries issued a joint ordinance creating notes of twenty to thirty livres, and of greater value, if necessary. These notes were to be given in payment of all the King's expenses and debts, and to be exchanged for all other papers, obligations, and bonds, so that they should speedily become the only currency of the colony. The French government received with astonishment the news that such a measure had been adopted, and expressed its disapprobation of it in very explicit terms. De Vaudreuil and Michel de la Rouvillière were energetically censured for having exercised a power which had never been delegated to them; they were ordered to withdraw all the paper they had issued, and to exchange these obligations for drafts on the treasurers-general of the Crown in France. The ministerial despatch on this subject contained these words:—" The experiment which was made in Louisiana, as to paper currency, ought to inspire great circumspection, in so delicate a matter, and it cannot be doubted but that the Governor's recent ordinance would soon produce the same disorders which were formerly the result of measures of the same kind." Such was the view taken of the subject by the French government, and De Vaudreuil and Michel de la Rouvillière were plainly told that their conduct, on that occasion, was without a shadow of excuse.

If the Marquis of Vaudreuil had the mortification of incurring the displeasure of his government in this particular act of his administration, he had the satisfaction, on the other hand, of succeeding, at last, in the application which he had made, during so many years, for the increase of the military forces of the colony. The King decreed that, for the future, there should be kept up in the colony thirty-seven companies of fifty men each, exclusive of officers. It was also decreed that the Governor could discharge, annually, two soldiers from each company, on condition that they should settle in the colony; and that, to all persons coming to establish themselves in Louisiana, there should be granted a supply of corn and rice for eighteen months, with the necessary implements to improve the lands that would be conceded to them. By the same royal ordinance, to mechanics, settling in cities, a supply of provisions for six months was allowed, with the instruments required for their trade. But the Governor was instructed to take special care that the liberality of the King should not be turned to improper and unprofitable uses; that the lands conceded should lie close to each other, and be well selected; and that the formation of villages be encouraged.

On the 12th of October, Livaudais, the chief pilot and portmaster, made an interesting report on the mouth of the Mississippi. The attention of the French government had always been fixed on this important subject, on which, from time to time, all the information which could be collected from careful observations was solicited, and filed in the archives of France.*

Towards the close of the year (1750), the colony was thrown into a state of excitement by the discovery, that a great deal of the paper currency of the country was counterfeited, and therefore entirely valueless. It gave rise to strict investigations, and a colored man, named Joseph, was tried, and convicted as one of the perpetrators of this crime. He was sentenced to be whipped by the public executioner, to have the mark of the flower-de-luce branded on his shoulder with hot iron, and to be transported for sale to one of the French West India islands.

On the 12th of January, 1751, the Marquis of Vau-

---

* See the Appendix.

dreuil wrote to his government to obtain the Cross of St. Louis for De Grand-Pré, as a reward for all the services which this distinguished officer had rendered in the wars with the Indians. The name of Grand-Pré, so well known in the oldest annals of chivalry, awakens stirring recollections of the past, and recalls to the mind the enlivening associations of history and of poetry. What says Shakspeare (King Henry V.)?

Messenger.—My Lord High Constable, the English lie within fifteen hundred paces of your tent.
High Constable of France.—Who hath measured the ground?
Messenger.—The Lord Grand-Pré.
High Constable.—A valiant and most expert gentleman. Would it were day! Alas! poor Harry of England! he longs not for the dawning as we do?"

The Grand-Prés of Louisiana descend from Pierre Boucher, who was Governor of Trois Rivières in Canada in 1653, and who published an interesting work on that country, then generally named New France. The title of the work is:—" Histoire naturelle et veritable des mœurs et productions du pays de la N'elle France, vulgairement dite le Canada."

Of the most remarkable men whose deeds will have to be recorded, when the history of Canada shall be written as it deserves to be, Pierre Boucher is to be ranked among the first. The study of his character shews a mixture, delightful to contemplate, of Spartan heroism, of Christian meekness, of the fiery enthusiasm of the knight, and the ardent faith of the martyr, of womanly tenderness, of unshaken fortitude, of worldly shrewdness, and of almost virgin artlessness, combined with a turn of mind productive of the energetic virtues of the feudal times—a baron and a saint—a man of aristocratic conceptions and bearing, with the utmost liberality of disposition, and the watchfulness of a sister of charity for destitution, sickness and affliction. De Muys, who was appointed Governor of Louisiana in 1707, and who died in Havana on his way to that French colony, was his son-in-law. Pierre Boucher left a large family, which divided itself into two branches. One of them, the Grand-Prés, has taken root in Louisiana, and the other, under the name of Boucherville, flourishes to this day in high social condition in Canada.

On the 18th of February, the Marquis of Vaudreuil and Michel de la Rouvillière published regulations of police, which, as forcible illustrations of the administration of the colony, and of the manners, ideas, customs, and morals then prevailing, are given in the appendix to this work. These regulations are also an evidence of the legislation which was, at that time, thought most appropriate to the state of the country. Hard labor, for life, on the King's galleys, was inflicted for offences which, in our days, would hardly be visited with the penalty of a few hours' imprisonment.

There is no doubt that Louisiana, under the arbitrary legislation of the despotic government of France, was frequently a sort of state prison or Bastile, to which were sent the victims of those orders of arrest, so well known under the name of *Lettres de Cachet*. In connexion with the exercise of this kind of authority, there is a curious despatch of the Marquis of Vaudreuil, dated on the 15th of May, 1751, in which he writes to the Minister in France:—" The situation of the Lady of Ste. Hermine, who came to this colony, thirty years since, by virtue of a *Lettre de Cachet*, obliges me to represent to you that this lady is at present unable to maintain herself here any longer, on account of the extreme destitution to which she is reduced by the death of Mr. de Loubois, with whom she had always lived.

I beg permission to send her back, gratis, to France, on one of the King's ships. Moreover, the Lettre de Cachet has expired, and the lady is very old." Under these cold lines, there lies, perhaps, a tale of deep woe and passion; and who knows how many such have passed by, unnoticed, on the far distant banks of the Mississippi, and in the discreet solitude of the boundless domains of the Father of Rivers!

During the year, 1751, the colony found itself in a better state of protection than it had ever been. This evidently proves the power of the Marquis at court; for more had been done for him than for any of his predecessors. His salary was greater than that of any of the preceding governors; and he had under his orders two thousand regulars—a larger force than had ever been seen in Louisiana. The distribution of these troops throughout the colony, was as follows:

District of New Orleans,	900 French,	75 Swiss,	975
" Mobile,	400 "	75 " "	475
" Illinois,			300
" Arkansas,			50
" Natchez,			50
" Natchitoches,			50
" Pointe Coupée,			50
" German Coast,			50
Total,			2000

This increase of troops and expenses was received as a demonstration that the French government intended to push on the work of colonization, with more energy than it had previously done, and with the expectation of better results. But it was soon discovered that it was a mere transient effort; that it had not originated from any deep laid and settled plan, or from any firm resolve in a persevering course of action; and that it was, either the offspring of accidental and ephemeral determination from those in power, or of personal considerations and favoritism. Whatever may have been the cause of this unusual grant of protection to Louisiana, the events which followed in a few years, prove it to have been one of those fitful, apparent revivals of strength and health, which frequently precede the last agonies of death.

Governor Vaudreuil and the Intendant-Commissary Lenormant had quarrelled, according to the good old custom prevailing in the colony since its foundation; and although the Marquis and Michel de la Rouvillière, the successor of Lenormant, had, at first, been on good terms, and had agreed on the issuing of paper money, which measure the French government had disapproved, they soon disagreed on every other act of administration. Hence followed, as usual, bickerings, recriminations, and mutual accusations, which disturbed the colony. These two high functionaries soon became more intent upon counteracting each other, than upon devising plans for the benefit of the colony; and the opposition which they made to each other, cramped and impeded the operations of their respective departments. On the 15th of May, 1751, Michel de la Rouvillière wrote to the French government :—

"At the English Turn, Mr. de Vaudreuil has stationed the Ensign, Duplessy, who is a raw recruit, without either capacity or experience. This officer, being drunk, ill-treated the store-keeper, Carrière. But the Governor sided with the officer; for, who says *officer* says *all*. When the word *officer* is uttered, the world must quake. Hence, when one of those gentlemen has any misunderstanding with a private citizen, he never fails to exclaim ; ' Are you aware that you are speaking to an officer ?' And if, by chance, the affair comes before me, the defence of the officer against whom the complaint is brought, may be summed up in these words, which he utters in a tone of astonishment: 'What! Sir! he dares thus speak to, or thus act toward an officer!' and although the officer may be in the wrong, judgment is always given against his adversary, because the military influence is predominant in the Council, through the Governor, the Major, and the Governor's flatterers.

"No justice is to be expected from Mr. De Vaudreuil; he is too lazy, too negligent;—his wife is too malicious, too passionate, and has too strong interests in all the settlements, and in the town of New Orleans, not to prevail upon him to keep on fair, and even on servile terms, with the body of officers, and with others."

"He was to destroy the abuses which sprung into existence during the sway of the India Company, but he has carefully abstained from doing so. Those abuses are too flattering to his vanity, since he is the absolute master of every thing, and they are too favorable to his interests to be eradicated. The army and the old members of the council find their advantage in this state of things, since they vex the public with impunity, as they have always done, through the protection they obtain from the Governor, by their servile courting of that functionary."

The Marquis of Vaudreuil, in his turn, did not, in his despatches, treat the Intendant Commissary, Michel de la Rouvillière, with more lenity. In a communication of the 20th of July, he complained that the Commissary did not furnish the several military posts in the colony, with the supplies of which they stood in need, and that it produced the worst effects on the troops, and provoked desertion. He said that the Choctaws were impatient at not receiving their customary presents; that this delay was much to be regretted, and might have the most fatal consequences; that he was even aware that they had had some conferences with the English, and that Michel de la Rouvillière was only intent on gratifying his self-love and his taste for despotism. On the very same day, Michel de la Rouvillière was also scribbling away denunciations against De Vaudreuil. He complained of the manner in which the King's merchandise was wasted, and declared that De Vaudreuil distributed it, capriciously, to his favorites at the different stations where they commanded, and that the Choctaws, through bad management, were a source of enormous expense to the government.

"There is no question,"—says he to the Minister,—"but that the Governor is interested, for one third, in the profits made at the post of Tombecbee, where De Grand-Pré commands, and that he has the same interests in all the other posts. Nobody doubts it here. Lenormant, my predecessor, must have proved it to you in his memorials, and in informing you that Mr. De Vaudreuil had gone security for the commanders at their respective posts, and for the traders who had taken, on lease, the privilege of trafficking with the Indians. The Marquis is too proud to have thus behaved, if he had not been prompted to it by self-interest. The commanders, at the posts, are all Canadians, who are his creatures, or who are kinsmen or relations of his own or of his wife."

"Mr. de Pontalba, the only one who does not belong to this gang, holds the government of Pointe Coupée, solely because he shares his profits with the Governor's lady. I have it from his own mouth, and, surely, he will not be called upon to draw lots with his brother officers, when the time shall come for the distribution of the troops which are to garrison our posts. There will be some pretext found to keep him where he is, and as specious a one will no doubt be discovered in favor of Mr. de Grand-Pré, who commands at Tombecbee, and who will not cast lots. In the meantime, the command of the English Turn has been withheld from Mr. de la Houssaye, who has given himself a great deal of trouble for the welfare of the new settlers at that point. As usual, *flour* was lately sent to Tombecbee, for the garrison; but it was *sold, also as usual,* and *corn* was given for food to the soldiers, of whom eight have deserted.

"Mr. Delino, an ensign, who is a kinsman of Mr. de Vaudreuil's, and who commands at the Arkansas, having heard that new troops had arrived, and that the officers of the colony were to cast lots for the distribution of the several posts among them, and being anxious to make sure of his own, which is one of the best in the colony, abandoned it, without permission, leaving a corporal in command. He arrived here, to the great astonishment of everybody. Mr. de Vaudreuil, who felt the consequence of such an act of insubordination, sent him back within forty-eight hours, but inflicted no punishment. On his return to the Arkansas, Mr. Delino found that the corporal and the rest of the garrison had swept everything clean, and had deserted, carrying away all that could be carried. Such are the causes which increase the expenses, beyond the Intendant Commissary's control."

"There is no discipline; the most indulgent toleration is granted to the soldiers, provided they drink their money at the licensed liquor shop, (cantine,) where they are given drugs, which ruin their health; for several months, there has never been less than a hundred of them at the hospital."

COMPLAINTS AGAINST VAUDREUIL. 61

" There are here at least sixty officers, who hardly do duty once in fifty days. Not one of them is required to visit the barracks, which are kept in the most filthy and disgusting manner; the soldiers are allowed to do what they please, provided they drink at the liquor shop designated for them; and they carry out of it wine and spirits, which they re-sell to the negroes and to the Indians. This has been proved ten times for one; everybody knows it, and yet the abuse is not stopped. I frequently spoke to Mr. de Vaudreuil on this subject. But this nefarious practice, instead of being checked, has grown more active. It is Mr. de Belleisle, the aid-major, who has the lease and administration of the liquor shop, and who gives for it a certain sum to the Major—others say to the Governor's lady. What is positive is, that Mr. de Vaudreuil has drawn upon the treasury for ten thousand livres of his salary as Governor, which he has given to Mr. de Belleisle, and it is with these funds that the supplies of the liquor shop have been bought."

" Moreover, Madam de Vaudreuil is capable of carrying on a still baser sort of trade. She deals here with everybody, and she forces merchants and other individuals to take charge of her merchandise, and to sell it at the price which she fixes. She keeps in her own house every sort of drugs, which are sold by her steward, and, in his absence, she does not scruple to descend, herself, to the occupation of measurement, and to betake herself to the ell. The husband is not ignorant of this. He draws from it a handsome revenue, to obtain which is his sole wish and aim."

" The first use which has been made of your Excellency's order to put a cadet in each company, was to bestow these favors on new-born children. There are some, between fifteen months and six years old, who come in for the distribution of provisions."

Michel de la Rouvillière enters into further details, as to the abusive acts of authority committed by the officers, and complains of the boundless power which they possess, through the protection of the Marquis of Vaudreuil and of the Council, wherefore many inhabitants are obliged to leave the colony, to avoid vexations. He complains, also, of the bad conduct of the Attorney-General, Fleuriau, whom he accuses of presumption, ignorance, and passion. But, from the tone of his letters, it cannot be inferred that he, himself, who reproaches Fleuriau for his passionate disposition, was free from a similar fault. His breast certainly does not seem to overflow with the milk of human kindness towards his brothers in authority, at whom he bites with the bitterest tooth of scurrility. If half of what he says be true, the colony must have been in a truly deplorable moral condition; for there prevailed in it the most shameful venality, and the stream of corruption originated and ran down from the upper regions of society. It must have been a miniature copy of what was then going on in France. These low, but graphic, details, which have been given here, will not, I hope, be deemed unworthy of being known, for they are the best illustrations of manners; nor is it to be forgotten that history, being the embodiment of human nature, in its past actions and feelings, is to be studied with more effect in the unguarded privacies of her bed-chamber, than in her stately halls of reception, where she appears only in her robes of dignity.

In 1732, a royal ordinance had exempted from the payment of duty, during ten years, all the merchan-

INTRODUCTION OF THE SUGAR-CANE.

dise and goods imported from France into the colony, and also the productions of the colony exported to France. In 1741, this ordinance had been renewed for ten years; and now, on the 30th of November, 1751, it was made known that the same privilege should continue in force until 1762. This was persevering in the right path; but the adoption of one liberal measure was not sufficient to establish the prosperity of the colony on a solid basis ;—it would have been necessary to co-ordinate, or to link together, a whole enlightened system of colonization, and to have put it into operation with steadiness, honesty, and ability.

It was in this year, 1751, that two ships, which were transporting two hundred regulars to Louisiana, stopped at Hispaniola. The Jesuits of that island obtained permission to put on board of those ships, and to send to the Jesuits of Louisiana, some sugar canes, and some negroes who were used to the cultivation of this plant. The canes were put under ground, according to the directions given, on the plantation of the reverend fathers, which was immediately above Canal street, on a portion of the space now occupied by the Second Municipality of the city of New Orleans. But it seems that the experiment proved abortive, and it was only in 1796 that the cultivation of the cane, and the manufacturing of sugar, was successfully introduced in Louisiana, and demonstrated to be practicable. It was then that this precious reed was really naturalized in the colony, and began to be a source of ever-growing wealth.

On board of the same ships, there came sixty girls, who were transported to Louisiana at the expense of the King. It was the last emigration of the kind. These girls were married to such soldiers as had distinguished themselves for their good conduct, and who, in consideration of their marriage, were discharged from service. Concessions of land were made to each happy pair, with one cow and its calf, one cock and five hens, one gun, one axe, and one spade. During the first three years of their settlement, they were to receive rations of provisions, and a small quantity of powder, shot, grains and seeds of all sorts.

Such is the humble origin of many of our most respectable and wealthy families, and well may they be proud of a social position, which is due to the honest industry and hereditary virtues of several generations. Whilst some of patrician extraction, crushed under the weight of vices, or made inert by sloth, or labor-contemning pride, and degenerating from pure gold into vile dross, have been swept away, and have sunk into the dregs and sewers of the commonwealth. Thus in Louisiana, the high and the low, although the country has never suffered from any political or civil convulsions, seem to have, in the course of one century, frequently exchanged with one another their respective positions, much to the philosopher's edification.

In 1752, the Chickasaws having renewed their depredations at the instigation of the English, the Marquis of Vaudreuil put himself at the head of seven hundred regulars, and a large number of Indians, with whom he marched against the enemy. But this expedition was not more successful than those undertaken by Bienville. The Chickasaws shut themselves up in some forts which the English had helped them to construct, and which proved impregnable. Contenting himself with setting on fire some deserted villages, and destroying the crops and the cattle of the Chickasaws, the

Marquis returned to New Orleans, after having considerably increased the fortifications at Tombecbee, where he left a stronger garrison. During this year, 1752, a Choctaw, happening to quarrel with a Colapissa, told him that he and all his tribe were no better than the fawning and mean-spirited dogs of the French. Whereupon, the Colapissa, resenting the insult, shot the Choctaw, and fled to New Orleans. The family of the dead claimed the fugitive, to have capital punishment inflicted upon him. The Marquis attempted, in vain, to persuade the Choctaws to receive presents in exchange for the blood they demanded, and found himself constrained to order that the fugitive be arrested. But nowhere could he be discovered. Whilst the search for him was on foot, his father went to the Choctaws, and offered to die for his son. His proposition was accepted, and his head, shattered by one blow of the revengeful tomahawk, redeemed the life for which he had so willingly forfeited his own. This event became the subject of a tragedy, composed by an officer named Leblanc de Villeneuve. It was one of the first literary productions of the colony.

On the 23d of September, the Intendant Commissary, Michel de la Rouvillière, made a favorable report on the state of agriculture in Louisiana. "The cultivation of the wax tree," says he, " has succeeded admirably. Mr. Dubreuil, alone, has made six thousand pounds of wax. Others have obtained as handsome results, in proportion to their forces; some went to the sea-shore, where the wax tree grows wild, in order to use it in its natural state. It is the only luminary used here by the inhabitants, and it is exported to other parts of America and to France. We stand in need of tillers of the ground, and of negroes. The colony prospers rapidly from its own impulse, and requires only gentle stimulation. In the last three years, forty-five brick houses were erected in New Orleans, and several fine new plantations were established."

A short time after writing this despatch, Michel de la Rouvillière died, and was succeeded by D'Auberville. Under the administration of the Marquis of Vaudreuil, the expenses of the colony kept steadily increasing, and amounted, for the year 1752, to 930,767 livres.

On the 9th of February, 1753, Kerlerec took possession of the government of Louisiana, the Marquis of Vaudreuil having been appointed Governor of Canada, where he distinguished himself, in 1756, by the skill and courage with which he resisted the invasion of the English.

The administration of the Marquis of Vaudreuil was long and fondly remembered in Louisiana, as an epoch of unusual brilliancy, but which was followed up by corresponding gloom. His administration, if small things may be compared with great ones, was for Louisiana, with regard to splendor, luxury, military display, and expenses of every kind, what the reign of Louis XIV. had been for France. He was a man of patrician birth and high breeding, who liked to live in a manner worthy of his rank. Remarkable for his personal graces and comeliness, for the dignity of his bearing and the fascination of his address, he was fond of pomp, show,. and pleasure; surrounded by a host of brilliant officers, of whom he was the idol, he loved to keep up a miniature court, in distant imitation of that of Versailles; and long after he had departed, old people were fond of talking of the exquisitely refined manners, of the magnificent balls, of the splendidly uniformed troops, of the high-born young officers, and of the many other unparalleled things they had seen in the days of the *Great Marquis.*

SECOND LECTURE.

ARRIVAL OF GOVERNOR KERLEREC—HE SHOWS HIMSELF FAVORABLE TO THE INDIANS—HIS DEALING WITH THEM—HIS OPINION OF THE INHABITANTS OF LOUISIANA—HIS DESCRIPTION OF THE STATE OF THE COUNTRY—HIS OPINION OF THE FRENCH AND SWISS TROOPS—REDUCTION OF THE FORCES AND OF THE EXPENSES OF THE COLONY—ARRIVAL OF SOME EMIGRANTS FROM LORRAINE—APPREHENSIONS OF AN ATTACK FROM THE ENGLISH—CRUELTY OF THE FRENCH COMMANDER AT CAT ISLAND—HE IS MURDERED BY HIS SOLDIERS—MANNER IN WHICH THEY ARE PUNISHED—HARD FATE OF BAUDROT—DEFENSIVE PREPARATIONS AGAINST THE ENGLISH—CURIOUS FACT AS TO BALIZE ISLAND—REVULSION OF KERLEREC'S SENTIMENTS IN RELATION TO THE INDIANS—HEAVY EXPENSES OF THE FRENCH ADMINISTRATION IN LOUISIANA—WARFARE BETWEEN THE CAPUCHINS AND JESUITS—THE ENGLISH CUT OFF ALL COMMUNICATION BETWEEN FRANCE AND LOUISIANA—DEFENCELESS STATE OF THE COLONY—MILITARY POWER OF THE CHOCTAWS AND ALIBAMONS IN 1758—ARRIVAL OF THE INTENDANT ROCHEMORE—PAPER MONEY OPERATIONS OF ROCHEMORE—HE IS BLAMED FOR THEM BY HIS GOVERNMENT—QUARRELS BETWEEN ROCHEMORE AND KERLEREC—ROCHEMORE IS DISMISSED FROM OFFICE AND HIS FRIENDS ARE EMBARKED FOR FRANCE—ATTEMPT TO MANUFACTURE SUGAR FROM THE CANE—NEW ORLEANS FORTIFIED WITH A DITCH AND A PALISADE—ARRIVAL OF FOUCAULT AS KING'S COMMISSARY—HIS DESCRIPTION OF THE COLONY—CESSION OF LOUISIANA TO SPAIN AND TO THE ENGLISH—PROTEST OF THE INDIANS AGAINST THE CESSION—KERLEREC IS RECALLED AND THROWN INTO THE BASTILLE—D'ABBADIE APPOINTED GOVERNOR—DESCRIPTION OF THE COLONY BY REDON DE RASSAC—THE ENGLISH TAKE POSSESSION OF MOBILE AND TOMBECBEE—BICKERINGS BETWEEN THE FRENCH AND ENGLISH—HOSTILITY OF THE INDIANS OF LOUISIANA TO THE ENGLISH—ENGAGEMENT BETWEEN THE ENGLISH MAJOR LOFTUS AND THE INDIANS ON THE RIVER MISSISSIPPI—EXPULSION OF THE JESUITS FROM THE COLONY—D'ABBADIE'S DESCRIPTION OF THE COLONY—PETITION OF THE MERCHANTS OF NEW ORLEANS TO D'ABBADIE—HIS OPINION OF THAT PETITION—MONOPOLY OF PRINTING GRANTED TO BRAUD—LETTER OF LOUIS XV. TO D'ABBADIE ON THE TREATY OF CESSION.

KERLEREC, the successor of the Marquis of Vaudreuil, was a captain in the Royal Navy. He was a distinguished officer, who had been in active service at sea twenty-five years, and who had been in four engagements, in which he had displayed ability and courage, and had received several wounds. He reached the

Balize on the 24th of January, 1753, New Orleans on the 3d of February, and was installed as Governor on the 9th of that month. Kerlerec began his administration by showing himself very well disposed towards the Indians, in whose favor he seems to have imbibed very decided impressions on his arrival in Louisiana. On the 11th of June, he convened a court-martial, to take into consideration the representations made by the Choctaws, on behalf of certain deserters who had been arrested by them and delivered up to the French, under the stipulations of a treaty, by which the Choctaws were bound to arrest all the French deserters, and the French, on the other side, had obligated themselves to pardon those that should be arrested and delivered up by the Choctaws. The Indians had faithfully complied with their part of the treaty; but the French seemed disposed to forget their obligations, and were detaining in prison, probably with the intention of proceeding to more rigorous means of punishment, three deserters who had been put in their possession under the treaty. The Indians had justly threatened to consider themselves as released from their obligation of arresting French deserters, if those that were in prison did not receive a full pardon. The court-martial, presided over by Kerlerec, decided in favor of the demand of the Indians, who were exceedingly gratified, when Kerlerec gave them the official information of that fact, and assured them that, for the future, the rights of the Indians and of the French would be impartially weighed in the same scales.

On the 20th of August, the new Governor wrote to his government:—"I am satisfied with the Choctaws. It seems to me that they are true to their plighted faith. But we must be the same in our transactions with them. They are men who reflect, and who have more logic and precision in their reasoning than it is commonly thought."

At a meeting of the Choctaw chiefs, Kerlerec reproached them, in a friendly tone, with their receiving, in their villages, English traders. He told them that, so long as they extended one hand to the French and the other to the English, they were to expect constant troubles, because they ought not to forget that the English were the originators of all the difficulties which had happened between the Choctaws and the French, and which had divided the Choctaws themselves into hostile parties. To these observations, the Indians replied, with a good deal of sense and truth: " The original wrongs and faults are on the side of the French. They are the first of the white race whom we have known, and who have inspired us with new wants, from which we cannot free ourselves, and for the satisfaction of which they are often but partially prepared, when not totally unprovided. The English study our tastes with more care than you do; they have a more diversified and a richer stock of merchandise. Hence are we driven to trade with them, when our hearts are with you. It is a matter of necessity, not of choice. Satisfy all our wants, and we shall, now and for ever, renounce the English."

Kerlerec admitted the strength of these observations, to which he called the attention of the French government, and he took this circumstance as a theme for requesting a larger supply than usual, of every sort of merchandise. He also convened the chiefs of the Arkansas, whom he feasted with great liberality, and whom he dismissed, much delighted with their reception at New Orleans, after having recommended them to send, all along the Mississippi, for about forty leagues

CHANGES AMONG THE OFFICERS.

up and down, war expeditions against the Chickasaws, the Cherokees, and the Chaouannons. With regard to the Chickasaws, although their numbers had been much curtailed, they were still very troublesome, and had lately killed all the men of a convoy destined for the Illinois district, sparing only one girl, ten years old, whom they carried away. Kerlerec betook himself to ransoming several prisoners, who had long been among the Indians. For the ransom of every male adult, the Governor gave one hundred pounds weight of deer skin, and proportionately less for females and children.

Kerlerec also proceeded to make some mutations among the officers of the several posts. "I have recalled," says he, in one of his despatches, "Mr. de Pontalba, who had the command of Pointe Coupée, although he ought to have been kept there for the good of that locality; but I was obliged to give way under the pressure of the calumnies of a gang of intriguers, who had spread the rumor that Mr. de Pontalba would retain his post, because he had annually paid to the Governor a stipend of twelve thousand livres; and that the same influence would be brought to bear upon me with the same results. Before the departure of Mr. de Vaudreuil, a petition signed by forty of the most respectable inhabitants of Pointe Coupée had been presented to me, to retain Mr. de Pontalba in the command. But I had to yield to malicious insinuations, and I must confess that this circumstance has filled me with grief, with humiliation, with contempt and disgust toward the people of this country."

The fact is that Kerlerec, in less than six months after his arrival, was beginning to see the tide of a sea of trouble and vexations rising fast upon him.

Many of the officers were discontented, and the Capuchins, whom he seems to have offended, were using against him all their priestly influence.

The state of the colony itself was not such as to present a very gratifying spectacle to its Governor, and, in connection with this subject, Kerlerec wrote to his government : " The German Settlement has not recovered from the unfortunate blow which it received from the Indians, in or about the year 1748. The inhabitants of that post withdraw from it insensibly, and therefore their numbers diminish every day. To those who remain nothing can inspire a feeling of security, and they are so disgusted with their present position, that many of them have petitioned me for lands elsewhere, unless I grant them an increase of troops for their protection. They even desire that those troops be Swiss, on account of the sympathies and affinities which they have with the men of that nation, and because the Swiss, being disposed to hard working, will help them in their agricultural labors, and will marry and settle among them, much more than the French are likely to do. Another reason is, that the troops of our nation, on account of the horrid acts of which they are known to be capable, have inspired the German settlers who have retained a proper sense of their worth and dignity, with a deep aversion to having with them any communication. I have sent to these Germans fifteen men of the Swiss company of Vélezand, and for the reasons here given, I solicit an increase of the Swiss troops. The Swiss behave exceedingly well : it would be necessary to carry their number to three hundred. I would prefer reducing the French troops and augmenting the Swiss; such is the superiority of the latter over the former!"

When reading the despatches of the governors of

CHARACTER OF THE TROOPS.

Louisiana for a series of fifty-four years, one is tempted to believe, that the French government used to select from the convicts in the King's jails, the men who were sent as soldiers to Louisiana. Bienville complained of the disgrace and grief inflicted upon him by putting under his command certain specimens of humanity, whose dwarfish size did not exceed four feet and a half, whose stunted and crooked proportions offended the sight, and whose vices were only equalled by their cowardice. Périer blushed at the necessity of confessing, that his soldiers usually fled at the first flash of an Indian gun. He even said, in one of his despatches, that his troops were so wretchedly bad, that they seemed to have been picked purposely for the colony, and that it would be much better to trust negroes on the battle-field, and use them as soldiers, were they not too valuable property, because they, at least, were brave men. Now comes Kerlerec, who, pouring out the last and bitterest drop remaining in the vial of vituperation, informs his government that it would be more expedient to send him Swiss instead of French troops, on account of the decided superiority of the former, and because the apprehension of the horrid acts of which the French troops were known to be capable, had induced the colonists to wish to avoid the contaminating and dangerous contact of such villains. What had become, one is tempted to exclaim, of the soldiers of Turenne and of Condé? What had become of the chivalry, that had threatened, under Louis XIV., to subdue the whole of Europe? What had become of the heroism, that had blazed uninterruptedly through so many centuries, and that had so freely spilt the noble blood of France, in every part of the world, from the days when the sword of a Gaul weighed so heavily in the Roman scales at the foot of the Capitol, down to the recently fought battle of Fontenoy? The fields of Canada were soon destined to show that the French soldiers, under Montcalm and others, had undergone no degeneracy. But the stern impartiality of the historian makes it his duty to record these words, which were written by a French officer (Périer) when giving an account of a panic : "*I am grieved to see that there is less of the French temperament in Louisiana than anywhere else.*" It is a relief, however, to remark that every Governor, although applying the most withering expressions of contempt to the colonial French soldiers, who, generally, were commanded by officers of distinguished abilities and great intrepidity, seldom fails to pay a flattering homage to the courage of the French colonists and of the few Creoles or natives of Louisiana.

After the departure of Vaudreuil, the troops were reduced to thirteen hundred and fifty men. The rest of the forces of the colony was composed of four companies of militia and one company of land waiters (gardes-côtes), the whole amounting to about five hundred men. The object of this reduction was to diminish the expenses, which for this year, 1753, rose to 887,205 livres.

The colony had been advancing in age, without having gathered strength enough to cease to be tributary to the Indians; for, at the beginning of the year 1754, Kerlerec wrote to his government : " I lack merchandise to trade with, and, particularly, to make to the Choctaws the customary presents which they expect, and of which three have now become due, without this debt having been discharged. This is the cause of their addressing me vehement and even insolent reproaches. They threaten to call in the English."

This year, the population of the colony was slightly

increased, by the arrival of some families from Lorraine. They were located at the German settlement, which, as we have seen, was undergoing a gradual process of depopulation, that was checked by this circumstance. They were industrious people, and proved a valuable acquisition.

The colony was, at this time, under great apprehension of being attacked by the English, and, on the 9th of July, Kerlerec wrote to his government in very strong language, to represent the utterly defenceless state of the colony, which was open on all sides, and destitute of everything. "And yet," said Kerlerec, "the English are moving everywhere about us, and threaten to interrupt our communications with the Illinois."

From the fear of danger coming from abroad, the attention of the colonists was diverted, for a time, by an event which filled them with horror, and the impression of which has been, in the traditions of the fireside, transmitted to us from generation to generation.

In Cat Island, there was a small garrison commanded by an officer named Roux, or Duroux, who was extremely cruel and avaricious. He used to employ his men making charcoal, which he sold for his private benefit; and for the slightest offence, ordering them to be stript stark naked, he had them tied to trees, in the midst of a swamp, and in the thickest of swarms of musquitoes. There he doomed them to endure the torments of a long night. The natural result ensued; the victims rose upon the tyrant, put him to death, fled to the mainland near Mobile, and, joining some English traders, endeavored to reach Georgia across the Indian territories. But, at the bidding of the French, a party of Choctaws pursued the fugitives, and made them prisoners, with the exception of one, who destroyed himself. They were taken to New Orleans, where they were tried. Two were broken on the wheel, and one of them, who was a Swiss, was, in conformity, it is said, with the penal code observed by the Swiss in the service of France, placed in a coffin, and (horresco referens) sawed asunder right across the waist, by two sergeants of the Swiss troops. In our days, it is more than doubtful, considering the provocation, whether these men would have been punished at all. So different are the judgments of man under the never-ceasing modifications produced by time!

The Indians, whose greediness and acuteness never lost an opportunity of obtaining some presents or indemnities from the French, pretended that their territory had been polluted by the suicide of the French soldier who had put an end to his life; and they claimed a present as an atonement for the crime. It was the Alibamons who urged this pretension, and Kerlerec, who wished to conciliate them, acceded to their demand.

When Roux was murdered by the soldiers under his command, there was, on Cat Island, a man named Baudrot, who had been thrown into prison by Roux, for disobedience to one of his arbitrary and oppressive orders. Baudrot had frequently been employed by the successive governors of Louisiana, to negociate with the Indian nations, and he had always shown himself worthy of the trust reposed in him. He was held in high estimation by the Indians, of whose languages he had acquired a perfect knowledge, and he was well acquainted with their manners, their customs, their laws, and the geography of the territories which they claimed as their own. Wonders were related of his physical strength, and had made him

FEARS OF INVASION.

known far and wide. The Choctaws, in particular, had conceived such respect and friendship for him, that they had adopted him, and had granted him all the privileges possessed by one of their race. The soldiers of Roux, after having murdered their commander, forced Baudrot to act as their guide, to a certain distance, through the territory of the Indians, and then sent him back, with a certificate that he had yielded only to violence on their part. He was tried, however, and found guilty, as an accomplice to the flight of the soldiers. To the horror of all the inhabitants of Louisiana, with almost every one of whom he had become acquainted in the course of his travels and wanderings, and whose sympathies he had gained, he was broken on the wheel, and his body, being denied Christian sepulture, was flung into the Mississippi, as if it had been the offensive carcass of the vilest animal. Such were the scenes acted in Louisiana in 1754! This barbarous deed struck with astonishment even the savages, and inspired them with an indignation which they did not fear loudly to express to Governor Kerlerec. The descendants of Baudrot are still in existence in Louisiana.

As already mentioned, the colony was under a lively sense of the danger of foreign invasion, and it became necessary to quiet the apprehensions of the inhabitants by defensive preparations. On the 20th of September, Kerlerec and the Intendant Commissary, D'Auberville, said, in a despatch to their government :—" The land, which is formed of alluvial deposits, at the mouth of the Mississippi, is so deficient in substance and solidity, that it is not possible, without considerable expenses, to establish thereon a settlement or durable fortifications. The fortifications which the India Company had caused to be erected there, and which were extensive, are destroyed. There are remaining but few vestiges of them, which are daily sinking into the mud, and are always under water when the tide rises, notwithstanding the repairs made to them in 1741 and 1742. It is important, however, to have at that locality a shelter for a small garrison, for pilots and their necessaries, and for those things of which the coming and departing vessels may stand in need."

"A fifty gun ship, with a solid bottom, a well caulked waist, and the rablets from stern to stem, up and down, starboard and larboard, lined with a sheet of lead, four inches wide, sheathed with nails and red cypress wood to preserve it from the worms, would last at least thirty years in the river. It would be the best substitute for a fort, which the nature of the soil renders impossible."

A fact of some importance is mentioned in this very same despatch:—"Balize Island, they said, which, twenty years ago, was half a league at sea, has now fallen back one league and a half on one side of the river, and joins that projection of land which the Mississippi gradually forms in carrying its waters into the Gulf. In this way, the island is now distant from the ships coming from sea. This circumstance makes it the more imperative to establish a floating post."

If there is no exaggeration in the assertion of the fact mentioned in this despatch, the Mississippi had gained on the Gulf, six miles in twenty years, and if his progress has ever after continued in the same proportion, the great Father of Rivers must be, in 1850, about twenty-nine miles farther than in 1754, in his career of conquest over the sea, and in his loving approach toward the fair Island of Cuba.

FEARS OF BRITISH INVASION.

In the month of December, there was at Mobile a great festival, given on the occasion of the distribution of presents to the Indians. Satisfied with their share, the Choctaws solemnly voted to Kerlerec the title of *Father of the Choctaws*. But Kerlerec seemed, at this time, to have a sad opinion of the virtues of his children, for he wrote to his government:—" I am sufficiently acquainted with the Choctaws to know that they are covetous, lying, and treacherous. So that I keep on my guard without showing it." This is a very different appreciation from the one made by Kerlerec the year preceding, when he said of the Choctaws :—" *I am satisfied with them. It seems to me that they are true to their plighted faith. They are men who reflect, and who have more logic and precision in their reasoning than it is commonly thought.*" Thus Kerlerec had changed his mind, as other men have done, and will do, on more than one subject.

Whatever was the real character of the Choctaws, they had remained true to the French in making war against the Chickasaws, who would have long been destroyed, if the Cherokees and Chaouannons, who were in the habit of marrying among them, had not supplied them with constant recruits. But their losses had been so heavy for a series of years, that it was evident that the triumph of the French was soon to be complete over these inveterate enemies.

Although the French government had recommended the strictest economy, and had diminished the number of the troops, the expenses of the year 1754 rose to 963,124 livres.

The year 1755 brought on an increase of the fear of British invasion. In the month of June, Kerlerec sent twelve men to Cat Island, to watch the approach of the English, who were expected soon to make their appearance at Ship Island; and these men were instructed to give him timely notice of the operations of the enemy. He also increased the fortifications at the English Turn, and he wrote to his government for an additional force of five hundred men. This year, the English had attacked the French in Canada, and Kerlerec had great fears for Louisiana, which the English had always coveted. He became therefore clamorous for help from the mother country. But France was then undergoing the deleterious influence resulting from the Orleans regency, and from the corrupt and pusillanimous reign of Louis XV. Her exhausted energies were not such as to enable her to protect effectually and to preserve her distant possessions.

At that time, there sprung up in the colony a sort of religious warfare, which added to the distraction produced by the expectation of perils from abroad. In 1717, the Capuchins of the province of Champagne, in France, had secured for their body exclusive ecclesiastical jurisdiction over New Orleans and a large portion of the territory of Louisiana. In 1726, the Jesuits had also obtained permission to settle in the colony; and in order to avoid all collision with the Capuchins, their jurisdiction had been confined to a remote region in the upper part of the colony. But they had taken care to procure, as an apparently insignificant favor, that their Superior might reside in New Orleans, *on condition that he should not discharge there any ecclesiastical function, unless it should be with the consent of the Superior of the Capuchins.* This was an entering wedge, which the well known and exquisite dexterity of the Jesuits turned to goodly purpose, so far as their interest was concerned. Enough had been granted to men in whom the energy of enterprise was

RELIGIOUS WARFARE. 81

equal to the sagacious daring of conception and to the artful readiness of execution. Thus they began with obtaining for their Superior, from the Bishop of Quebec, in whose diocese Louisiana was included, a commission of Grand Vicar, to be carried into effect within the limits of the ecclesiastical jurisdiction of the Capuchins, with which they had no right to interfere, in virtue of the stipulated conditions of the contract entered into between the Capuchins and the India Company, in 1717. The Jesuits pretended that this was not a violation of that contract, because their Superior did not assume to act as *Jesuit*, but as *Grand Vicar* and *representative* of the Bishop of Quebec in his diocese of Louisiana. But the Superior Council, siding with the Capuchins, had refused to admit and to record the nomination made by the Bishop. Nevertheless, the Jesuits had gradually usurped many of the functions of the Capuchins, in spite of the strenuous opposition of the latter, and had carried their audacity so far as to threaten to interdict their rivals altogether. The poor Capuchins, who were completely bewildered, and who were wanting in the spirit and ability necessary to cope with such adversaries, contented themselves with uttering loud complaints, and clamoring for the help of the government. Unluckily for their cause, they had committed the fault of acting with too much expansion of good nature towards the Jesuits. For instance, on the 9th of March, 1752, Reverend Father Dagobert, the Superior of the Capuchins, had had the imprudent courtesy of inviting Father Baudoin, the Superior of the Jesuits, to give his benediction to the Chapel of the Hospital, built for the poor of the parish of New Orleans. Father Baudoin, the Jesuit, assented with pious alacrity to the proposition of Father Dagobert, the Capuchin, which alacrity was stimulated by the circumstance that Father Dagobert, on that occasion, had, with Christian meekness, offered to act, and did act, as aid, or assistant, to the proud Jesuit, that is, in an inferior capacity. Father Baudoin availed himself of this circumstance as a weapon against the Capuchins. He said that he had published his letters patent as Grand Vicar, immediately after having received them, and that, although he had assumed this title, and announced his determination to act as such, no objection had been raised to his causing, in this capacity, certain publication to be made, on the 26th of February, 1752, with regard to the celebration of the Jubilee in the parish of New Orleans; that, subsequently, he had given his benediction, in the same capacity, to the Chapel of the Hospital, and that, having thus been openly recognized Vicar General of Lower Louisiana, it was now too late for the Capuchins to dispute his title and the prerogatives thereto appertaining. This was the question which had agitated the colony for several years, and which still remained undecided in 1755. It was called the *War of the Jesuits and the Capuchins*, and produced much irritation at the time. It gave rise to acrimonious writings, squibs, pasquinades, and satirical songs. The women, in particular, made themselves conspicuous for the vivacity of their zeal either for one or the other party.

The year 1756 passed off without leaving in its course anything worth recording. Kerlerec continued to complain of the grievous state of destitution from which the colony was suffering, and of the intrigues of the English, whom he represented as gaining much ground and influence with the Indians. In a despatch of the 1st of April, he says:—"The governors of Virginia and Carolina have offered rewards for our heads. I believe that the English government is not aware of it; otherwise, it would be an abomination. Our Indians have frequently proposed to bring to me English scalps, and I have always rejected their offer with indignation." Notwithstanding the destitution in which the colony was represented to be, its expenses went up, this year, to 829,398 livres.

On the 14th of March, 1757, the Intendant Commissary, D'Auberville, died, and was succeeded, *ad interim*, by Bobé Desclozeaux.

The English had nearly cut off all communication between France and Louisiana, and Kerlerec found himself so much in want of ammunition, that he sent to Vera Cruz for powder, but all he could obtain from the Governor of that place, was twenty-one thousand six hundred and twenty-three pounds of an inferior quality.

On the 21st of October, Kerlerec informed his government that he had written fifteen despatches in cypher without receiving an answer, and that the colony was so defenceless, that it would yield to the first attack, particularly if the French were abandoned by the Indians, who, so far, had been their allies, and who were showing much dissatisfaction. "The English," Kerlerec wrote, "have taken very efficacious means to capture all ships bound to Louisiana. They have established a permanent cruise at Cape St. Antonio de Cuba, and their privateers, spreading desolation among our coasters, pounce upon them at the very mouth of the Mississippi. In a word, we are lacking in everything, and the discontent of our Indians is a subject of serious fears. So far, I have quieted them, but it has been at considerable expense. Had it not been for the distribution among them of some merchandise, procured from small vessels which had eluded the vigilance of our enemies, some revolution fatal to us would have sprung up among the Indians."

Three critical years had elapsed, during which Louisiana seems to have been severed from all communication with France, when, in August, 1758, a new Intendant Commissary, De Rochemore, arrived from the parent country, with some of the supplies which had been so long prayed for. Never had help been more opportune; for the Choctaws, impatient at not receiving their customary presents, had begun acts of hostility against the French. According to a statement made by Kerlerec, the Choctaws could then bring into the field four thousand warriors, and the Alibamons three thousand. "These two nations," said Kerlerec, "are the bulwarks of the colony, and they must be conciliated, cost what it may."

Kerlerec also informed his government that his plan, for two years, had been to unite all the Indians of the South and West into a great confederacy, to march at their head against the English settlements, and thus to operate a diversion in favor of De Vaudreuil, who was struggling at the North in the defence of Canada, but that he had, in vain, waited two years for the necessary means to carry his plan into execution.

On the 20th of December, Kerlerec applied for the Cross of St. Louis in favor of Captain Aubry, who was destined, at a future period, to be Governor of Louisiana, and who was to play a conspicuous part in the drama by which her destinies were closed as a French colony. This officer had recently distinguished himself at Fort Duquesne, and previously, on several other occasions. It seems that, on the 14th of September, at six o'clock in the morning, Fort Duquesne had been attacked by an English detachment of nine hundred men. Aubry, who commanded the Louisiana troops, sallied out at their head to meet the enemy. Notwithstanding three murderous discharges of artillery and musketry, he fell upon the English troops with fixed bayonets, and crushed them entirely. The English left upon the battle ground three hundred men, dead or mortally wounded; many were drowned, and two hundred made prisoners. Such is the French report.

The year 1759 was marked in Louisiana by one of those paper money operations, from which she had already suffered so many evils at different times. Hardly had Rochemore been installed in his office as Intendant Commissary, when he called in one million eight hundred thousand livres of paper money which circulated in the colony, and converted it into drafts on the treasury in France. He replaced the withdrawn currency by another emission of paper money to the same amount, under the singular pretext of making his administration distinct from that of his predecessor. In so doing, he had the hardihood to act in direct opposition to his instructions, and was justly and severely reprimanded for it by his government.

Rochemore seems to have cared very little for the blame he had incurred, and did not hesitate to engage in bitter hostility against Governor Kerlerec, whom he accused of being guilty of an illegal and corrupt traffic with the Indians, secretly carried on under cover of the Governor's Secretary, Titon de Sibèque. He also complained of the extravagant expenses in which the Governor indulged, and informed the French government that the costs of the administration of the colony would, this year, rise to one million of livres.

It appears, however, that Rochemore had irregularities enough of his own to be forgiven, and that he ought not to have felt justified in looking too closely and too critically into the conduct of others; thus, not only had he assumed the power of issuing paper money, but he had also annulled certain concessions of lands, to bestow those lands on members of his own family. He proceeded to dispose, in the most arbitrary manner, of the King's merchandise, to the safe keeping of which he had appointed his brother-in-law. He whimsically appointed to the office of Comptroller his friend and adviser, Destréhan, who was Treasurer of the colony : so that Destréhan, the Comptroller, was expected to supervise, direct, and control the acts of Destréhan, the Treasurer. He went into suspicious partnerships with certain individuals, to whom he had granted the execution of the public works, and to whom he had made considerable and injudicious advances. For these reasons, and on account of his hostility to Kerlerec, Rochemore was dismissed from office by a ministerial resolution of the 27th of August, 1759. His Secretary, Bellot, a sort of pettifogger, was arrested and sent to France. In the possession of Bellot was found forty thousand livres, which, considering his small salary, could not have been honestly acquired in the course of one year, elapsed since his arrival in the country. Destréhan was ordered back to France, as being *too rich and dangerous.* All those who had supported Rochemore in his opposition to the Governor, and they were numerous, highly connected and powerful, incurred displeasure, reprimand, or dismissal from office, at the hands of the French government, and some of them were forcibly embarked by Kerlerec and transported to France.

There is but too much evidence that, from the foundation of the colony, the French government, the princely merchant Crozat and the India Company had

INTRODUCTION OF THE SUGAR CANE. 87

been shamefully defrauded. Thus, two of the King's ships, which had been sent to Louisiana with merchandise, having arrived on the 17th of August, 1758, were not ready to depart before the 2d of January, 1759, and their expenses, during this unaccountable delay, amounted to 194,099 livres. The Minister of the Marine department made it a ground of energetic complaint against the administration of Louisiana, and he, no doubt with reason, suspected that gross fraud had been practised on the King. The fact is that the fate of Louisiana, as a French colony, was rapidly approaching a crisis, and that the French government had grown disgusted with a possession which had been, for more than half a century, the cause of heavy expenses, without giving even a faint promise of adequate compensation in the future. It is not, therefore, astonishing that the King, for the sake of economy, suppressed at once thirty-six companies of the Louisiana troops, and thereby reduced to almost nothing the forces of the Colony. The colonists, however, were striving to increase their resources and to ameliorate their condition, by engaging with more perseverance, zeal, and skill in agricultural pursuits. Dubreuil, one of the richest men of the colony, whose means enabled him to make experiments, and who owned that tract of land where now is Esplanade street, and part of the Third Municipality of New Orleans, seeing that the canes, introduced by the Jesuits in 1751, had grown to maturity, and had ever since been cultivated with success, as an article of luxury, which was retailed in the New Orleans market, built a sugar mill and attempted to make sugar. But the attempt proved to be a complete failure.

Although an order had been issued in France, on the 27th of August, 1759, to recall Rochemore, he was still in office on the 2d of January, 1760, and, as Intendant Commissary, he took part in a Court Martial, in which it was unanimously resolved that it was expedient to surround New Orleans with a ditch and palisade, in conformity with a plan made by the engineer Devergès. These fortifications were to be erected at the King's expense, because the inhabitants of New Orleans were too poor to undertake such works, and would be sufficiently taxed with the obligation of keeping them up. This Court Martial was composed of Kerlerec, as Governor, of Rochemore, as Intendant Commissary, and of the following officers : Devergès, D'Herneuville, Grand-Pré, Grand-Champ, Maret de la Tour, Bellehot, Favrot, Pontalba, Dorville, and Trudeau. On the 21st of December of the same year, 1760, the projected fortifications were completed, but Kerlerec wrote to his government that, to render them efficient, he wanted artillery, men, and ammunition.

The officers who had sided with Rochemore against Kerlerec, and whom Kerlerec had forcibly sent back to France, had been so clamorous against the Governor and had advocated the cause of Rochemore with such zeal, that they had succeeded in suspending the execution of the ministerial order dismissing the Commissary from office. Among these officers, the most active and influential were Grondel and Marigny de Mandeville, and it was not long before Kerlerec perceived that they were no contemptible enemies.

But, in 1761, new complaints, which were countenanced by the Superior Council, having been made against Rochemore, he was definitively recalled, and Foucault, his successor, arrived in June of the same year. Describing the state of the colony in a despatch addressed to his government, Foucault said : " I have found the King's warehouses entirely empty, merchan-

HELP SOLICITED FROM SPAIN. 89

dise selling at enormous prices, the papers and registers of the administration scattered about and intrusted to clerks, some of whom are no longer in the employment of the colony. There is afloat more than seven millions of paper money. Drafts on the treasury in France are discounted at 400 and 500 per cent."*

Hence it is difficult to imagine a more painful and precarious situation than that in which the colony found itself at the time. A few words, extracted from a despatch written by Kerlerec, on the 12th of July, will complete the picture : " The Choctaws and the Alibamons," said he, " harass us daily, to have supplies and merchandise. They threaten to go over to the English, if we cannot relieve them, and, in the mean time, by their frequent visits, they devour the little that remains of our provisions and exhaust our meagre stock of merchandise. We have just ground to fear and to expect hostilities from them. Therefore our situation is not tenable, and the whole population is in a state of keen anxiety."

Whilst Kerlerec was drawing up such a delineation of Louisiana, the Ambassador of France at the Court of Madrid presented to that government, on the 31st of October, 1761, a memorial in which he made the humiliating confession, that France was unable to protect Louisiana any longer, and solicited the help and co-operation of Spain, to supply the necessary wants of that colony, and to prevent her from falling into the hands of the English. The principal argument used to awaken the sympathy of Spain and to elicit favorable action on her part, was, that Louisiana was then the only bulwark between the English and her

---

* This means that four or five livres of the paper currency, or of drafts on the Treasury, were given for one livre in specie.

own colonies. "*This circumstance alone*," said the French ambassador, " would be deserving of the attention of Spain, if his Catholic Majesty was not disposed, as he is, to afford to France all the assistance in his power." The Ambassador concluded his memorial with the declaration, that France would reimburse Spain, with the greatest punctuality, for all the pecuniary advances which she would make, and for all the supplies and ammunition with which she would furnish Louisiana.

Kerlerec was made acquainted with this application to the Spanish government, and sent couriers in every direction to inform the Indians that, as the Spaniards were going to join the French in the protection of Louisiana, he would soon be in a situation to supply all their wants, and to trade with them on the largest scale. He therefore counselled the Indians to show, on all occasions, their friendship and gratitude to the Spaniards. With a view to strengthen his administration and to prevent opposition to his measures, he proceeded to make some considerable changes among the officers in command. Thus, he gave the command of New Orleans to De la Houssaye, in the place of Belleisle, a friend of Rochemore, and put De Grand-Pré in command of Mobile, removing the incumbent on account of some partiality shown to Rochemore.

But Kerlerec was doomed to see all his hopes blasted, and to break all his promises. Spain, with her customary prudence, was pondering or dozing on the application made by the French government, and had not allowed herself to be betrayed into any departure from her usually slow mode of acting. She had remained passive so far, and had left Louisiana to her fate, and to the ineffectual protection of France. In 1762, however, some ships arrived at New Orleans

DEPARTURE OF ROCHEMORE.

from the parent country, but contributed very little to the relief of the colony. Alluding to these ships, Kerlerec wrote on the 24th of June : " They have brought none of the articles we wanted most, and hardly any of the things mentioned in the invoices. What they have brought is either not to the taste of the Indians, or is of so inferior or bad a quality, that it is without value. I am, therefore, under the shameful and humiliating necessity of not keeping my plighted faith to the savages. What shall I do with those Indian tribes I had convened, under the expectation of the supplies which I was led to believe would soon be at hand? What will be their feelings? How shall I keep them quiet? I am in a frightful position. Is the province of Louisiana destined to be the sport of cupidity and avarice?"

Rochemore, who had remained in the colony since his removal from office in 1761, left, this year, in July, for France. In a despatch to his government, Kerlerec said : " Rochemore has departed in the Medea, with a pocket-book full of bills of credit, which are drawn in favor of another name than his, but which will secure to him a brilliant fortune in France. The object of this substitution of name is to prevent the government from knowing the truth." This despatch contained bitter complaints against certain officers of the colony, such as Belleisle, Grondel, Grand-Champ, D'Hauterive, Marigny de Mandeville, Rocheblave, Broutin, &c. Kerlerec transmitted also to his government a certificate as to the mal-administration and evil doings of Rochemore, which was signed by sixty of the most respectable citizens and by the members of the Superior Council.

Foucault, who had succeeded Rochemore, was the very personification of treachery. He managed to keep on good terms with the Governor, and this functionary, in his despatches, bestowed the highest commendation on the new Commissary. But, whilst Kerlerec was acting so kindly towards Foucault, this individual was far from returning the favor, and, on the contrary, secretly accused Kerlerec of every sort of malfeasances, of a wasteful expenditure of the public monies, and of their appropriation to his own uses and purposes.

Thus matters stood, when, on the 3d of November, 1762, the Marquis of Grimaldi, the Ambassador of Spain at the Court of Versailles, and the Duke of Choiseul, the premier in the French ministry, signed at Fontainebleau, an act by which the French king *ceded to his cousin of Spain, and to his successors, for ever, in full ownership and without any exception or reservation whatever, from the pure impulse of his generous heart, and from the sense of the affection and friendship existing between these two royal persons, all the country known under the name of Louisiana.* This apparent act of generosity had been so spontaneous and unforeseen on the part of the French king, that the Spanish minister had no instructions on the subject, and accepted the gift conditionally, that is, *sub spe rati*, subject to the ratification of his Catholic Majesty.

On the 13th of the same month, the King of Spain declared that, in order the better to cement the union which existed, between the two nations as between the two kings, he accepted the donation tendered to him by the generosity of his Most Christian Majesty.

These acts of donation and acceptance were kept secret, and the King of France continued to act as sovereign of Louisiana. Thus, on the 1st of January, 1763, he appointed Nicholas Chauvin de la Frénière, Attorney General, and, on the 10th of February, he

TREATY OF PEACE SIGNED AT PARIS. 93

appointed, as Comptroller, Foucault, who already held the office of Intendant Commissary.

On the same day, a treaty of peace was signed at Paris, between the kings of Spain and of France on the one side, and the King of Great Britain on the other, with the consent and acquiescence of the King of Portugal. The Art. 7 said:

"In order to re-establish peace on solid and durable foundations, and to remove for ever all causes of dispute in relation to the limits between the French and British territories on the continent of America, it is agreed that, for the future, the limits between the possessions of his Most Christian Majesty and those of his Britannic Majesty in that part of the world, shall be irrevocably fixed by a line drawn along the middle of the River Mississippi, from its source to the River Iberville, and from thence by a line in the middle of that stream and of the Lakes Maurepas and Pontchartrain to the sea; and to that effect, the Most Christian King cedes, in full property and with full guaranty, to his Britannic Majesty, the river and the port of Mobile, and all that he possesses, or has a right to possess, on the left side of the Mississippi, with the exception of the town of New Orleans and the island on which it stands, and which shall be retained by France, with the understanding that the navigation of the Mississippi shall be free and open to the subjects of his Britannic Majesty as well as those of his Most Christian Majesty, in all its length from its source to the sea, and particularly that part of it which is between said Island and New Orleans and the right bank of the River, including egress and ingress at its mouth. It is further stipulated that the ships of both nations shall not be stopped on the river, visited, or subjected to any duty."

94 TREATY OF PEACE SIGNED AT PARIS.

By this treaty, the King of France renounced his pretensions to Nova Scotia or Acadia, and guarantied the whole of it with its dependencies to Great Britain, ceding also Canada with its dependencies, and whatever remained of his ancient possessions in that portion of North America.

The King of Spain ceded also to Great Britain the province of Florida, with the fort of St. Augustine and the Bay of Pensacola, as well as all the country he possessed, on the continent of North America, to the east and south-east of the River Mississippi.

It will be observed that, by this treaty, the King of France transferred to Great Britain, in 1763, part of what he had already given to Spain in November, 1762. But, probably, Spain had very little objection to resign a portion of an acquisition which had been forced upon her, and to which she did not at the time attach much value.

Thus France, with one stroke of the pen, found herself stripped of those boundless possessions which she had acquired at the cost of so much heroic blood and so much treasure, and which extended in one proud, uninterrupted line, from the mouth of the St. Lawrence to that of the Mississippi. The adventurous and much-enduring population which had settled there, and had overcome so many perils under the flag of France, and for her benefit, was coldly delivered over to the yoke of foreign masters. Tradition points to the spot, called "*El ultimo suspiro del Moro*," "the last sigh of the Moor," where the Infidel king, driven away from his fair city of Granada, looked back on her white towers glittering in the distance, and wept like a woman for the loss of that which he had not defended like a man. But he of France, the most Christian majesty, did he sigh at the immensity of his oss, he who never had either the tenderness of a woman's heart, the pride of a king, or the courage of a man! The English called West Florida that portion of territory they had acquired from Spain. George Johnston, having been appointed Governor of West Florida, soon arrived at Pensacola, in company with Major Loftus, who was to take command of the Illinois district, and they both lost no time in sending detachments to take possession of forts Condé, Toulouse, Baton Rouge, and Natchez. Thus, the British Lion had at last put his paw on a considerable portion of Louisiana, with no doubt a strong desire and with a fair prospect of grasping the rest at no distant time.

On the 16th of March, the King of France, who still acted as Sovereign of that part of Louisiana which he had not ceded to Great Britain, but which he had given away to Spain, announced, through a Royal ordinance, that he had determined to disband the troops serving in Louisiana, where his intention was to keep only a factory, with four companies of infantry for its protection and police. D'Abbadie was appointed Director of the factory, with the powers of a military commander.

The Indians were much incensed, when they heard of the treaty of cession. They said that the King of France had no right to transfer them over to any white or red chief in the world, and dispose of them like cattle, and they threatened resistance to the execution of the treaty. Several of the small nations, that were much attached to the French, when they saw the French flag pulled down, abandoned their lands, and came down to New Orleans. The Governor praised their fidelity, and granted them lands on the West bank of the Mississippi.

On the 2d of May, Governor Kerlerec wrote to his government, that it was expedient to make the customary presents to the Indians, notwithstanding the state of penury in which the treasury then was—1st. Because the government was pledged to it according to its promises, in return for which promises, real services had been performed. 2d. Because this honest and loyal dealing would secure for ever the attachment of the Indians, which would be handed down from generation to generation, and which might be of great help to the French, in case, on a favorable occasion, France should ever attempt to recover by force that of which she had been deprived by force. He added that the Cherokees, the Choctaws, and the Alibamons, when united, might set afoot more than twelve thousand warriors, and, therefore, that they would be no despicable auxiliaries in case of need.

On the 29th of June, 1763, D'Abbadie landed at New Orleans, and Kerlerec soon after departed for France, where, on his arrival, he was thrown into the Bastile. He had been Governor of Louisiana about ten years and five months. He was accused of several violations of duty and assumptions of power, and he was reproached, in particular, with having spent ten millions in four years, during the administration of the Intendant Commissary, Rochemore, under the pretence of preparing for war.

When Kerlerec and Rochemore accused each other with such virulence, the colony became divided into two camps, and the French government hesitated between the conflicting testimony adduced by the contending parties; but it is a matter of little importance to posterity, to know which of the two was right, or whether both had not acted with impropriety. It is enough to be informed that their dissensions, like those of their predecessors, proved injurious to the colony; and when each of them, being weighed in his turn, was found wanting in the scales, and alternately kicked the beam, it is probable that both of them deserved the treatment which they received at the hands of their government.

In the archives of the Department of Marine in France is to be found a memorial, written on the 15th of August, 1763, on the situation of Louisiana, by one Redon de Rassac, who seems to have occupied an official position in the colony. Among the causes which he gives, as having operated as obstacles to the prosperity of Louisiana, are the three following, described in his own style:—

"1. Says he, under Mr. De Vaudreuil, half of the married women sent to Louisiana had no children, and were between fifty and sixty.

"2. A good many families were located below the English Turn, on marshy and unwholesome ground, requiring incessant labor to make and keep up embankments. To this must be added the deleterious influence of poverty, and of every variety of misery, the abjection of the men and the prostitution of the women.

"3. The officers, addicted to trading, and converting their soldiers into slaves; a shameful system of plunder, authorized by the governors, provided they had their share of it; the dissolute morals of the military; drunkenness, brawls, and duels, by which half of the population was destroyed."

What a frightful synopsis in these few words! What a picture, if it be a representation of truth!

On the 20th of October, Robert Farmer took possession of Mobile, in the name of his Britannic majesty, and Tombecbee was delivered up to Thomas Ford, on the 23th of November. Hardly had the English set foot on their newly-acquired territory, when the French perceived that they had to deal with neighbors of a very exacting disposition. Thus, on the 5th of Dec., Colonel Robertson wrote to D'Abbadie, to claim the artillery which had been withdrawn from Mobile, because it belonged, said he, to Great Britain, in virtue of the treaty of cession.

On the 7th of the same month, D'Abbadie answered that *his* construction of the treaty was different from that of Colonel Robertson, because, in his opinion, the words : " The most Christian King cedes to his Britannic majesty the river and the port of Mobile, and all that he possesses or has a right to possess on the left side of the River Mississippi, with the exception of New Orleans and the island on which it is situated," could apply only to the soil and to the structures standing thereon. He said, however, that, as a favor, he would not remove the guns from Fort Tombecbee and from the fort at the Alibamons, on account of the difficulty which the English might experience in supplying their place ; and also that he would leave a few guns at the Illinois, in case the English wanted them, but that it should be under a strict inventory, and with the promise on their part to give them back, if he was supported by the French and English governments in his construction of the treaty.

Thus the French governor was acting with a courtesy which does not seem to have been acknowledged by the English, who made for it but a sorry return. " They never fail on every occasion," wrote D'Abbadie, " to harass me with innumerable objections and artifices of the pettiest and most groundless chicanery. For instance, among other things, they maintain that we are bound to protect them against the incursions of the Indians !"

OPPOSITION OF THE INDIANS TO THE ENGLISH. 99

In the Illinois district, the Indians showed a disposition to resist the English, and to prevent them from taking possession of the country. Nyon de Villiers, who was the commander of that district, wrote to D'Abbadie that it was the fault of the English if the Indian nations manifested such enmity to them. " The English," said he, " as soon as they became aware of the advantages secured to them by the treaty of cession, kept no measure with the Indians, whom they treated with the harshness and the haughtiness of masters, and whose faults they punished by crucifixion, hanging, and every sort of torments. They wish to wipe away from the minds of the Indians the very recollection of the French name; and, in their harangues to these people, in order to induce them to forego their old attachment for us, they use, in reference to our nation, expressions which are very far from being respectful, not to say gross and rude. I will, however, endeavor to dispose the Indians favorably towards the English, although their hostility to them is very great, and although they refuse to listen to words of peace on this subject. I doubt, therefore, whether the English will be able, for some time, to take possession of this district."

An amiable man this Nyon de Villiers was, who carried Christian humility and charity so far as to attempt to dispose the Indians favorably towards the English, by whom they were *crucified and hung*, to punish them, no doubt, for the fault, among others, of regretting the French! It is, indeed, curious to observe such anxiety in a Frenchman to serve the English, who, not satisfied with having stript the French of almost all their magnificent American possessions, used, in speaking of their vanquished foes, *gross and disrespectful expressions !!* The conduct of Villiers was the more remarkable, from the fact that this gentleman was a chivalrous officer, who had highly distinguished himself in battle against the English, and who had had the honor to force Washington to capitulate, at Fort Necessity, on the 4th of July, 1756. When it is considered that, in the opinion of Villiers, his brother Jumonville had been basely assassinated by the English, it must be admitted that his letter, as recorded here, is a monument of his moderation and magnanimity, and is one of the proofs of the more than good faith with which the treaty of cession was executed by the French officers, and another demonstration that the complaints of the English about the obstacles thrown in their way by those officers, were not well founded. The circumstances accompanying the death of Jumonville de Villiers had produced in France, at the time, a considerable degree of excitement, and became the subject of a short epic poem by the well-known French author, Thomas.

It will be remembered that the Capuchins had been struggling against the encroachments of the Jesuits, since 1755. But, in 1764, they were rid of their redoubtable adversaries, in consequence of the famous order of expulsion issued by the French government against this celebrated religious order. All their property in Louisiana was seized, confiscated, and sold for $180,000, a large sum at that time. It is well known that the Jesuits of Spain and Naples shared the same fate with those of France, and that they were almost simultaneously expelled from all the domains appertaining to these three kingdoms. It was thought that these men, who held, it was said, every consideration secondary to the prosperity of their association, and whose attachment to it did not yield to that of Horatius, Scævola, or Brutus for Rome, had become too powerful; and even kings had been taught to fear their doctrines, which were represented as dangerous, and their ambition which had expanded in proportion to the vast wealth of their order. When it was subsequently abolished by the Pope himself, in 1773, the shallow multitude, whose look does not penetrate beyond the epidermis of things, thought that the mighty society created by Loyola was really dissolved. But those who were better acquainted with the prodigious organization of the Company of Jesus, and with the vitality it derives from it, smiled at the ignorant credulity of mankind. Were they not right? Does not the year of our Lord, 1850, find the Jesuits in full resurrection everywhere, and is it not likely that they now possess more property in Louisiana than in 1764?

D'Abbadie, in a letter of the 10th of January, 1764, continued to complain bitterly of the conduct of the English. " Immediately," said he, " after the delivering up of Mobile to Mr. Farmer, who took possession of it in the name of his Britannic Majesty, this officer issued a captious decree, which is calculated to produce the greatest anxiety in the minds of the French inhabitants.

" 1. He requires the French inhabitants to take the oath of allegiance within three months, if they wish to be protected in their property. What right has he to impose any such obligation on those inhabitants, since the treaty grants them a delay of eighteen months to emigrate, if they choose, and since it is stipulated that they shall be, under no pretext, subjected to any restraint whatsoever?

" 2. The French inhabitants are prohibited from disposing of any land or real estate, until their titles thereto are verified, registered, and approved by the commanding officer. No titles are accepted as good, except those which are founded on concessions in due form, given by the governors and the Intendant Commissary of New Orleans, when, on account of the small number of the inhabitants, and of the immense extent of public lands, the mere fact of taking possession and the continuation of it, on permission given to select a tract of land and to clear it of its timber, has always been looked upon as a sufficient title."

On the 7th of April, Aubry, who commanded the four companies left in New Orleans, wrote to the French government: "The English being prevented from going to the Illinois by the way of Canada, on account of the hostile attitude of the Indians, have been driven to attempt to ascend the Mississippi up to that territory. Consequently, a number of officers, with three hundred and twenty soldiers, twenty women, and seventeen children, left New Orleans on the 27th of February, under the command of an officer named Loftus, in ten boats and two pirogues. Mr. D'Abbadie had caused the Indians to be harangued in favor of the English, and had ordered the French commanders stationed at the several posts on the bank of the river, to afford aid and protection to Loftus and his party, and had given them Beaurand as interpreter. He had thus done all that he could to ensure the success of their expedition."

On the 15th of March, the convoy had arrived, without accident, at Pointe Coupée, save the desertion of eighty men. When the English were at Pointe Coupée, something turned up which was very near bringing them into collision with the French. It seems that an Indian slave had fled from New Orleans, and taken refuge on board of one of the English boats. At Pointe Coupée, this Indian was recognised by one of his former masters, and claimed as a slave. The demand was backed by several persons who knew the man to be a slave, and the French commander granted the order to arrest him, but gave courteous information of the fact to Loftus, before permitting the order to be executed. Loftus, however, disregarding all the reasonings assigned to justify the arrest, declared haughtily that he would protect the slave at all risks, and ordered his detachment to betake themselves to their arms in support of the position he had assumed. The French commander, wishing to avoid a conflict, the consequences of which might be exceedingly serious, had the prudence to yield, and the slave remained free, in spite of the justice of the claim set up to him, in violation of the right of the master, and much to the annoyance and vexation of the inhabitants of Pointe Coupée and of the neighboring Indians, who would have been glad of an opportunity to give, by hard blows, substantial evidence of their feelings towards the English.

At the upper limit of the Parish of Pointe Coupée, Beaurand, the interpreter, took his departure, as it had been agreed upon, but not before having warned the English to beware of the Indians. The advice was kindly meant, but the English took it for an ironical and treacherous show of sympathy.

The English had come up to Davion's Bluff, or Fort Adams, when, on the 19th of March, at ten o'clock in the morning, some Indians, who were in ambuscade on both sides of the river, fired at the two pirogues, which were reconnoitring ahead of the bulk of the convoy, killed six men and wounded seven. The pirogues fell back on the main body of the English, who, without firing a shot, slunk back to New Orleans, where they arrived on the 22d. The Indians who had attacked them did not number more than thirty men, and might easily have been repulsed. But Loftus and his party were frightened by the bugbear of French treachery, and were under the impression that whole Indian tribes had been instigated to lie in wait for them on their way to the Illinois. But no fears can have been more groundless, as demonstrated by the correspondence of the French officers, who acted not only with strict good faith, but also with something like a wonderful abnegation of sensitiveness, of pride, and of long-nourished prejudice towards an hereditary foe.

"On the return of the English commander to New Orleans," says Aubry, in one of his despatches, "Mr. D'Abbadie expressed to him his regrets at the untoward event which had happened, and tendered all the assistance in his power. But the English officer, far from answering this act of kindness as he should, and far from showing any gratitude for it, said that Mr. D'Abbadie was the cause of the failure of the English expedition, that the Indians had attacked his party in obedience to the orders of D'Abbadie, who afterwards, as he alleged, received from the chief of the Indians in person an account of what had been done. There never was a blacker or more atrocious calumny. Mr. D'Abbadie used his best efforts to induce the Indians to remain quiet, and the English commander seeks in vain to excuse himself for the weakness of his nerves, and the little determination and judgment which he showed on that occasion."

Much to the displeasure of the English, some of the Indian tribes continued to emigrate and to settle among the French. Two hundred Taensas and about as many Alibamons were allowed to form two villages on Bayou Lafourche. In relation to these emigrations,

CONDITION OF LOUISIANA.

D'Abbadie said to his government that they were productive of a good deal of expense, but that it was inevitable, and that he took care that it should be as moderate as possible. He further observed that these Indians could be turned to useful purposes, and might help in the defence of the colony, which therefore would receive the equivalent of the money they cost the government. But he severely animadverted on other sources of expense.

"The expenses of the several posts in the colony," said he, "are analogous to those incurred in Canada, where, as here, everybody has some sort of justification for everything. It is a chaos of iniquities, the cause of which must be traced up to the chiefs, who ought to have been the first to check all abuses, and who have not done so. I cut down every claim on the government to one fourth, &c., &c.

"With regard to the possession of that part of the colony which has remained ours, I shall always consider it very precarious, until it is made sure by new arrangements; for, how can I keep it without troops, without ammunition, and without ships to protect the navigation of the Gulf, and to defend the mouths of the Mississippi?"

On the 7th of June, D'Abbadie wrote to his government a very interesting letter, containing his views on the situation of the country:

"I have the honor," said he, "to submit my observations on the character and dispositions of the inhabitants of Louisiana. The disorder long existing in the colony, and particularly in its finances, proceeds from the spirit of jobbing which has been prevalent here at all times, and which has engrossed the attention and faculties of the colonists. It began in 1737, not only on the currency of the country, but also on the bills of exchange, on the merchandise in the King's warehouses, and on everything which was susceptible of it. It is to this pursuit that the inhabitants have been addicted, in preference to cultivating their lands, and to any other occupation, by which the prosperity of the colony would have been promoted. I have entirely suppressed the abuse existing in connexion with the King's warehouses, out of which merchandise was extracted to be sold to individuals, and frequently to the King himself.

" The old paper currency, not having been converted by the government into bills of exchange on the French treasury, has no fixed value, but only that which public confidence assigns to it; and it has fallen so low, that it loses three hundred per cent. when exchanged for bills of credit on the treasury at home.

" If the inhabitants of Louisiana had turned their industry to anything else beyond jobbing on the King's paper and merchandise, they would have found great resources in the fertility of the land and the mildness of the climate. But the facility offered by the country to live on its natural productions, has created habits of laziness. The immoderate use of Taffia (a kind of rum), has stupefied the whole population. The vice of drunkenness had even crept into the highest ranks of society, from which, however, it has lately disappeared.

" Hence the spirit of insubordination and independence which has manifested itself under several administrations. I will not relate the excesses and outrages which occurred under Rochemore and Kerlerec. Every one knows how far they were carried. Notwithstanding the present tranquillity, the same spirit of sedition does not the less exist in the colony. It re-appears in the thoughtless expressions of some madcaps, and in the anonymous writings scattered among the public. The uncertainty in which I am, with regard to the ultimate fate of the colony, has prevented me from resorting to extreme measures, to repress such license; but it will be necessary to come to it at last, to re-establish the good order which has been destroyed, and to regulate the conduct and morals of the inhabitants. To reach this object, what is first to be done is, to make a thorough reform in the composition of the Superior Council. I have already had the honor of expressing my opinion on the members of the council, and particularly on the Attorney-General Lafrénière. Subjects chosen in France, to fill up the offices of Counsellors and of Attorney-General, would assist me in the intention I have, to devote myself exclusively to promoting the welfare of this colony, which has been ruined by the effects of jobbing, that first cause of all the evils from which we suffer here. Three fourths, at least, of the inhabitants are in a state of insolvency. But everything will again be set to rights, and with some advantage, through that severity which is required, to enforce the observation of the laws and to maintain good order.

"As I was finishing this letter, the merchants of New Orleans presented me with a petition, a copy of which I have the honor to forward. You will find in it those characteristic features of sedition and insubordination of which I complain. Its allegations are false in every respect, &c., &c."

D'Abbadie concludes his letter with the observation, that the complaints set forth in this petition of the merchants are presented in a style and manner which deserve *to be treated by the minister with the utmost severity*. In the petition to which D'Abbadie alludes, the merchants complained of the frightful condition of affairs in the colony, of the repeated postponement of the liquidation of the paper currency, and of the concession by which D'Abbadie granted to a company the exclusive right of trading with the Indians. This petition, which had ruffled D'Abbadie so much, was signed by the principal merchants of New Orleans.

Whilst D'Abbadie was thus addressing the French government, his predecessor, Kerlerec, who was still detained in the Bastile, was striving to excite the sympathies of that same government in his favor, and to prevent himself from being forgotten in his dungeon. To accomplish this object, he laid before the ministry a memorial, in which he attempted to show the utility for France to convert Louisiana, in concert with Spain, into a commercial depot, in order to turn that colony to some profitable account. The minister, to whose consideration this document was specially referred, endorsed it with this note:

"Considering that there are in this memorial some details, which might point out to the Court of Madrid proximate causes of conflict with the English, and therefore render the cession of Louisiana less acceptable to Spain, it seems proper that this memorial be recast, so as to produce a favorable impression upon that government."

It is evident from this circumstance, and from many others, that the French government considered Louisiana as a burden, of which it was anxious to disencumber itself, and that it was so fearful of the King of Spain's altering or withdrawing his act of acceptation, that it took every precaution to prevent his Catholic Majesty from rejecting the gift tendered to him.

It is not to be wondered at, after all, that France felt inclined to fling away Louisiana, in despair at her

ANXIETY OF THE FRENCH GOVERNMENT. 109

want of success in colonizing that distant possession. Louisiana had proved a dead weight in the hands of the great merchant, Crozat, who had buried several millions in her wilderness. The India Company had, with the same result, devoted over twenty millions to carry into execution, on the banks of the Mississippi, the grand scheme in which her charter originated. With regard to the French Government, it does not seem an exaggeration to suppose, that it had squandered from forty to fifty millions of livres in the attempt to colonize Louisiana. Thus, an enormous capital had been disbursed, no return had been made for it, and what was still more discouraging, was the conviction brought home to France, that, if she retained possession of Louisiana, she would be under the necessity of incurring still more considerable expenses, for, at the very moment when the cession of that colony was made to Spain, D'Abbadie was informing his government, in repeated despatches, that that French possession was in a *state of complete destitution;* that it was a *chaos of iniquities;* and that to re-establish order therein, it would be necessary to have recourse to *measures of an extreme character.* Hence the anxiety of the French government to part with a territory which, at a later period and in abler hands, was destined to astonish the world by its rapid and gigantic prosperity.

In presenting his memorial on Louisiana, the object of Governor Kerlerec had been, no doubt, to show that, although laboring under the displeasure of his government, and immured between the four walls of a prison, he was disposed to act as a useful servant, and he probably hoped, in this way, to procure his release. But his enemies, or at least those who thought they had been his victims, were, at the same time, and in a manner not calculated to help him, calling the attention of the government to his acts whilst Governor of Louisiana. Thus Philippe Marigny de Mandeville, an officer of the marine troops sent to Louisiana, who had been arrested by Governor Kerlerec, and dismissed back to France, was petitioning the Prime Minister, the Duke of Choiseul, to know the cause of the illtreatment inflicted upon him, and accusing Kerlerec of abuse of power, and other violations of duty. To this petition Marigny had annexed two certificates, one from Bienville and the other from Vaudreuil, in which the highest commendation was bestowed upon him by these functionaries, under whom he had served. He was the son of Marigny, who had died in command of New Orleans, as major, and who was a Knight of St. Louis.

On the eve of losing his faithful subjects of Louisiana, the King, to reward some of them for their good services, distributed a few favors among them, and granted the Cross of St. Louis to Favrot, a captain of foot, who had been wounded in the attack on the Village of Ackia, in 1736, and to Nyon de Villiers, who had long been commander of the Illinois District. An individual, named Braud, obtained, on the recommendation of D'Abbadie, the exclusive privilege of printing and of selling books in Louisiana. It was the last monopoly conceded by the French government.

On the 21st of April, 1764, the King wrote to D'Abbadie a letter containing an official communication of the cession of Louisiana to Spain. To this document were annexed copies of the act of cession and of the act of acceptation. The letter of the King ran thus :

LETTER OF LOUIS XV. TO D'ABBADIE.

"*Louis XV. to Mr. D'Abbadie:*

"Monsieur D'Abbadie, by a private act passed at Fontainebleau, on the 3d of November, 1762, having, of my own free will, ceded to my very dear and beloved cousin, the King of Spain, and to his successors and heirs, in full property, completely, and without reserve or restriction, all the country known under the name of Louisiana, and also New Orleans, with the island in which it is situated; and by another act, passed at the Escurial, and signed by the King of Spain, on the 13th of November of the same year, his Catholic Majesty having accepted the cession of Louisiana and of the town of New Orleans, as will appear by copies of said acts hereunto annexed, I write you this letter to inform you, that my intention is, that, on the receipt of it, and of the documents thereto annexed, whether they are handed to you by officers of his Catholic Majesty, or, in a direct line, by the French ships to which they are intrusted, you deliver up into the hands of the Governor, or of the officer appointed to that effect, the said country and colony of Louisiana, with the settlements or posts thereto appertaining, together with the town and island of New Orleans, such as they may be found on the day of said delivery, it being my will that, for the future, they belong to his Catholic Majesty, to be governed and administered by his governors and officers, as belonging to him, fully, and without reserve and exception.

"I order you, accordingly, as soon as the Governor and the troops of that monarch shall have arrived in said country and colony, to put them in possession thereof, and to withdraw all the officers, soldiers, or other persons employed under my government, and to send to France, and to my other colonies of America, such of them as will not be disposed to remain under the Spanish dominion.

"I desire, moreover, that, after the entire evacuation of the said port and town of New Orleans, you gather up all the papers relative to the finances and administration of the colony of Louisiana, and that you come to France to account for them.

"My intention is, however, that you deliver up to said Governor, or other officers duly authorized, all the papers and documents which concern specially the government of that colony, either with regard to the limits of that territory, or with regard to the Indians and the different posts, after having obtained proper receipts for your discharge, and that you give to said Governor all the information in your power, to enable him to govern said colony to the mutual satisfaction of both nations.

"My will is, that a duplicate inventory of all the artillery, warehouses, hospitals, vessels and other effects which belong to me in said colony, be made and signed by you and the Commissary of his Catholic Majesty, in order that, after your having put said Commissary in possession of the same, there be drawn up a verbal process of the appraisement of such of said effects as will remain in the colony, and the value of which shall be reimbursed by his Catholic Majesty, in conformity with said appraisement.

"I hope at the same time, for the advantage and tranquillity of the inhabitants of the colony of Louisiana, and I flatter myself, in consequence of the friendship and affection of his Catholic Majesty, that he will be pleased so to instruct his Governor, or any other of his officers employed by him in said colony and said town of New Orleans, that all ecclesiastics and religious communities shall continue to perform their functions of curates and missionaries, and to enjoy the rights, privileges, and exemptions granted to them; that all the Judges of ordinary jurisdiction, together with the Superior Council, shall continue to administer justice according to the laws, forms, and usages of the colony; that the titles of the inhabitants to their property shall be confirmed in accordance with the concessions made by the Governors and ordaining Commissaries (Commissaires Ordonnateurs) of said colony; and that said concessions shall be looked upon and held as confirmed by his Catholic Majesty, although they may not, as yet, have been confirmed by me; hoping, moreover, that his Catholic Majesty will be pleased to give to his subjects of Louisiana the marks of protection and good will which they have received under my domination, and which would have been made more effectual, if not counteracted by the calamities of war.

"I order you to have this letter registered by the Superior Council of New Orleans, in order that the people of the colony, of all ranks and conditions, be informed of its contents, and that they may avail themselves of it, should need be; such being my sole object in writing this letter.

"I pray God, Monsieur D'Abbadie, to have you in his holy keeping.

(Signed) LOUIS.
(Countersigned) DUKE DE CHOISEUL."

Thus ended, in Louisiana, the reign of Louis XV., which was as fatal to France itself, as to its colonial possessions in America.

When D'Abbadie published the instructions he had received, the colony of Louisiana was plunged into the deepest consternation. So far, mere surmises had been afloat as to the misfortune which threatened the colonists; there had been alternate fits of fear and hope, but hope, as is generally the case, had predominated; when, suddenly, truth came in a shape not to be questioned, and sad reality put to flight all the fond delusions of the heart. Although partially prepared for the present evil by the dismemberment of Louisiana, which had been effected so recently in favor of the English, the fortitude of the colonists had not been steeled to meet this new blow. As Frenchmen, they felt that a deep wound had been inflicted on their pride by the severing in twain of Louisiana, and the distribution of its mutilated parts between England and Spain. As men, they felt the degradation of being bartered away as marketable objects; they felt the loss of their national character and rights, and the humiliation of their sudden transformation into Spaniards or Englishmen, without their consent. As colonists, as property owners, as members of a civilized society, they were agitated by all the apprehensions consequent upon a change of laws, manners, customs, habits, and government. Such was the state of feeling in Louisiana, when D'Abbadie published the letter of Louis XV. in October, 1764.

THIRD LECTURE.

Execution of the Treaty of Cession to the English—Smuggling Trade carried on by the English—Meaning of the phrase, "I am going to Little Manchac"—Death of D'Abbadie—Aubry, his successor—Arrival of the Acadians in Louisiana—Causes of their expulsion from Acadia or Nova Scotia—Their settlement in Louisiana—The Mississippi, a common thoroughfare for the English and French—Inconveniences thereof—Construction of English Forts at Manchac, Baton Rouge, and Natchez—Introduction of Negroes by the English—Curious Despatch from Aubry on the difficulties encountered by him—Origin of the name of Baton Rouge—Representations to the King made by the Louisianians on the treaty of Cession—They send Jean Milhet as their delegate to France—Interview of Jean Milhet and Bienville with the Duke of Choiseul—Death of Bienville—Ulloa appointed Governor of Louisiana by the King of Spain—His letter to the Superior Council—His arrival and reception—Gayarre appointed Contador, or Comptroller, by the King; Loyola, Commissary of War and Intendant; Navarro, Treasurer—Disagreement between Ulloa and the Superior Council—He refuses to show his powers—His reasons for it—He visits the different posts and settlements of the Province—He orders a Census to be made—Its result—Biographical sketch of Charles III., Ulloa, Loyola, Gayarre, and Navarro.

With regard to that part of the Treaty of Cession which concerned the English, the French were executing its provisions with as much celerity as was permitted by the obstacles resulting from the hostility of the Indians to these new European lords and masters. Nyon de Villiers, who had the command of the Illinois District, abandoned it on the 15th of June, 1764, and arrived at New Orleans on the 2d of July, with six officers, sixty-three soldiers, and eighty of the inhabitants, including women and children. The English were indeed eager to avail themselves of all the advantages and acquisitions they had lately secured, and their ships, much to the mortification of the French, were seen proudly parading up and down on the bed of the old father of rivers. They used to stop, after having passed New Orleans, at the spot where is now situated the city of Lafayette, and they sold contraband goods to the inhabitants of the town and of the neighboring country. The wants of the colony were so pressing at the time, that D'Abbadie overlooked this illegal traffic, which was as advantageous to the colonists as to the English. As it was under the pretext of proceeding to their possessions of Manchac and Baton Rouge, that the English continued to make a stay at the place above designated, it became customary for one to say, when repairing to it for the purpose of smuggling: "I am going to Little Manchac." This phrase became proverbial, and the spot on which is now the city of Lafayette, long retained the name of "Little Manchac."

On the 4th of February, 1765, D'Abbadie died, and Aubry became his successor.

During the course of that year, the population of that part of Louisiana remaining to France, was increased by a considerable emigration from the Alibamons and Illinois Districts, which had been ceded to the English, and from the province of Acadia, or Nova Scotia.

The discovery of this province, in 1497, has been attributed to the Cabots, but no settlement was formed in it before 1604, when it was colonized by De Monts and a party of Frenchmen, who, it is said, called it Acadia, from the Indian name of one of its rivers. They were not allowed, however, peaceful possession of the far distant and wild home, which they had selected in the rugged country, where frowned an almost perpetual winter. The English claimed it as their own domain, in virtue of the discovery of Sebas-

EXPULSION OF THE ACADIANS.

tian Cabot, and sent a force which succeeded in driving away those whom they looked upon as intruders. In 1621, a grant of the whole of this peninsula, under the name of Nova Scotia, was made to Sir William Alexander. But the French regained a footing in it a second time, and retained it until the strong and ever victorious arm of Cromwell, extended across the Atlantic, reduced them to subjection in 1654. This subjection was not of long duration, and, in 1667, Nova Scotia, or Acadia, was resigned back into the hands of the French by the treaty of Breda. Next came the treaty of Utrecht, in 1713, which expressly conceded Nova Scotia, or Acadia, in its full extent, to England. Then the treaty of Aix la Chapelle, in 1748, *re-established all things as they were before the war.* But hence arose the perplexing questions—What was the state of things before the war? What was the extent of the territory forming the province of Nova Scotia, or Acadia? What were the limits between that province and Canada? From this source sprung claims which brought on, at first, partial collisions between the French and the English colonies on the North American continent, and those collisions were speedily followed by a war between France and England.

By the treaty of Utrecht, it had been stipulated that the French colonists of Acadia should retain their possessions. So far, they had refused to take the oath of allegiance as British subjects, except with the condition that it would not obligate them to bear arms against the French, even in defence of the province. The English government had not consented to this modification of the oath of allegiance, but had employed no means of coercion against a poor and scattered population, from which it anticipated no hostility, beyond that which consisted merely in the secret feelings of the heart. When, however, war broke out between the French and the English, the Acadians, who were on the disputed territory, openly sided with the French, and those who were within the unquestionable and avowed limits of Acadia, such as it was admitted by the French themselves to have been ceded by the treaty of 1713, assumed the character and the name of *neutrals*.

"They dwelt principally," says Williamson in his History of Maine, "about Annapolis, Chignecto, Bay Verte, the Basin of Minas, Cobaquid Bay, and in that vicinity—and altogether, made a population of 18,000 souls. They were an industrious, frugal people, strongly attached to the French interest and the Catholic religion. So desirous were they of throwing off the yoke, that they had secretly courted the visit of the French troops, and furnished them and the Indians with intelligence, quarters, provisions, and every assistance, and a part of them had actually taken arms in violation of their oath of neutrality. Nay, all of them, as heretofore, utterly refused to take the oath of unqualified allegiance to the British crown, though such as had not appeared openly in arms, were assured, if they would take it, that they should still be allowed the unmolested enjoyment of their lands and houses.

"Perceiving the indissoluble attachment of the Acadians, or '*French neutrals*,' to their parent nation, Lieutenant-Governor Lawrence, and the Provincial Council, with advice of Admirals Boscawen and Mostyn, finally determined that the whole of them should be removed and dispersed among the British colonies, where they, being unable to unite in any offensive measures, would become naturalized to the government and the country. Without knowing their destiny, they were summoned to meet in their chapels,

FATE OF THE ACADIANS.

September 5th, 1755, to hear their doom. At Grand Pré (Minas and Horton), assembled 1923 persons, aged and young, whom General Winslow met, and after animadverting upon their disloyal conduct, said to them: 'I now declare to you his Majesty's orders. Know then, that your lands, tenements, cattle, and live stock of all kinds, are forfeited to the Crown, with all other effects of yours, excepting your money and household goods, which you will be allowed to carry with you: and that yourselves and families are to be removed from this province to places suiting his Majesty's pleasure; and in the meantime, to remain in custody, under the inspection and control of the troops I have the honor to command. In a word, I now declare you all the King's prisoners.' Shocked and petrified at this thrilling decree, some of them burst into tears, and some fled to the woods, whose houses were committed to the flames, and country laid waste, to prevent their subsistence. Indeed, every possible measure was adopted to force them back into captivity.

"When the transports arrived at Annapolis, to convey away the ill-fated people from that place and vicinity, the soldiers found the houses entirely deserted by the inhabitants, who had fled to the woods, carrying with them their aged parents, their wives, and children. But hunger, infirmity, and distress soon compelled the return of numbers, who surrendered themselves prisoners at discretion. The more athletic penetrated into the depths of the wilderness, and encamped with the savages; and a few wandered through the woods to Chignecto, and thence escaped to Canada.

"In Cumberland, the summons were generally disobeyed, and hence it was found necessary to resort to the most severe measures. Here, 253 of their houses were set on fire at one time, in which a great quantity of wheat, flax, and other valuable articles were consumed: the country presenting, for several days and several miles, a most direful scene of conflagration. As the different Acadian settlements were too widely extended to admit of an actual subjugation at once, only 7,000 were collected at this time and dispersed among the several British colonies. On the 10th of September, 1755, one hundred and sixty-one young men, taken from among the prisoners belonging to the district of Minas, were driven by a military guard on board of five transports, stationed in the River Gaspereaux. The road from the chapel to the shore, one mile in length, was lined with women and children, all of whom, bathed in tears, knelt and uttered, amid deep heart-broken sighs—farewell! as the dejected prisoners advanced with slow and reluctant steps, weeping, praying, and singing hymns as they passed. These were followed by their seniors, who passed through the same heart-rending scene of sorrow and distress; and when other vessels arrived, they carried away also their wives and children. About 1,300 arrived in Massachusetts and Maine, and became a public charge, principally in consequence of an irreconcilable antipathy to their situation. Also, 415 were sent to Pennsylvania, and some were transported as far south as Georgia. Such was the wretched fate of the French *neutrals*."

A few pages farther, the same author goes on saying: "An act passed the next day (to wit, the 24th of December, 1755,) for the distribution of the French neutrals through the province (Massachusetts), and the support or relief of them in the different towns, as beneficiary paupers. A number were assigned to Maine. The overseers of the poor were required to make suitable provision for them at the charge of the province, unless they were remunerated by the Crown, or by the Government of Nova Scotia. Bigoted to the Romish religion, necessitous, disaffected, and unhappy, they entertained a settled, unconquerable dislike of the English, their habits and sentiments —and being exiles from their native land, which they loved and longed to see, they were neither enterprising nor industrious, but an intolerable burden to the government. According to a committee's report, Jan. 25, 1760, there were, even at that time, 1,017 of this miserable people within the province."

Thus, the Messenians, after their noble and protracted struggle for independence against the Spartans, being subjugated, were remorselessly driven away by their implacable foes from their blood-stained hearths and the honored graves of their ancestors, to wander through Greece in search of pity and assistance, and of a new home for the houseless exile in the land of the stranger. Thus at a later period, and by a more awful decree, Jerusalem was torn from her foundations, and the Jews sown broad-cast over the face of the earth, to be the beasts of burden, the dogs, the footstools of every nation, or rather to be the swine of the human species, herding through so many centuries in the troughs and sewers of society, and battening upon its dregs and offals.

The miserable outcasts who, by an English decree, had been made the Messenians and the Jews of America, could never be reconciled to their fate, and, in the words of Williamson, *retained an unconquerable dislike of the English.* The race which, in Acadia, had deprived them of everything, of all that is dear to the human heart, was the very same race they met in Massachusetts, in Pennsylvania, in Virginia, in all the English colonies to which they were transported. It was the race of their oppressors, and the bread which pity or charity presented to them, was English bread offered by an English hand! How could they not be broken-hearted, when the very words of encouragement and consolation in which they were addressed, were in a language hateful to their ears! How could they be industrious, when their industry would have brought them into more immediate contact with those they cursed as the authors of their misery! How enterprising, in a land from which they longed to flee! How could they forget their wrongs, and labor on English ground! How could they plough the soil that England owned, unless it were with the hope of sowing the Dragon's teeth, destined to spring up in hostile array, and to shed the blood that vengeance claimed! During ten years, the Acadians thought of nothing else than finding the means of seeking some genial clime, where they could be gathered under the flag of France, and kept their eyes steadily fixed on the French West India Islands, and particularly on Louisiana. Luckily for them, they proved, as they wished, and as the historian of Maine says, *an intolerable burden to the English colonies*, and, after ten years of sufferings and of vain longings, many of them were permitted, encouraged, and assisted to execute their deeply cherished design of moving to the French colonies.

Thus, between the 1st of January and the 13th of May, 1765, about six hundred and fifty Acadians had arrived at New Orleans, and from that town had been sent to form settlements in Attakapas and Opelousas, under the command of Andry. In one of his despatches to his government, the Commissary, Fou-

SETTLEMENT OF ACADIANS IN LOUISIANA. 123

cault, observed that these settlements would, in a few years, rise to considerable importance, should Bayou Plaquemine be cleared, and should thereby a free communication be opened from the River Mississippi to the Gulf of Mexico. The arrival of these emigrants threw the provincial authorities into a great state of perplexity, by forcing them into expenses which they could not well meet, on account of the deplorable condition of the colonial treasury, and which were incurred to increase the population of a province no longer belonging to France. They felt no less anxiety about their responsibility, in making disbursements and in contracting obligations, which their government might not approve. But the claims of the unfortunate exiles who had come to seek an asylum in Louisiana and under the French flag, were too strong to be resisted, and they obtained all the assistance which the public purse, aided by private charity, could afford.

This, however, was the least of all the difficulties which Aubry and Foucault had to encounter in their administration of the colony. By making the Mississippi a common thoroughfare for the English and the French, a wide door had been opened to jealousies, apprehensions, misunderstandings, and conflicts of every kind. The French saw, with distrust, the frequent transportation of English troops, through the very heart of the poor remnant of their once so extensive and magnificent possessions. They heard, with uneasiness, the morning and evening guns which the English fired, as they went up and down the river. This gun-firing greatly alarmed and excited the Indians, who took it as a sign of hostility or triumph. They could hardly be persuaded that it was no more than a military usage, and they had imbibed the impression, that the French admitted their inferiority, or showed cowardice, in not resenting this provocation offered to them. But the acts of English sovereignty were not confined to empty demonstrations and the parade of naval strength. A frigate was sent to the mouth of Manchac, where she was to remain until a fort should be constructed. It was also known that another frigate was to ascend to Natchez, where the erection of a fort was contemplated.

On the 16th of May, Aubry wrote to his government: "It is for us a new and even an alarming spectacle, to see constantly passing before New Orleans, ships of war and foreign troops. Although we are in full peace, and although it seems that we have nothing to fear, yet I feel inwardly, and, as it were, in spite of myself, alarms on this subject, considering that I have neither ships, nor troops, nor ammunition, to oppose hostile designs, should any such be formed. It seemed to me indecorous not to have any battery on the river; consequently, I had twenty pieces of artillery put on their carriages in front of the barracks. In this way, we shall return more decently the salutes; and, besides, it commands respect.

"The English had flattered themselves to open, with ease, the communication which had long been stopped between Lake Maurepas and the Mississippi, through the River Iberville (now Manchac), which is thirty-five leagues from this town, and where begins the island of New Orleans. But this enterprise is more difficult than they had thought, and Du Parc, an inhabitant of this colony, who had undertaken this task, with the consent of Mr. D'Abbadie, is likely to fail in its execution.

"The government of this colony is more embarrassing than it ever was. It is exceedingly difficult to conciliate, at the same time, the English, the French, and the Indians, who are here pell-mell.

"The correspondence which I am obliged to have with the English, who write to me from all parts, and particularly with the Governor of Mobile, gives me serious occupation. This governor is an extraordinary man. As he knows that I speak English, he occasionally writes to me in verse. He speaks to me of Francis I. and Charles V. He compares Pontiak, an Indian chief, to Mithridates; he says that he goes to bed with Montesquieu. When there occur some petty difficulties between the inhabitants of New Orleans and Mobile, he quotes to me from the Great Charter (Magna Charta) and the laws of Great Britain. It is said that the English Ministry sent him to Mobile to get rid of him, because he was one of the hottest in the opposition. He pays me handsome compliments, which I duly return to him, and upon the whole, he is a man of parts, but a dangerous neighbor, against whom it is well to be on one's guard.

"The ordinary communication from Mobile to New Orleans is through the Lakes and Bayou St. John. So far, we have always permitted the English to pass in that direction. I have lately, however, refused this privilege to Mr. Farmer, who is going to the Illinois with three hundred men. He has the river; let him use it." And so did the English, in no sparing manner, and much to their commercial advantage. At the fort they had constructed at Manchac, and which they called Fort Bute, in compliment to Lord Bute, the celebrated favorite of their King, as well as at their settlements of Baton Rouge and Natchez, they were carrying on a large contraband trade with the inhabitants of French Louisiana, who used to repair to these places for all their supplies. Besides, the English ships, in going up and down the river, were actively engaged in smuggling, and especially, unladed at every point a peculiar kind of commodities in the shape of negroes. This became the source of the fortune of more than one planter. As the colony was on the eve of being transferred away from France, and was no longer a mart for her trade, the government winked at these illicit transactions.

The settlement of Baton Rouge, which had been ceded to the English, and which they had converted into a depot of contraband trade with the portion of Louisiana that was destined to become Spanish, was then composed of nothing better than a miserable fortlet, and some huts which were scattered about in its neighborhood. The future had in store higher destinies for that locality, which is now one of the most agreeable and loveliest sites in the State of Louisiana. It boasts, in 1850, of a pretty town of four thousand inhabitants, where the federal government of the United States has erected an arsenal and barracks, on a large scale and of imposing aspect. There the State penitentiary works its looms, teaches convicts the usefulness and morality of honest industry, and makes guilt itself subservient to the purposes of trade and to plans of reform, if not to the prevention of crime. There the ever-wonderful order of the Jesuits has established a College, and is to locate, it is said, the head-quarters of that spiritual province or circumscription in which Louisiana is included. As a climax of good fortune, the seat of State Government was transferrred to that favored spot, on the 1st of December, 1849; and to serve as the capitol of the State, a castellated building has been erected, which is intended to imitate the Anglo-Norman style of architecture, and which seems to look down, with the air of a feudal baron, on the town, and on the mighty river rolling majestically at the foot of its snow-white towers.

The capital of Louisiana deserves that the origin of its name of Baton Rouge, or Red Stick, be recorded. It is well known that the cypress tree, in this southern climate, rises to a prodigious height, and that its bark is of a reddish hue. Its trunk is shorn of branches, and its head alone wears a leafy crown. In nature's book of architecture, it represents the pillar with its chapiter. Le Page du Pratz relates that, in his time, there was yet to be seen, on the present site of the capital of Louisiana, a famous cypress tree, out of which a carpenter had offered to build two boats, one of sixteen tons, and the other of fourteen. "As the wood of the cypress tree is red," says Le Page du Pratz, " one of the first travellers who arrived at this locality, exclaimed that this tree would make a fine stick! Hence the name of Baton Rouge (Red Stick) given to this place. With regard to the tree, its height has not as yet been measured. It towers almost beyond sight."

If this description be true, this red stick would have deserved to have been handled by one of the Titans of old Greece. The ancient Romans, who used to see omens and presages in everything, would hardly have failed to believe that this prodigy of the vegetable kingdom was the sure sign of some extraordinary destiny, for the sacred spot on which it had been planted by the Gods.

When the inhabitants of Louisiana had been informed of the treaty of cession to Spain, they had resolved to make representations to the French governmen. They hoped that the king of France, when made aware of their love and devotion, would retract his donation, and that they would thus prevent what they all dreaded so much. Consequently, every parish had been invited to send delegates to New Orleans. The invitation was not fruitless, every parish responded to it, and a numerous assembly, composed of some of the most distinguished inhabitants of the colony, met at New Orleans. The principal and most active members were: Lafrénière, the Attorney-General Doucet, St. Lette, Pin, Villeré, D'Arensbourg, Jean Milhet, the wealthiest merchant of the colony, Joseph Milhet, his brother, St. Maxent, De La Chaise, Marquis, Garic, Masan, Massange, Poupet, Noyan, Boisblanc, Grand-Maison, Lalande, Lesassier, Braud, the King's printer, Kernion, Carrère, Dessales, &c.

The Attorney-General, Lafrénière, after having depicted in a very energetic and eloquent speech, the sad situation of the colony, presented a resolution by which the colonists, in a body, supplicated the King of France not to sever them from the mother country. The resolution was unanimously adopted, and Jean Milhet was selected to carry it to the foot of the throne.

The first care of Jean Milhet, on his arrival in Paris, was to wait on Bienville. That distinguished man was then in his 86th year, still retaining, however, almost unimpaired, the moral and intellectual faculties which had characterized him through life. The body was nothing but the wreck of a goodly ship, which, after having been long buffeted by the storms of the world, was now fast sinking into the yawning abyss. But the spiritual commander, the soul, unscorched by the fury of the contending elements, fatigued, not subdued or dismayed, could be seen proudly standing on the deck, serenely surveying the desolating scene and the approaches of desolation, and ready to spring up, at

PRESENTATION OF THE PETITION.

the last moment, from where it stood, to the shore of eternal peace and safety. Deeply grieved was he to have lived long enough to see the gradual abasement of France, and the partition of Louisiana between England and Spain. What had become of Canada, his native country? What of half of Louisiana, that colony which he had founded in concert with his beloved brother Iberville? What had become of that splendid creation of his youthful days? Was France now to give up the last inch of that immense territory, which he had acquired for her, at the cost of so many perils and so much endurance? Was it for the Spaniards that he had called New Orleans into life? Were the Louisianians, were the numerous members of his family, whose home he had selected in the cradle of his future fame, were his many friends and the old companions of his labors, to be no longer his countrymen? Well may it be imagined, with what readiness Bienville accepted the proposition of Milhet, to call with him on the Prime Minister, Duke of Choiseul.

Introduced into the Duke's closet, they laid before him the petition of the inhabitants of Louisiana. Milhet, their delegate, was the first to address the Minister, and urge upon him all the considerations which, he thought, ought to induce France to retain that important possession. Then, Bienville, with the authority of his age and past services, and with an eloquence inspired by the deep feelings which overflowed his heart, made a pathetic appeal, not only to the reason, but also to the sensibility of the powerful man who held in his hands the fate of Louisiana. Eloquent indeed he was, for he spoke like a father suing for the life of his child. The Duke listened with courteous attention, but said in reply, and in few words, that he regretted his inability to change the course of things. Jean Milhet, despairing of success, and with a look of profound affliction, had risen to depart, when Bienville gave way to the emotions which, so far, had been pent up in his heart. Tears gushed from his eyes, his tremulous hands seized those of the Duke, he bent his knee, and in this humble posture, with an almost sobbing voice, he prayed for a reconsideration of the decree issued against the colony. This was too much even for the minister. He appeared greatly moved; he hastily raised up the octogenarian suitor, whom he embraced with respect, and, as it were, in token of the sympathy he felt for a distress he could not relieve. But his resolution was not shaken, and he said in a soothing tone: "Gentlemen, I must put an end to this painful scene. I am deeply grieved at not being able to give you any hope. I have no hesitation in telling you that I cannot address the King on this subject, because I, myself, advised the cession of Louisiana. Is it not to your knowledge that the colony cannot continue its precarious existence, except at an enormous expense, of which France is now utterly incapable? Is it not better, then, that Louisiana should be given away to a friend and faithful ally, than be wrested from us by an hereditary foe? Farewell—you have my best wishes. I can do no more." Thus dismissed, the noble veteran, Bienville, staggered out of the minister's room, leaning on the arm of Milhet. Grief had loosened the feeble chords which bound him to life, and, a short time after, he was no more. He had departed to meet his favorite brother Iberville, in a better world.

Although Milhet duly informed his fellow-citizens of the result of his mission, yet they continued to flatter themselves with the hope that the treaty of cession would not be carried into execution. This hope was founded on circumstances, which were interpreted by the colonists in a manner favorable to their wishes. For

ULLOA APPOINTED GOVERNOR OF LOUISIANA. 131

instance, one year had elapsed since the receipt of the letter, in which the King had instructed D'Abbadie to deliver up the colony to the first Spanish officer, who should present himself with the necessary powers. Such an officer had not as yet arrived, and it seemed that the King of Spain was making no preparation to take possession of the province. Thus, the lowering clouds, which had darkened the horizon, were fast sinking away from the sight of the colonists, when they reappeared with a blacker shade, at the news that Don Antonio de Ulloa had been appointed Governor of Louisiana, and had reached Havana. Soon after, on the 10th of July, this officer wrote to the Superior Council at New Orleans the following letter:

GENTLEMEN,—" Having recently been instructed by his Catholic Majesty, to repair to your town and take possession of it in his name, and in conformity with the orders of his most Christian Majesty, I avail myself of this occasion, to make you acquainted with my mission, and to give you information, that I shall soon have the honor to be among you, in order to proceed to the execution of my commission. I flatter myself beforehand that it will afford me favorable opportunities, to render you all the services that you and the inhabitants of your town may desire; of which I beg you to give them the assurance from me, and to let them know that, in acting thus, I only discharge my duty and gratify my inclinations.   ANTONIO DE ULLOA."

At the moment when the country was thus on the eve of changing its old livery of colonial bondage for another one, the King of France thought proper to drop, from the table of royal favors, crumbs of consolation for some of the faithful servants whom he was abandoning, and sent the decorations of the Cross of St. Louis to Marest de la Tour, Bonille, D'Arensbourg, and Lavergne.

August, September, October, November, December, passed away, and Ulloa did not come! What detained him, when so near? Had counter orders arrived? And hope, that feeling happily so congenial to human nature, of so rapid growth and of so slow decay, began to revive in the breasts of the colonists. The year 1766 had begun its onward march, and had brought no Ulloa! Many of the colonists now adopted the conviction, that the Treaty of Cession was nothing but a sham instrument, concealing some diplomatic manœuvering.

In the month of February, 216 Acadians arrived in Louisiana. The families, who had first sought refuge in the colony, had set up an example, which others had been eager to follow. Implements of husbandry were distributed to them at the cost of the government, and they were authorized to form settlements on both sides of the Mississippi, from the German Coast up to Baton Rouge, and even as high as Pointe Coupée. Hence, the name of *Acadian Coast*, which a portion of the banks of the river still bears. To these refugees, during the first year of their settlement, were given the same rations which were allowed the troops of the colony.

On the 5th of March, 1766, the town of New Orleans was thrown into a great state of excitement. The long expected Ulloa had arrived at last, and had landed with two companies of infantry commanded by Piernas. He was accompanied by Loyola as Commissary of War and Intendant, Gayarre, as Contador, or Comptroller, and Navarro, as Treasurer. Besides their respective attributions, Gayarre and Navarro were made joint commissioners with Loyola, to take possession of the colony, and to appraise all the objects belonging to the King of

France, which the King of Spain might think convenient to keep for his own account. The reception of Ulloa was respectful, but cold and sullen, betokening clearly the discontent of the population. Having been requested by the Superior Council to exhibit his powers, he refused, on the ground that he intended to postpone taking possession of the country, until the arrival of all the Spanish forces which he expected. He added that he had nothing to do with the Superior Council, which was nothing else than a civil tribunal, by which he could not possibly be called to any account; and that, with regard to the delivery of the province into his hands, he had to deal only with Governor Aubry, whom he recognized as the sole competent authority in that matter. Here was a bitter pill to swallow; it was the first but decided intimation to the Superior Council, that, henceforward, it was no longer to be, what it had been—one of the ruling powers of the colony. The members of that body had been used to believe that they were very great personages; and to be suddenly told by a new-comer, that he had not of them the same exalted opinion, which they themselves entertained, was gall and wormwood. Nothing can be more unforgiving than the wounded pride and self-love of petty functionaries; and there is no doubt but that the cavalier and unconciliating manner, in which the members of the Council thought they were treated by Ulloa, was one of the causes of subsequent events.

Ulloa, although he refused to show his powers, and to take formal possession of the colony, proceeded, however, to visit its different posts and settlements. At Natchitoches, particularly, he remained a considerable time, studying the locality, and making inquiries as to its facilities of communication with the Mexican provinces. He ordered a census to be made of the whole population of Louisiana, and the result was found to be: 1893 men able to carry arms, 1044 women, married or unmarried, 1375 male children, and 1240 of the other sex. Total, 5562. The blacks were about as numerous. But the population was somewhat reduced by an epidemic which prevailed in that year (1766), and which, it is said, closely resembled the disease now so well known here, under the name of yellow fever.

The monarch, whose subjects the inhabitants of Louisiana were destined to be, was far superior, as to the qualifications of a man and of a king, to the feeble and corrupt Louis XV. Charles III., who wore the crown of Spain and of the Indies, was the son of Philip V. and Elizabeth Farnèse, and was born in January, 1717.* Called to the succession of Tuscany, when the last of the Medici had died without leaving heirs to that illustrious name, Charles, before the dawn of adolescence had shaded his chin, appeared in Italy in 1730, at the head of the armies of his father, the Catholic King. Four years after, he invaded the kingdom of Naples, and made a triumphant entry in its noble capital, whose gates had been thrown open at the sight of the heroic bands of Spain. Proud of his son, Philip V. ceded to him all his rights to the kingdom of the two Sicilies. But the imperial troops of Germany were advancing, to wrest from the youthful warrior the fair prize he had grasped so boldly. The battle and victory of Bitonto secured to him the crown of which he was worthy, and the Duke of Montemar, who commanded the troops of his Catholic Majesty, received the title of Duke of Bitonto. After having firmly established his authority in the kingdom of Naples, Charles invaded Sicily, and, in less than one year, conquered the whole

* Biographie Universelle de Michaud.

island. Then, in 1735, he was recognized as King of the two Sicilies by Louis XV., and his ambassador was openly received at the court of that monarch. In 1738, the treaty of peace, signed at Vienna, left him the undisputed master of an Italian kingdom. He had well fought for, and deserved, the splendid acquisition. After having used the sword with distinguished valor, he knew how to wield the sceptre with moderation, and the wisdom and magnanimity of his administration won to him the deep attachment of his subjects.

War again broke out between the great continental powers of Europe, and Italy became, as for ages it had been, the devoted battle ground for the armies of France, Spain and Germany. Very naturally, Charles joined his forces to those of his father. When the jarring elements of strife are at work, England is never far off; and the English admiral Martin presented himself before Naples with a fleet. He threatened to bombard the city, if Charles did not bind himself to remain neutral and not to assist his father. The first impulse of the young King was to refuse the unnatural request. Martin drew his watch, and gave Charles one hour to determine, whether he would yield to the humiliating demand addressed to him, or see his capital battered down. Unfortunately, Naples was in so defenceless a state, that no resistance could be made; and Charles had to obey the stern laws of necessity. But he never forgot the insult, whilst he waited for better times. As soon as the English disappeared from his sight, he devoted all the means he could command, to shelter himself against the repetition of what had so humbled his proud spirit. When from the state of the fortifications he had erected and the implements of defence he had gathered, he thought he was no longer exposed to succumb, in his own palace, to the dictation of an English officer, he marched at the head of his troops to join those of his father, of which he was appointed commander-in-chief, jointly with the Duke of Modena. After some partial success, the combined armies of Spain and Naples were surprised in Velletri by the Prince of Lobkowitz, who commanded the Imperialists. Charles was very near being made prisoner; but the Spaniards speedily repaired the disorder into which they had been thrown, and, in their turn, charged with impetuosity the enemies, who had not known how to profit by their momentary advantage. They retrieved by prodigies of valor the negligence which had been so fatal to them, and the defeated Imperialists, in their flight, during which they were hotly pursued to some distance, abandoned a considerable number of cannons and flags, to those whom they had, on the first onset, driven away before them in confusion. After this campaign, Charles enjoyed, during fifteen years, the fruits of his good fortune and of his labors. He governed the Kingdom of Naples with the kindness and wisdom of a good and intelligent man, until the 10th of August, 1759, when being called to succeed, on the throne of Spain, his brother Ferdinand VI., he left the Kingdom of Naples to Ferdinand, his third son. Charles, finding himself at the head of a powerful nation, remembered Admiral Martin, and never failed to avail himself of every opportunity, to show the English that he had a tenacious memory. In 1761, he formed with Louis XV. the celebrated *family compact*, which guarantied the rights, and gathered up in close union all the forces, of the different branches of the house of Bourbon. He did not hesitate to join France in the two wars which she had to wage against England. That of 1762 was not favorable to the two allied powers; Spain lost Havana, twelve ships of the line, immense treasures, the Philippine Islands, and was completely foiled in the campaign which she attempted against Portugal, whose resistance was made effective by the assistance of the English. Charles was obliged to give up Florida in exchange for peace. The war of 1778 was followed by more satisfactory results. The French Duke of Crillon, the commander of the troops of his Catholic Majesty, took possession of Mahon, in 1781, and by the treaty of peace, Minorca and Florida were restored to Spain. Released from the struggle with so potent an enemy as England, Charles attempted to check the depredations and to punish the insolence of the pirates of Algiers. Count O'Reilly was intrusted with the command of that important expedition. This officer had military talents and zeal, which were admitted even by his enemies; but he was an Irishman by birth, and Spanish pride ill brooked that the services of a foreigner should be preferred to those of so many worthy sons of the land. The death of the Marquis of La Romana, who perished in a skirmish, in which he became the victim of his fiery imprudence, gave rise to unfounded suspicions and to seditious clamors. The temper and the situation of the army became such, that O'Reilly had to reembark it with precipitation. This expedition was as fatal to Charles III., as a similar one had been to Charles V. His only consolation was, to be able to say that he had not been there in person. Probably, if he had headed his army, his royal presence would have prevented the dissensions and jealousies which ruined the expedition.

This brief abstract of the events which marked the military career of Charles III., proves that it was not inglorious. But this prince showed himself still greater in the civil administration of his Kingdom. He carried into execution with indomitable perseverance the plans of useful reforms which he had conceived on ascending the throne. His was the noble conception to revive the energies of that ancient and once so powerful nation, and to rekindle the sacred light of the arts and sciences, which the Austrian dynasty of the monarchs of Spain had allowed to be extinguished. His ambition was, to be the Peter the Great of his nation. But his first operations produced a feeling of discontent, which soon ripened into violent opposition. The attachment of the Spanish people to their usages, to their prejudices, and above all, to their national costume, went, at the time, far beyond all that can be imagined and described. The Castilians, of all classes, were clad in black, and besides, in all seasons, were wrapped in cloaks up to their eyes; a large, broad brimmed hat was carried in such a way as to complete the concealment of their faces. This mysterious and gloomy costume not only shocked the sight and awakened apprehensions, but also, materially assisted felons in eluding the vigilance of the police. In imitation of the Russian reformer who had commanded his subjects to shave their chins, Charles III. ordered his to lay aside their cloaks and hats. Not so submissive the Spaniards were, as the Muscovite serfs. They revolted at what they thought to be a trespass on their rights, and an unwarrantable interference with their taste and comfort. The Wallon guards, who were on duty at the royal palace, were slaughtered by the populace; but they had made so obstinate a resistance, that they had given time to the King to fly to Aranjuez, where he collected fresh troops. This cloak and hat insurrection produced a ministerial change; the Count of Aranda was appointed President of the Council of Castile, and reestablished good order; the favorite minister of Charles, the Marquis of Squilace, an Italian by birth, was dismissed, as being odious to the populace and to the nobility, and a sort of compromise took place between the King and his people as to the hats and cloaks. To gratify their Sovereign, the people gave up their broad brimmed hats; but in return, to please his loyal subjects, the King had to tolerate the cloaks, provided they should be somewhat curtailed in their length and width. On the faith of these transactions, good harmony was restored, and the royal parent and his children were as loving as ever.

Many are the useful establishments and the public monuments which, at the present day, are to be traced up to the reign of Charles III. The high roads in Spain, the Custom House, and the Post Office building in Madrid, the works which have embellished that capital, and secured the health of its inhabitants, the Cabinet of Natural History, the Botanical Garden, the Academies of Painting and Drawing, the canal of Tudela, that of Madrid, abandoned since his death, and many other improvements, either originated with, or were perfected by him. He loved an upright and enlightened administration of justice, and he selected, with rare discrimination, his magistrates and public functionaries among the most virtuous and learned citizens. From those whom he once tried and found honest and capable, he never withdrew his confidence on any insidious delation or unfounded and vague accusations. The Counts of Florida Blanca and of Campomanes were raised to the first offices of the Kingdom from a state of obscurity; and, although they were rivals and hostile to each other, they both enjoyed, at the same time, the esteem of their Sovereign, who did not allow himself to be prejudiced by one against the other. Charles had the good sense of employing these two men, each in the department to which he was suited, and never permitted himself to be influenced by their passions. It is by such means that this prince succeeded in rousing Spain from the lethargy in which she had been so long plunged, since Philip III. Certainly, nothing but the energetic will of a despotic sovereign, could have stirred into action a nation benumbed in its faculties, concentrated within itself, and chilled into petrifaction. Obstacles of all sorts were to be conquered, and Charles did not shrink from the unpleasant task. We have of him some sayings, which describe perfectly the situation of Spain, the injustice of public opinion, and the turn of mind of that monarch. "My subjects," said he, "are like children who cry when cleansed." Whenever he heard of a love affair, a political intrigue, or a family quarrel, he used to ask: "What monk is there at the bottom of it?" He liked to speak of the dangers and fatigues he had undergone in war, and always treasured up faithfully the recollection of the least service which had been rendered him. The corps of royal Carabineers had distinguished itself in the campaigns of Italy. At Velletri, when Charles was in danger of being made prisoner, the Carabineers saved him. Years had elapsed since that event, when, one day, the Minister of War, proposing to him retrenchments and economical reforms in his military household, summoned up all his eloquence to demonstrate that the corps of Carabineers had a vicious organisation, and was more onerous than useful. Charles seemed not to have heard his remarks, and gave no answer. The Minister renewed his attacks, and spoke with more decision and pertinacity. The King who, all the while, was brooding over his anger, thundered out, "If any one dares again speak against my Carabineers, I will have him hung."

In 1759, when he took possession of the throne of Spain, he was surprised to see a grandee of the kingdom presenting himself to perform the functions of Great Chamberlain, which a gentleman of the name of Losada had been accustomed to discharge near his person, for many years past. " Where is Losada ?" cried out the King impatiently. The answer was : " Sire, Losada is not a grandee of Spain. The etiquette of the court requires that he who has the honor of serving your Majesty as Great Chamberlain, be invested with that dignity." " Well," said the King, " I make Losada a Duke. Let him come, and give me my shirt." He had, through the benevolence of his nature, retained almost all the servants of his predecessor, and, among others, a valet of the royal chamber, who continued to wait on him for seventeen years. One day, the King heard of his death. " God bless his soul," said he, " for an honest man he was ; although, since the first time I saw him at Barcelona, I never could bear him." Charles was the most methodical man of his kingdom, and could, in his actions, have challenged the regularity of a clock. From the 1st of January to the 31st of December, the precise hour for every occupation and every pleasure was set down and minutely observed. Years in advance, every Spaniard knew when the King would go to bed, when he would leave it, and the exact day when he would undertake a particular journey. He was a sort of almanac in flesh and blood, indicating the rising and setting of the sun. Charles was certainly not gifted with the brilliant qualities of a hero, but possessed a sound judgment, a wise firmness of mind, an excellent understanding, and above all, those qualifications which constitute a good and useful man. The Spaniards still cherish the memory of his paternal administration and of his private virtues. He died in Madrid, on the 14th of December, 1788, at the age of seventy-two, not without having foreseen the storms which threatened Europe and given judicious advice to his successor. When King of Naples, he had created the decoration of the order of St. Janvier, and when King of Spain, that of the Immaculate Conception or Charles III.

Such was the prince into whose hands Louisiana was to pass. He certainly paid her a great compliment, and gave her the measure of his regard, by the selection which he made of her first governor. He could hardly have sent her a more distinguished character than Don Antonio de Ulloa, who had made himself illustrious in the republic of letters, and who was one of the brightest ornaments of Spain in the eighteenth century, by his scientific labors and travels, and by his long and useful services as a naval officer and an administrator.

Antonio de Ulloa* was born in Seville, on the 12th of January, 1716. His family was already distinguished in the maritime annals of the country, and took care to fit him for their hereditary career, by making him go through the best course of studies. He entered the navy as a midshipman, in 1733, and he soon acquired a reputation which surpassed the hopes of his friends and family. The first commission with which he was intrusted, was to join the learned expedition concerted between the governments of Spain and France, to measure an arc of the meridian at the equator, which was an operation desired by the Academy of Sciences of Paris, in order to determine the configuration of the earth, and which was to be executed by three members of that body, Bouguer, La Condamine, and Godin.

It being thought that the province of Quito in Peru offered the equatorial station most favorable to that enterprise, which would be a long and a laborious one, it had been found necessary to apply to the Spanish government, to obtain leave for foreigners to penetrate into that rich country, as the pioneers of science. Spain

---

* Biographie Universelle de Michaud.

had always jealously guarded her provinces of America against foreign intrusion, and against the investigations of curiosity. But the friendship which then united the two courts, and a generous emulation in favor of science, prevailed on every other consideration. It was decided that two officers of the royal navy, capable of assisting the French academicians in their labors, should be sent with them for their protection, and to recommend them to the local authorities, as well as to share, in the name of their country, in the honor of that important operation. The King left the choice of the two officers to the Royal Academy of Midshipmen, and the young Antonio de Ulloa, who was hardly nineteen years old, was selected with another officer, named George Juan, who had acquired celebrity as a mathematician. Both worthily executed their commission, worked together with the greatest harmony, and kept themselves free from those bickerings and quarrels, which occurred among their French associates. On their return, thirteen years after their departure, and one year before the academicians of Paris, they published the results of that great expedition. George Juan, having more specially reserved to himself the digesting and editing of the geometrical, physical and astronomical observations, made either in common, or by each of them separately, published in 1748, at the cost of the Spanish government, his volume of " Observations," &c. Madrid, in 4to.; and a few months after, Ulloa published also at the cost of the King, the " Historical relation of a voyage made to South America, by order of the King, to measure some degrees of the meridian, and ascertain the true configuration and size of the earth, with divers astronomical and physical observations," &c. Madrid, 1748.

Departing with the grade of lieutenant of a ship of the line, on two vessels of war, one of which transported to Carthagena the new Viceroy of Peru, they awaited, during five months, in that city, the arrival of the French sloop, which, at last, brought Bouguer, La Condamine, and Godin. This long detention enabled them to make numerous observations on the natural history, the statistics of the country, and the manners of its inhabitants, which are fully set forth in the relation of Ulloa, who showed himself possessed of an observing, logical, and judicious mind. The members of the expedition, having thus been brought together, departed with a rich supply of mathematical instruments, and repaired to Quito by the way of Porto Bello, Panama, and Guayaquil. From the beginning of their trigonometrical labors, in June, 1736, to their completion, Ulloa never ceased contributing to them, with a zeal which elicited the praises of his colleagues; he participated in all the operations of Bouguer and La Condamine, whilst George Juan and Godin were engaged, on their side, in making separate calculations and pursuing a series of triangles. The geometrical measurements were completed, only after the lapse of four years, during which these distinguished men, willing to be the martyrs of science, were exposed to innumerable fatigues and perils, either by their long sojourning on snow-covered mountains, amidst dangerous precipices, or by their suddenly passing from those frozen regions to the burning temperature of the plains, or finally by their running foul of the ignorance or prejudices of the inhabitants of those regions, which came very near being fatal to the expedition, in 1739. Ulloa describes, in the most interesting manner, and with touching simplicity, all the sufferings which he and his companions had to endure. What is characteristic, is the indifference he shows in recording all that occurred to himself, and he almost omits to mention a very serious illness which brought him to the very verge of the grave, in one of the mountainous regions of that country. He illustrates the prejudices of the natives by several humorous anecdotes, and, among others, that of an Indian who, taking these learned men for magicians, fell on his knees before them, and supplicated them to reveal to him who had stolen his ass. Towards the end of September, 1740, when they were making astronomical observations, at one of the extremities of the arc of the meridian which had been measured, an order of the Viceroy of Peru obliged the two Spanish officers to proceed suddenly to Lima. War had just broken out between England and Spain, and Vice-Admiral Anson was threatening the coasts of the Spanish possessions. Ulloa and Juan were intrusted with the care of putting in a state of defence the sea-coast in the latitude of Lima and Calao. When this was executed, they were permitted to return to Quito, and resume their scientific labors. But soon after they had reached their destination, they were called to Guayaquil. The sacking of Payta by the English fleet had scattered terror far and wide. It is impossible to form an adequate idea of the fatigues attending their goings forward and backward, without knowing fully the difficulty of travelling through the mountains of Peru. In every trying circumstance in which they were placed, and whatever were the obstacles they had to overcome, Ulloa and Juan discharged their duties with a zeal and fortitude which cannot be too highly appreciated.

When they had provided for the safety of Guayaquil, only one of them was permitted to depart, and it was Ulloa who, although the season was extremely unfavorable to travelling, hastened back through every fatigue and danger to Quito. On entering that city, he met an order to return in all haste to Lima, whither he went with Juan, who joined him on the way. There they took the command of two frigates, to cruise on the coasts of Chili and of the island of Juan Fernandez. Fortunately, on the arrival of reinforcements, Ulloa and George Juan were permitted to resume their scientific mission at Quito, where, of all the French academicians, they found only Godin, with whom they observed the comet of 1744. At last, impatient for a return to Europe with the fruits of their labors, they embarked at Callao, each in one of two French ships, which were to go round Cape Horn on their way to Brest. These ships were separated in a stress of weather; and the one on which Ulloa was, overtook two French ships, with which she was navigating in concert, when they were attacked by English privateers, much superior to them in force. After very hard fighting, the two vessels, which had on board three millions of dollars, were captured, and Ulloa's ship escaped with difficulty. To avoid new dangers, it was thought necessary to proceed in a totally different direction, and the ship sailed towards North America. When she entered Louisbourg, at Cape Breton, all on board congratulated themselves on having escaped from so many dangers; but this feeling of exultation was not of long duration, and they were obliged to surrender to the English, who had just taken that town, and who had designedly kept hoisted up the French flag as a decoy. A prisoner of war, Ulloa was transported to England, where he was treated with much consideration. It is the privilege of the votary of science who has acquired celebrity, to excite universal sympathy. Kindred spirits he meets everywhere, who are linked to him by the freemasonry of learning. So it was with Ulloa, in whose favor many distinguished personages interested themselves, and, among others, the celebrated Vice-President of the

Royal Society of London, Martin Folkes. Through their protection, he soon recovered his liberty and papers. Martin Folkes presented him to his colleagues, and had him elected a member of the Society.

Bidding adieu to his English friends, he embarked for Lisbon, whence he proceeded to Madrid, where he arrived in 1746, at the commencement of the reign of Ferdinand VI. He met with the most flattering reception, and was made the Captain of a frigate and a commander in the order of St. James. To the relations of his voyage to, and observations in, South America, he joined an historical summary of the Peruvian monarchs, from Manco Capac, the first of them, to the latest kings of Spain and of the Indies. Shortly after, Ulloa travelled through a considerable part of Europe, by order of the King, and the information he gathered in his travels was happily applied to the service of the State and to the benefit of the nation.

During the remainder of his active career, Ulloa endeavored to conciliate his taste for study with the numerous commissions with which he was intrusted in the Naval department, and later, in the department of the Interior, where his learning was taxed for the improvement of the domestic industry of the nation. The superintendence of the quicksilver mine of Guancavelica, in Peru, was his reward; but the products of that mine had been greatly curtailed by the avarice and embezzlements of those who had the privilege of working it. Ulloa had the daring to denounce the depredations of some men in power, and the consequence was that he lost his place.

When Charles the Third ascended the throne, his able ministers, who showed great discriminating zeal and patriotism in bringing out all the native talents which Spain possessed, raised Ulloa to the grade of Commodore, and gave him the command of the fleet of the Indies. When, by the treaty of peace of 1762, Louisiana was ceded to Spain, Ulloa was appointed to take possession of that province, to govern it, and to organize, on a proper footing adapted to the wants of the country, the different branches of the Spanish administration. This was a difficult task, and one requiring both the knowledge of the world and the learned wisdom of the closet. Ulloa arrived at New Orleans, as we have seen, on the 5th of March, 1766, and we shall soon have to relate the events which preceded and followed his expulsion from that province.

In the intervals of his campaigns at sea, Ulloa used to correspond with all the men who had acquired celebrity by their learning, and was elected one of the associate members of the academies of Stockholm and Berlin. Since 1748, he had been one of the regular correspondents of the Academy of Sciences of Paris. In 1772, he published in Madrid, in 1 vol. in 4to., a collection of observations under this title: " Noticias Americanas, entretenimientos physico historicos sobre la America Meridional, y la Septentrional Oriental." In this work, he reviews the soil, the climate, the vegetable, animal, and mineral productions of those vast countries. His disquisitions on marine petrifactions, on the Indians, their manners, usages, antiquities, languages, and their probable origin, are full of interest, although some of his hypothetical remarks will hardly be sanctioned by the sobriety of logical deductions. In 1773, he presented to the Spanish ministry another valuable work on the naval forces of Europe and Africa. In 1778, he published, at Cadix, his observations at sea of the eclipse of the sun which took place in that year. They made known a singular fact, which, for some time, engaged the attention of all the astronomers. The author assures having seen, for one minute, during the eclipse of the sun, and to have caused to be seen by several other persons, a brilliant spot on the moon, which he considers to be a real hole through that planet. " According to my calculations," said the celebrated astronomer, Lalande, " that hole ought to be forty-five miles in depth, and three hundred and twenty-seven in length. But it cannot be looked upon as a volcano." In the judgment of the same Lalande, Antonio de Ulloa was one of the greatest promoters of astronomy in Spain, and it was particularly through his exertions that the observatory of Cadix was constructed. This brief sketch is sufficient to show what high grade Ulloa had attained in the hierarchy of the princes of science.

But Ulloa, although possessing in the most eminent degree the theory of navigation, did not rise above mediocrity in its practical application. He, at different times, commanded fleets without flattering results to his fame. He had reached, however, the grade of Lieutenant General of the royal navies of Spain, when he was ordered, in 1779, to cruise in the latitude of the Azore islands, to capture eight English vessels belonging to the India Company, and returning loaded with the wealth of Asia. He was next to proceed to Havana, where he was to be provided with additional forces, to attack the provinces of Florida. His orders were to break the seal of his letters of instructions only in a certain latitude ; but Ulloa, absorbed in astronomical observations, or some deep study, forgot to open his letters of instructions in time, and returned at the expiration of two months, after a useless cruise. He was accused of having allowed the eight English ships to pass without noticing them, and of having suffered a Spanish frigate and a merchant ship from Manilla to be captured within sight of his own fleet, without interfering. These were grave accusations, which caused his being arrested and brought, in 1780, before a court martial, which, it must be said, was convened at his own request. Either because the accusation was not proved, or because his superior merit and the eminent services he had rendered to his country, disposed his judges to be indulgent for a fault which had resulted from mere absence of mind—of a mind abstracted in the pursuit of science,—he was honorably acquitted, and retained his grade, titles, and decorations. But he ceased to be employed at sea; he served only as the Commander of maritime departments, and was director general by interim of the naval armies of Spain. In this capacity, he was intrusted with the examination of the students at the school of marine artillery of Cadix. Ulloa became also minister of the Junta General of Commerce and of the Mint, and died in the island of Leon, on the 3d of July, 1795, at the advanced age of eighty. Townsend, the English traveller, who had visited him in Cadix, eight years before, has left of him the following portrait:

"The Spaniard whose conversation interested me most, was Don Antonio de Ulloa. I found in him a true philosopher,* full of wit and learning, sprightly in his conversation, free and easy in his manners. He is of a small size, extremely thin, and bending under the weight of years; he was dressed like a farmer, and surrounded by his numerous children, the youngest of whom, two years old, was playing on his knees. In the room where he used to receive his visitors there could be seen, lying confusedly scattered, chairs, tables, trunks, boxes, books, papers, a bedstead, a printing press, umbrellas, articles of clothing, carpenter's tools, mathematical instruments, a barometer, a clock, weapons, paintings, mirrors, fossils, minerals, shells, a kettle, basins, broken

* In the absence of the original, this is a re-translation, from a French translation.

pitchers, American antiquities, silver ingots, and a curious mummy of the Canary islands." This at once gives a key to Ulloa's character. His heart must have been as amiable as his head was profoundly learned.

It is not solely by services rendered to the state, and by his superior acquirements in the highest departments of science, that Ulloa has left a name deservedly honored in his country. Spain owes to him the creation of the first cabinet of natural history, and the first laboratory of metallurgy it possessed; the conception of the canal of Old Castile, for navigation and irrigation, commenced under Charles III. and abandoned after the death of that monarch; the knowledge of platina and its properties; of electricity and artificial magnetism. It is he who perfected the art of engraving and printing in Spain; who directed the Spanish geographers of the time in the composition of a correct map of the Peninsula, who made known the advantages of the wool called *churla*, which resembles that of Canterbury in England; and the secret of manufacturing superfine cloth by mixing this wool with the merino wool. In order to demonstrate the advantages of his discovery, he established at Segovia, with the authorization and on the account of the king, a manufactory, out of which came cloths as superfine as any of those produced in foreign countries. Finally, it was on his earnest representations that young men were sent to different parts of Europe, to be instructed in the liberal and mechanical arts, which he wished to introduce into his own country. Such was the first Spanish Governor given to Louisiana, and well might the most refined and fastidious community have been proud of the choice.

The companions of Ulloa and his associates in power were not unworthy of their chief, and might, at least, have challenged comparison with any of the French rulers who preceded them in the colony.

Don Juan Joseph de Loyola, the commissary of war and military intendant, was, it is said, of the family which boasted of having produced Ignatio de Loyola, the celebrated native of the province of Guipuscoa—at first the noble cavalier, the brilliant courtier, the poet, the intrepid hero; at last, the saintly enthusiast, the extraordinary compound of piety and genius run mad; in a word, the originator of the most powerful association the world ever knew—the founder of the prodigious order of the Jesuits. Don Juan Joseph de Loyola was no unfit representative of the name he bore. He had the elegance of manners, the high breeding, and the knightly bravery of his namesake; nay, to make the resemblance stronger, and as it were in proof of the kindred blood he pretended to have in his veins, he seemed to have inherited, as an heirloom, the poetical mind, the heated imagination, and the religious enthusiasm which colored his life, which gleamed like a subdued fire under the crust of his most worldly actions, and marked him as an interesting object of study to the observer, and as a man of no ordinary stamp.

Don Estevan de Gayarre, the contador, or royal auditor and comptroller, was a younger son of a patrician house of the kingdom of Navarre, in Spain. At the age of nineteen, on the 1st of November, 1741, he had sought to better his fortunes by the chances of war, and by enlisting in the army. From 1742 to 1748, under the command of his Royal Highness Don Felipe, he served with distinction in Italy. In his first campaign in Piemont, he was in the engagements of Aygabel and St. André; in the second, he shared the dangers of the retreat through the defile of Lañell;* in the third, he

* This is the Spanish orthography of these names in the documents which I possess.

was at the attack of the trenches and batteries of Nice; at the storming of the citadels of Villa Franca and Montalban, in the county of Nice, which were built amidst almost inaccessible rocks, and which could be approached only through narrow gorges and yawning abysses, commanded by a formidable artillery, and defended by a numerous army occupying the neighboring heights. Villa Franca, which is perched on a rock rising up twelve hundred feet, and bristling with guns, was garrisoned by ten thousand Piemontese, assisted by the English Admiral Mathews, with a portion of the marines and gunners of his fleet. Both these fortresses, which seemed impregnable, were carried by a simultaneous assault of the French and Spaniards; the Piemontese were cut to pieces, and the English put to flight. Twenty thousand prisoners, among whom was the Count de La Suze, the commander-in-chief, one hundred and seven pieces of artillery, and the conquest of the county of Nice, were the results of these two glorious expeditions.

Don Estevan Gayarre was also at the taking of the Post of the Barricades, a passage of eighteen feet wide, between two mountains towering to the sky, protected by the Stura, which the king of Sardinia had turned from its natural course into the precipice, and by three intrenchments and a covered way; at the siege of Demont, a fortress built at an immense cost on the top of an isolated rock, in the midst of the valley of Stura, and which was taken on the 17th of August, 1744, after a siege of one month; at the siege of the fortified town of Coni, and at what the Spaniards called the *glorious battle of the Campo de la Madona del Holmo.* This battle, in which he was dangerously wounded, is the one which occurred under the walls of Coni, when the combined armies of Spain and France were attacked, on the

30th of September, 1744, by the king of Sardinia at the head of superior forces to those of his adversaries. The Piemontese, with a loss of five thousand men, were beaten back by the French and Spaniards, who fought with the generous emulation of old rivals in feats of arms and deeds of glory. In the campaign of the year 1747, in the county of Nice, Don Estevan Gayarre attracted the notice and obtained the commendation of his superiors, by the zeal and intelligence which he displayed in several perilous sallies and partial expeditions, which he led through the country.

On the 1st of December, 1751, after having served ten years, he applied to the court to be permitted to retire from the army; and considering, said his certificate of discharge,* that among the other causes of the step he had taken, was that of his having exhausted his patrimony, by his just inclination to, and love of, the military career, and, above all, the permanent injury done to his health by the serious wound he had received at the battle of the Madona del Holmo, in 1744. He was graciously granted what he sued for, and was strongly recommended to the royal favor. Probably in consequence of it, he obtained, in January, 1752, one of the most important offices at La Coruna, under Don Francisco de Mendoza y Sotomayor, general Contador, or auditor and comptroller, for the army and kingdom of Gallicia. On the 31st of May, 1765, he received a letter from the Marquis of Piedra Buena, asking him whether he would, as Contador, or royal comptroller of the province of Louisiana, accompany Ulloa to that colony. His answer to this proposition is remarkably in harmony with the reluctance which Spain felt to take possession of the territorial present tendered to her by

---

* La de haver extinguido su patrimonio en justa inclinacion y amor de las armas, y la principal, de la minoracion de su salud por la gravedad de su herida.

France, and is a characteristic specimen of the light in which was considered a mission to a country, not then of very good fame, and certainly of very little importance, at the time, in European estimation. In his reply to the Marquis of Piedra Buena, Don Estevan Gayarre says that, "after having had the honor of serving the king twenty-four years, his devotion and fealty to the royal person cannot permit him to refuse to discharge any duties, which his majesty might think of imposing upon him." But, on signifying his acceptance to the Marquis of Piedra Buena, he dwells upon the merit which he thinks he deserves by it, and stipulates that his going to America must be understood as not interfering with his promotion in the Peninsula. On the 10th of June, 1765, he was finally appointed by the king: *Contador princpial del Ministerio de Guerra y Real Hacienda*, in the province of Louisiana. Thus far go the public documents concerning this gentleman. There are others of a private nature, testifying to his many virtues, to the excellence of his mind, and showing that, in those qualities which adorn the soul, he could hardly be excelled. He possessed, in an eminent degree, all the noble traits of character which distinguish the healthy and hardy race of mountaineers, among whom he was born, in the valley of Roncal in Navarre, amidst the impressive scenery of the Pyrennean heights. To those qualifications he owed, no doubt, the many testimonials of respect and esteem he received, in the different situations in which he was placed, during the course of a long life vouchsafed to him by providence.

Don Martin Navarro, the treasurer, represented among his colleagues the democratic element, which, in later days, was to exercise so powerful an influence over the destinies of mankind. He was the son of a poor tavern-keeper, and had risen, by dint of industry, perseverance, and address. Shrewd, active, and honest, he deserved to be trusted; and being withal a boon companion, and skilful in the ways of the world, he had those qualifications which mollify envy, conciliate opposition, and render smooth and easy the path to success. Like water, which seeks its level, his talents and acquirements had, by slow degrees, raised him to the position in society which was his due.

Such were the men, who, in 1766, had come, in the name of Charles III., king of Spain, and of the Indies, to take possession of the country ceded to him in 1762.

FOURTH LECTURE.

ULLOA'S SALARY—HIS INSTRUCTIONS—HIS EFFORTS TO KEEP UP THE DEPRECIATED FRENCH PAPER MONEY—THESE EFFORTS ARE COUNTERACTED BY THE COLONISTS—REFUSAL OF THE FRENCH TROOPS TO PASS INTO THE SERVICE OF SPAIN—CAUSES FOR WHICH ULLOA DOES NOT TAKE FORMAL POSSESSION OF THE COLONY—HIS IMPRESSIONS, UNFAVORABLE TO THE POPULATION—FRANCE REFUSES TO PAY THE EXPENSES OF THE COLONY SINCE MARCH, 1766—THEY ARE ASSUMED BY THE SPANISH GOVERNMENT—AUBRY RETAINS THE NOMINAL COMMAND OF THE COLONY, BUT GOVERNS ACCORDING TO ULLOA'S DICTATES—SPANISH COMMERCIAL DECREE, ON THE 6TH OF MAY, 1766—APPOINTMENT OF FRENCH COMMISSARIES TO PURCHASE ARTICLES OF EXPORTATION—ULLOA VISITS THE SEVERAL POSTS AND SETTLEMENTS—OTHER SPANISH DECREE OF COMMERCE IN SEPTEMBER, 1766—EFFECTS OF THAT DECREE—REMONSTRANCES OF THE COLONISTS AGAINST IT—ITS EXECUTION, SUSPENDED BY AUBRY—FOUCAULT'S LETTER TO HIS GOVERNMENT ON THE SUBJECT—THE COLONISTS ARE UNDER THE IMPRESSION THAT THEIR ANCIENT RIGHTS AND PRIVILEGES ARE SECURED UNDER THE TREATY OF CESSION—ULLOA SOJOURNS SEVEN MONTHS AT THE BALIZE—HIS MARRIAGE WITH THE MARCHIONESS OF ABRADO—AUBRY'S DESCRIPTION OF ULLOA'S CHARACTER—COMMUNICATION OF THE MARQUIS OF GRIMALDI TO THE COUNT OF FUENTES ON SPAIN'S DELAY TO TAKE POSSESSION OF LOUISIANA—RETURN OF JEAN MILHET, THE DELEGATE OF THE COLONISTS TO FRANCE—SIGNS OF HOSTILITY TO THE SPANIARDS—INTENSE COLD IN 1768—INCREASE OF EXCITEMENT—ULLOA'S TASTES, HABITS, AND DISPOSITIONS—HIS WIFE GIVES OFFENCE—AUBRY'S OBSERVATIONS ON HIS OWN EXTRAORDINARY POSITION—CONSPIRACY AGAINST THE SPANIARDS—PROCEEDINGS OF THE CONSPIRATORS—CHARACTER OF LAFRENIERE, THE KING'S ATTORNEY GENERAL—THE CONSPIRATORS TAKE POSSESSION OF NEW ORLEANS AT THE HEAD OF THE ACADIANS AND GERMANS—GENERAL INSURRECTION—AUBRY'S CONDUCT—ULLOA RETIRES ON BOARD OF THE SPANISH FRIGATE—LOYOLA, GAYARRE, NAVARRO, AND THE OTHER SPANIARDS, ON THE POINT OF BEING EXTERMINATED—THE COLONISTS DEMAND OF THE SUPERIOR COUNCIL THE EXPULSION OF THE SPANIARDS—SPEECH OF LAFRENIERE IN THE COUNCIL—DECREE OF THE COUNCIL AGAINST ULLOA, GAYARRE, LOYOLA, AND NAVARRO—AUBRY'S PROTEST AGAINST IT—OPINION EMITTED BY FOUCAULT IN THE COUNCIL—DINNER AT FOUCAULT'S HOUSE—THE COUNCIL VISITS THE INSURGENTS IN A BODY—TUMULTUOUS REJOICINGS OF THE PEOPLE—REFLECTIONS.

THE annual salary allowed to Don Antonio de Ulloa, as governor, in 1766, of a colony of ten thousand whites and blacks, was $6000. The same sum is granted, in 1851, as a sufficient remuneration for his services, to the present governor of Louisiana, with a population of more than 500,000 souls. Considering the difference of circumstances, and of the relative value of money at that time and in our days, it cannot but be seen that there was, in reality, a striking difference between the two salaries. Under the French government, the salary of the governor had risen, from two thousand dollars given to Bienville, to ten thousand allowed to the Marquis of Vaudreuil.

Acting with the usual benevolence which formed one of the well known features of his character, and taking into consideration the habits, customs, prejudices, wants, and wishes of his new subjects, Charles III. had given to Ulloa the following instructions :

"I have resolved that, in that new acquisition, there be no change in the administration of its government, and therefore, that it be not subjected to the laws and usages which are observed in my American dominions, from which it is a distinct colony, and with which it is to have no commerce. It is my will that it be independent of the ministry of the Indies (ministerio de Indias), of its council, and of the other tribunals annexed to it ; and that all which may be relative to that colony, shall pass through the Ministry of State (ministerio de Estado), and that you communicate to me, through that channel alone, whatever may be appertaining to your government."

It will be recollected, that there were in the colony seven millions of paper currency, which had been issued by the French government. When the rumor spread that the Spaniards were coming up the river, among the other causes of consternation, was the uncertainty existing as to that currency. Would the Spanish government reject it altogether? Would it be suppressed in private transactions? Or would the new government step into the place of the old, and assume its obligations? In that case, would the paper currency be redeemed at par, or only at the discount of 75 per cent., which the French government had established as the legal amount of its depreciation, although, in fact, in the common run of business among individuals, four dollars in that paper currency represented only one dollar in specie. So intense became the excitement on the subject, that, on the very day of Ulloa's arrival, the intendant commissary Foucault, thought himself justified, in his first interview with the Spanish governor, to lay before him the apprehensions of the colonists. Ulloa returned the gracious answer, that he perfectly understood the distress which would result from the suppression of that currency, and that, in order to keep it in circulation until he received instructions to stop it by its conversion into some other currency, he would, immediately after having taken possession of the colony, order that the paper issued by the French government be received as well among the Spaniards as among the French, at the rate of 75 per cent., which was the rate of depreciation acknowledged by the government of France. Aubry and Foucault hastened to make public this liberal declaration. But the colonists were not satisfied, and clamored that the paper ought to be taken at par.

So anxious was Ulloa to conciliate those over whose destinies he had come to preside, that, having been informed of their complaints, he resolved, in order to put an end to their discontent, to show them that his intention was that the Spaniards' should fare no better than the colonists. To accomplish this object, he bought with dollars, at a discount of seventy-five per cent., all the paper he could get in the market, and tendered it to the Spanish troops, in discharge of one-third of their pay. But these troops obstinately refused to receive it, and Ulloa found himself opposed in this scheme, both by the French and the Spaniards. The inhabitants of Louisiana, who were in the habit of losing three dollars in four of the paper currency, in meeting the current expenses of life, and who had been eager to furnish the French government with as much of it as it had chosen to redeem at seventy-five per cent., refused to part with it on the same terms when offered by Ulloa; and although it was to please them and to show his impartiality, that this functionary was attempting to give it in payment to his troops, yet it was with considerable difficulty that he could procure the small quantity which he had tendered to his troops, and at which they had scouted. The colonists gave as a reason, that the king of France would, if Louisiana had not been transferred to Spain, have called in all his paper at par, and that his Catholic Majesty was bound to do the same; they further pretended, that although the colony had ceased to belong to the most Christian king, yet that, true to the plighted faith of his royal word, he would pay to the last cent the full amount of the depreciated paper. But the whole financial history of the colony gave the most emphatic contradiction to these assertions, and the pretensions of the colonists were provokingly unjust and unreasonable. They originated from the desire of throwing every obstacle in the way of the new government, and this was the true reason why Ulloa's liberality met with so singular a return. This was the first trial which the philosophy of the man of science had to undergo in Louisiana; and it is not unfair to suppose that he came to the conclusion, that he had to deal with a very intractable set of people.

Another cause of irritation for the Spaniards soon

DIFFICULTY WITH THE FRENCH TROOPS. 161

followed. France, in order to induce Charles III. to take charge of the burdensome colony of Louisiana, and in order to soften the prospect of the fruitless disbursements with which he was threatened, in case of his accepting the donation pressed upon him, had represented to that monarch that it would not be necessary for Spain to go to the immediate expense of transporting troops, ammunition, &c., to that colony; and had promised that the three hundred men of infantry she had in Louisiana would remain there at the service of his Catholic Majesty, as long as he pleased to retain them. This was the cause of Ulloa's having come only with ninety men to take possession of the province. But the French troops, having for some time past been entitled to their discharge, peremptorily refused to pass into the service of Spain. It was in vain that Aubry, Ulloa, and Foucault assured them that their engagement would not be of long duration, because troops were expected from the Peninsula; it was in vain they were informed that the wish of their king was that they should so enlist, and that a promise to that effect had been made by his most Christian Majesty; it was in vain that their officers, at least ostensibly, urged them to continue to be on military duty under the Spanish banner. They answered that their time was out; that they were willing, however, not to avail themselves of their right to be discharged, but that it was a sacrifice which they would undergo only to serve their legitimate king under the national flag. Aubry convened all the French officers, laid before them the instructions which he had received from his government, to put the military forces of the colony at the disposal of the Spanish governor, and consulted them on the practicability of coercing the troops into the service of Spain; but the officers unanimously declared that the attempt would be exceedingly dangerous. Such being the state of affairs, Ulloa gave up all idea of taking possession of the colony for the present; rented, at the extremity of the town, some houses, in which he lodged his two companies of foot, and sent immediate information to his government of the circumstances in which he was placed.

The pay of the Spanish soldiers in Havana was thirty-five livres per month; but Ulloa, on his arrival in Louisiana, reduced to seven livres a month the pay of the ninety men he had taken at that city, on his way to New Orleans. This was the pay of the French soldiers in Louisiana, and Ulloa had, no doubt, taken this step with a good intention—that of putting the Spanish troops on the same footing with the French, and of preventing any invidious comparison. But it was a stroke of bad policy; it was an act of injustice to the Spanish troops, who became discontented; and it was wanting in liberality to the French, who railed at the ill-timed economy. Probably if Ulloa had raised the French pay of seven livres to the Spanish pay of thirty-five per month, the temptation to enlist would have been so great, that the aversion of the French would have yielded to the allurement tendered to them. Ulloa's course, on this occasion, must certainly be blamed, unless he acted under special instructions.

These were the difficulties he met on the threshold, and they produced on him very unfavorable impressions, to which other circumstances had contributed to give a deeper shade. The influence of physical and external objects, even on the strongest mind, is well known; and it is not therefore astonishing that the gloomy scenery of the Balize, of the heavily timbered and uncultivated banks of the Mississippi, as well as the

WRETCHED CONDITION OF LOUISIANA. 163

miserable appearance of the hamlet of New Orleans, which then numbered no more than three thousand inhabitants of all color and condition, should not have predisposed in favor of Louisiana a man who had revelled, for so many years, amidst the most gorgeous productions of nature and art in Spain, in Peru, and many other parts of the earth. On the 5th of March, when he landed at New Orleans, it was in the midst of a storm, through which the new comers saw, for the first time, the capital of the province lately added to the dominions of the Catholic King, and its aspect looked dismal enough. The inhabitants frowned upon the representative of the majesty of Spain; the French troops spurned the idea of serving under the proud flag of Castile, in spite of the assurance given by their king, that their assistance would be secured to the Spaniards, in taking possession of the ceded territory. The French government had, therefore, in the opinion of the Spaniards, been unfaithful to, or unmindful of, its engagements. It was negligence, or breach of faith, and it was resented as such by those whom it had placed in a position full of difficulties.

It must be admitted, and it is abundantly proved by the despatches of the highest functionaries, as well as by the documents containing the written complaints of the inhabitants, that Louisiana had been, since its foundation, that is for sixty-six years, in a starving condition; that being deficient in the knowledge of its internal resources, or rather in energy or will to develop them, it had been almost entirely dependent, for its very food and for everything else, on the mother country, which could no longer supply its wants; and that the tenure by which the French king held this possession was so precarious and burdensome, that he had pressed the acceptance of it, as a present, on the

Spanish king, who had hesitated to receive the onerous donation, and had consented to it merely to oblige *his beloved cousin of France*. Now when the Spaniards had come, at the urgent invitation of France; when they certainly could not make matters worse for the colonists, than they had been so far; when, on the contrary, there was the prospect of a change for the better; when the dollars of Spain were to be introduced, instead of the stamped paper rags which had constituted the currency of the country; when Ulloa, on the very day of his arrival, had hastened to relieve the uneasiness of the inhabitants, by promising to keep up the present rate of the depreciated paper, such as it had been fixed by France; when he had made known his instructions, that no changes would take place in the civil organization, in the laws, customs, and usages of the province; when he had professed in his letter from Havana to the Superior Council, and since, in repeated verbal declarations, that it was both his duty and his most anxious wish to do all in his power to be useful and agreeable to the people; when to remove national prejudices, he had put the Spanish troops on the footing of the French, with regard to their pay, it surely was passing strange, as he thought, that under these circumstances he and his companions should be guests so unwelcome, nay, should meet with so much and so ill concealed hostility. He felt it keenly.

Ulloa, a few days after his arrival, had sought information from Aubry, as to the resources, the wants, and the character of the province he had come to govern. From certain expressions, which perhaps had dropped imprudently from the French governor, and from a perusal of the documents to which he was allowed access, Ulloa drew conclusions, which may explain his subsequent acts, and some of the reproaches

CHARACTER OF THE INHABITANTS. 165

to which they gave rise. He saw that, from the earliest day of the existence of the colony, from Lamothe Cadillac to D'Abbadie, almost all its governors and high dignitaries had represented its inhabitants as a set of reprobates, infected with the *rebellious spirit of republicanism;* that it had been, without interruption, the prey of intestine dissensions, one half of the functionaries and of the population having hardly ever ceased to be arrayed against the other; and that they agreed only in one thing—that is, in accusing each other of the most shameless corruption and hateful malfeasances. Thus he found on record, under the hand and seal of his predecessors, through a long series of years, that Louisiana was, in the words of D'Abbadie, *a chaos of iniquity and discord;* and Aubry, the last of the French rulers, far from having said one word in extenuation of the sweeping condemnation, had given Ulloa to understand, that between the perversity and the insubordination which prevailed in the past, and that which existed in the present, there was no perceptible difference. As if this was not enough, Kerlerec, who was still detained in the Bastile, wrote to Ulloa a letter, in which he gave him a frightful picture of Louisiana, which he had administered ten years, and he concluded, saying: *From the bottom of my heart I pity you for having been sent to such a country!* The Superior Council, the king's attorney general, and others, who, by their offices, their rank, or their wealth, occupied a high position, had those enemies whom men, under such circumstances, generally meet in their path, and who are generated either by envy, or by the resentment resulting from the existence of real or supposed wrongs. These and other malcontents, who are always to be found in every community, poured also their denunciations into the ears of Ulloa, upon whose mind and temper it is easy to conceive the effect produced by these informations, coupled with what he had seen and experienced since his arrival.

If Ulloa could not take possession of the colony, for the causes already known, the French authorities had no longer the means of carrying on the old government, because they had been informed by the French ministry, that their drafts on the Treasury of France, for colonial expenses, would no longer be accepted. Not only were they not permitted to issue any further drafts, but, also, even those they had given to meet the expenses of the years 1763, 1764, 1765, had been kept in abeyance by the French government, on the ground that the province had become Spanish since the very day of the cession, although the Spaniards had delayed taking possession; and that the French had only administered as trustees, on the account and for the benefit of Spain; wherefore, that power was bound to pay all the expenses made by the French authorities. To relieve the officers of his Most Christian Majesty from their embarrassments, and the colony from the state of misery to which it had been reduced by this decision of the French court, Ulloa agreed to loan to Foucault the money necessary to discharge some of the most pressing obligations contracted by the French government before his coming to the colony, and assumed to take for the account of Spain all the expenses of the administration since the 5th of March 1766, when he had landed at New Orleans. Governor Aubry and the Intendant Commissary Foucault greedily assented to this proposition, and all the public functionaries and the troops, as well as the rations given to the Acadians, and all the other expenses, were provided for out of the Spanish treasury, as if Ulloa had taken formal possession. It was further understood that, considering that the French troops refused to obey the Spanish governor, Aubry would remain the apparent and nominal chief of the colony, but would govern according to the dictates of Ulloa. This expedient having been hit upon, the wheels of the government, which had threatened to stop, resumed their rotation. Ulloa commanded, and Aubry faithfully executed; the one was the head, and the other the arm. The leaders of the party opposed to the Spaniards set up a cry of indignation, at what they called a shameful compromise, a slavish surrender of the dignity and independence of their nation, in the person of the French governor. But the middle course adopted by the French and Spanish authorities seems to have been the wisest, nay, the only one that could have been followed. What else could have been done? Ulloa held the purse, and Aubry the sword. Without some compromise between the two, it is evident that no government could have subsisted.

On the 6th of May, the Spanish government issued a decree permitting, by a special favor, a direct commerce between the French colonies and its American possessions, from which, on the fulfilment of certain formalities, cattle and grains might be exported, provided it should be in Spanish ships from Caraccas. To prevent smuggling and other frauds, there was to be a port designated in every province, where two French commissaries were to reside, and be authorized to purchase the articles allowed to be exported. There was a duty of five per cent. to be paid on all exportations. From Louisiana, lumber, rice, corn, and other productions of the soil, were permitted to be exported. Favre d'Aunoy and Villars were appointed French commissaries at New Orleans, with a salary of 4000 livres, or 800 dollars, each.

After having made this decree public, Ulloa departed to visit the several posts and settlements. In relation to those establishments, Captain Pitman, in his work, published in London in 1770, on the European settlements on the Mississippi, relates an anecdote illustrative of the state of things and manners existing at the time. "This settlement (Opelousas) was made," said he, "under the direction of Mons. D'Abbadie, in the year 1763, and was governed by a French officer, named Pélerin, till the year 1767, when the inhabitants, who had been oppressed by the tyranny which has been always exerted by officers of that nation commanding outposts, complained to Don Antonio de Ulloa and Mons. Aubry, accusing him (Pélerin) also of sacrilege, he having forcibly taken possession of the plate destined to the use of the altar, and used it at his own table, under pretence of keeping it in security. This worked his ruin more effectually than his ill treatment of the inhabitants, and he was threatened with excommunication. However, he was punished by undergoing severe penances enjoined by the priests, and rendered incapable, by a sentence of a court martial of French officers, of any employment military or civil. The government of this settlement was afterwards vested in a magistrate to be chosen annually by the inhabitants from among themselves. One company of militia was also raised for the defence of the establishment, and the officers received pay from the Spanish government."

On the 6th and 7th of September, a score of soldiers, with fixed bayonets, and preceded by a drum, whose solemn and loud beating attracted the attention and excited the anger of the inhabitants, paraded the streets of New Orleans, and proclaimed, by the order of Aubry, an ordinance, which had been dictated by Ulloa, in conformity with the instructions he had received from Spain. It contained commercial regulations; and among others the following :—French ships had leave to bring from Martinique and St. Domingo wine, flour, and other supplies, provided they carried back in return the lumber and other productions of the colony. Passports were to be given to French ships exporting from the kingdom of France the merchandise and other supplies necessary to Louisiana; but "whereas," said the ordinance, "these permissions have been granted only with a view to benefit the inhabitants of the colony; and whereas the merchants have asked for their goods, and particularly for their wines, an extraordinary price, and have refused to receive in payment any other currency than dollars, which pretension is very prejudicial to the inhabitants; now in consequence of the orders of his Catholic Majesty, addressed to Mr. de Ulloa, and by him communicated to us, we, Philip Aubry, &c., &c., have decreed that all captains coming from St. Domingo, as well as from France, and provided with a passport from his excellency, the secretary of state of his Catholic Majesty (for otherwise they would not be admitted into the colony), shall be bound, on their arrival, to present themselves to Mr. de Ulloa, with their bills of lading and passports, and are prohibited from unloading any portion of their goods without, beforehand, obtaining his permission, in writing, at the bottom of their passports or bills of lading; and the agents for those goods are also ordered to present themselves before Mr. de Ulloa, and to furnish him with a note indicating the price at which they intend to sell their goods, which goods shall be examined and appraised by impartial and intelligent persons residing in the colony; and should the prices demanded be excessive, the owners of the goods shall not be allowed to sell them here, and shall be obliged to go to another market. The merchants shall be bound to receive the currency of the country in payment for their goods, and to take one-third of their return cargo in lumber and other productions of the colony."

A sudden jar in a beehive would not have produced more buzzing and stirring than did this ordinance in New Orleans. Although it seems to have been framed in the interest of the consumers, yet it certainly was a severe blow to the importers, and they resented it as such. On the 8th of September, two days after its promulgation, the merchants of New Orleans, in a body, presented to the Superior Council, through the attorney general, Lafrénière, a petition, in which they begged that the execution of Aubry's decree be suspended, until they should be heard on the subject, and sued for the grant of a delay, to prepare their remonstrances, which were submitted to the council on the 12th; and also all the captains of ships in the colony presented a document of the same nature.

The remonstrances of the merchants and captains were founded on the belief of the existence of certain restrictions imposed on the government of Spain by France, when she ceded Louisiana. The commissary Foucault seemed to have been himself under a similar impression; for on the 29th of September, he wrote to the minister of the marine department: " It has not been the intention of his majesty, on making the cession, to strip, for the benefit of Spain, his loyal subjects of the privileges and exemptions which they had always enjoyed. I beg your excellency to transmit to us the necessary orders, to confirm the subjects of the king in the belief that they have suffered no diminution of the advantages granted to them by his majesty."

DOUBTS AS TO THE ACT OF CESSION. 171

The petitions laid before the council were not acted upon. A verbal declaration made by Aubry, that, on reflection, he would suspend the execution of his ordinance, was considered by that body as sufficient for the time. " But," said Foucault, in one of his despatches, " the revocation of the ordinance not having been made in due form, gives no security. Several persons have written to the other colonies, to suspend all shipments to this one. For several months past there have come but few French ships, and none belonging to the English. These last had always been of great assistance, by furnishing us with flour, of which their cargoes were generally composed; and as my supplies are very limited, I shall be reduced to the necessity of giving nothing but rice to the troops, and to the other persons entitled to rations."

It seems as if nothing could convince the colonists that the cession of Louisiana to Spain was serious and conclusive. Yet they must have been prepared for it, by the transmission of half of the territory to the English, who had already taken final possession. Would France have abandoned so rich a portion of her domain, if she had not determined to part with the rest? Was it not to the knowledge of all, that the French government had refused to accept the drafts issued for the expenses of the colony during the years 1763, 1764, 1765, on the ground that those expenses were to be paid by Spain? Was not then the cession an accomplished fact, a bonâ fide transaction; and therefore was not France holding Louisiana only as a mere trustee, until the new owner should take possession?

It is evident that the colonists were bent upon giving to the king's letter to D'Abbadie much more importance than it really had, and looked upon it as a sort of

Magna Charta, binding on the king of Spain, whilst it could have no such effect. When the king of France, informing the inhabitants of Louisiana that he had placed them under the domination of Spain, told them that he hoped that his Catholic Majesty would maintain them in the enjoyment of all their rights and privileges, and would make no innovation in the order of things to which they were accustomed, and in the laws to which they had always been subjected, it is apparent that he had no other object than that of gilding the bitter pill which they had to swallow. Besides, the colonists had been made acquainted with the acts of donation and acceptation, and the mere perusal of those documents ought to have convinced them that the cession was without reserve and condition. The very letter on which they were basing their pretensions and remonstrances had been addressed by the French king to one of his own officers, after the unconditional alienation of the colony. The King of Spain was not a party to that instrument, and could not even be supposed to know of its existence. After all, had it been officially communicated to him, it contained merely the expression of wishes on the part of the King of France, which the King of Spain might or might not take into consideration. Those wishes could not be construed into imposing any binding obligation on the Spanish government, and therefore could not constitute rights, of which the colonists could avail themselves. Nevertheless, although they could not claim anything of *right, and in law,* by virtue of the French king's letter to D'Abbadie, yet they might have relied on it, *in equity,* as having some moral force, when making an appeal to the generosity and magnanimity of the King of Spain.

Whilst the colonists were in that state of excitement,

lloa left New Orleans, and departed for the Balize, in e month of September. At first it was rumored that had gone to meet the Spanish troops which he pected; and this rumor kept alive the anxiety which d so long agitated the colony. But when October d November had elapsed, the people began to onder at what might detain the Spanish governor in e dismal spot to which he had retired. The month December came on with its freezing northern blasts, t did not drive away Ulloa back to New Orleans, in arch of more comfortable quarters. January and ebruary swept by with their dreary train of howling orms, and sharp edged cold, and piercing sleet, con-lsing the broad bosom of the Mexican gulf; and yet seemed that a spell kept Ulloa rooted, in the midst of hat, to every other, must have looked as the worst ode on earth. At a loss for discovering a motive, fficiently strong to warrant so strange a conduct on e part of the unpopular Spaniard, the colonists came the settled conviction, that the hatred he had con-ived for them was such, that rather than live among em, and purposely to show his feelings, he had taken e step which astonished them so much, and their sentment rose in proportion to the enmity which they pposed to exist against them.

Loyola, Gayarre, and Navarro had, alternately and ccessively, visited their chief at the Balize, and, henever they returned to New Orleans, earnest tempts were made to draw from them some informa-on as to the motives, the feelings, and the plans of lloa. But these officers had answered in a manner hich had parried and silenced all inquiry. Aubry mself paid a visit to Ulloa at the Balize. Ulloa then oposed to him that he, Ulloa, should take possession the colony at the Balize, and that the French flag be withdrawn, to be succeeded by the Spanish flag. This proposition surprised and embarrassed Aubry, who observed that the inhabitants, and even the strangers who were in the colony, would be astonished if such an out of the way place were chosen for the theatre of so important a ceremony. He remonstrated that it was proper that it should be performed with all the requisite pomp and dignity in the capital itself, and in the presence of all the inhabitants, who would come to take their oath of allegiance, and who would assure him of their inviolable fidelity to the service of his Catholic Majesty. But Ulloa persisted in his proposition, and although it seemed singular to Aubry, this officer, after some difficulties, finally consented to it. Accordingly, in the evening, an instrument was drawn in writing, by which Aubry declared that he had delivered up the colony to Ulloa, but retained its government, until the arrival of the Spanish troops. This document was signed by these two high functionaries. However, on the next morning, which was the time fixed for the formal taking possession of Louisiana by the Spaniards, Ulloa declared that he had reflected during the night on what had been done the day previous, and that he now thought that it would be better to postpone the contemplated ceremony, until the arrival of the Spanish troops; but that although the engagement they had concluded together had not been completed, yet he would send a copy of the document they had signed to his court, and that Aubry might do the same with regard to his government, should he deem it necessary. Two days after, on Aubry's preparing to return to New Orleans, Ulloa requested him to order the French commander at the Balize to pull down the French flag, and to hoist up the Spanish, whenever he, Ulloa, should desire it. Aubry acquiesced in this request, and went back to New Orleans; where, to the disquietude and indignation of the inhabitants, he related what had occurred between Ulloa and himself, and sent a detailed account of it to the French court.

But still the inquiry remained unanswered. What could have induced Ulloa, during so many months, and even in the depth of the winter, to lock himself up in a miserable shed at the Balize? It is true that when he left New Orleans for the mouth of the Mississippi, he had given it to be understood that his object was to establish a Spanish post at that locality; but that was, at farthest, the work of a few days, and it certainly was not an object of sufficient importance to detain the Spanish governor more than a very short time. Whatever his motives might be, people were amazed at the fortitude which Ulloa must have possessed to have remained so long at such a spot. How did he pass his time? How could he live there at all? How is it that he did not die, either from want of comfort and of company, or from weariness of spirit and despair? Was he mad? How could anybody but a prejudiced ascetic and iron willed Spaniard forego the conveniences of a home in New Orleans to perch, like a sea bird, during the wintry season, on the shaking piles driven into the mud and amidst the reeds of the mouth of the Mississippi? These were the reflections and inquiries.

But such a mind as that of Ulloa carried within itself a world of enjoyments, which few dreamed of. The man who, when in command of a fleet, became so abstracted in scientific pursuits as to forget the instructions which ordered him to capture eight English ships loaded with the wealth of India, could live apart from the world, forgetting, and perhaps happy to be forgotten. He had carried to the Balize his books, his manuscripts, his mathematical, astronomical, and other scientific instruments; and when surrounded by them he could bid defiance to the cares of office, to time itself, and to the other foul fiends which persecute mankind. His body was at the Balize, but his mind was diffused through space and through the universe. What did he care for the moaning reeds, for the shrieking winds, for the pitiless storms, for the roaring waves, for the tottering shelter, for the humble abode, for the dark face of nature? Could he not light it up and change it at will? Had he not the enchanter's wand? Had he not Aladdin's lamp? Was he confined by place or time? Could he not go back to the creation of the earth, study it in its primitive and almost chaotic state, and follow it up, through its infinite modifications, to its present organization? Could he not, when it suited his pleasure, live for days among the Persians, the Egyptians, the Greeks, and the Romans of old, and pursue through centuries the mighty revolutions of empires—the births, the struggles, and the deaths of nations? Could he not dive into the bowels of the earth, to revel in its mysteries? Could he not, on the wings of imagination, return to the gorgeous sceneries of Peru, or to the Arabian palaces of Spain? Could he not sail with the clouds, to mark the formation of lightning, and the other prodigies of the air? Were not the elements his companions, holding with him such converse as unfits one for the inane talk and flat communion of man? Towering far above the flight of the eagle, could he not ascend among the planets, to solve some great problem of the Deity, or

> To follow through the night the moving moon,
> The stars, and their developments?

Far happier, indeed, was he, the gifted son of science, in the solitude of the Balize than in New Orleans, where he was constantly dragged back from the heaven of the student to the petty miseries of earth, and recalled to a painful sense of his official duties and of their annoyances.

In the month of March, 1767, a piece of news reached New Orleans, which became the wonder of the day, and explained the enigma of Ulloa's sojourn at the Balize. For seven months the illustrious companion of La Condamine, the celebrated member and correspondent of so many learned academies had, with the romantic gallantry of the time of Ferdinand and Isabella, been awaiting the arrival of his bride, who was no less than the young and beautiful Marchioness of Abrado, one of the richest women of Peru, whom he had known when travelling in that country. Ulloa was then fifty-one years old, and possessed few of those attractions which, in the common estimate of the world, are supposed to be valued by the daughters of Eve. The good luck of the hated Spaniard excited envy, and gave fresh fuel to the hostility already existing against him. He was married at the Balize by his chaplain, and immediately after came up to New Orleans with his Peruvian wife.

It seems, from several of Aubry's despatches, that, in his opinion, the Spanish Governor was deficient in those qualifications, which endear a man to those over whom he is called to rule. In a communication of the 30th of March to his government, he said: "The Governor, whom his Catholic Majesty has sent here, is a man full of merit, of learning, and of talents, but, as an exception to the well known temperament of his nation, he is exceedingly hasty, and it seems to me, that he does not listen sufficiently to the representations addressed to him. It is a cause of discontent in those who have to deal with him.

"Considering the change of government which the colony has to undergo, I had wished that the officer sent to assume its command, had possessed the art of managing the public mind, and of gaining the hearts of the inhabitants. Men are not to be ruled with haughtiness and pride, with threats and punishments. Marks of kindness and benevolence, with judicious promises, would have been necessary, to reconcile the colonists to the change of dominion which has come upon them. This was the only course to be pursued, in order to win the affection of new subjects, who regret their former master. If the Spaniards do not act with mildness, and if they attempt to govern this colony like a Mexican Presidio,* most of the inhabitants will abandon their lands, to cross over to the English, who are on the opposite side, and who will neglect nothing to attract them. In this way, the Spanish portion of Louisiana, which had remarkably increased in population for the last few years, will soon become a desert." He concluded with informing the French Court, that the measures adopted by Ulloa, were not calculated to give popularity to the Spanish government.

In relation to the reproaches which were addressed to the Spaniards, as to their delaying so long the taking possession of Louisiana, and in relation to the expenses of the colony, which France wished Spain to pay, back to 1763, the Marquis of Grimaldi, who was a member of the cabinet of Madrid, wrote as follows, on the 11th of May, 1767, to the Count of Fuentes, the ambassador of Spain at Versailles:

"Ulloa arrived at New Orleans, only on the 5th of March, 1766. He did not then take possession, for the motives already explained. The Duke of Praslin† will

* A Presidio is both a Spanish and Mexican establishment, half barracks and half jail for refractory soldiers and unfortunate convicts.
† One of the French Ministers.

recollect that there were doubts on our part, as to the acceptation of the donation tendered by his most Christian Majesty. But, as the same reasons which had made France believe in the necessity of the cession, prompted Spain to accept it, the king gave it his assent, although it was well known that we were acquiring nothing, but an annual incumbrance of two hundred and fifty to three hundred thousand dollars, in consideration of a distant and negative utility—which is—that of possessing a country to prevent its being possessed by another nation.

"After all, there never was any stipulation, as to the time when Spain should take possession of Louisiana, and it ought not to be a matter of astonishment, if we have not been in a hurry to do so, because, if the colony is profitable, we have been the sufferers by the delay; and if not, what reason could we have to change our ordinary way of proceeding, and to run after an onerous burden? This, sir, is the cause of our surprise at the Duke of Praslin's insinuation, that we may be called upon to pay all the expenses of the colony, from 1763, when the cession was made. France would have as good grounds, to ask us to pay all her expenses in Louisiana since its foundation. What makes this pretension still more singular is, that, from the date of the cession to Ulloa's arrival at New Orleans, it is France which has had the absolute enjoyment of all the commercial advantages of that colony, which advantages she continues to enjoy to the present day, when the expenses of administration are no longer hers. Not a single Spanish vessel has as yet gone to Louisiana, with a cargo of merchandise. So far, that trade is monopolized by French ships. Would it be just that France, when reaping all the profits that the country can afford, should require of us to pay the expenses which had been incurred, before Spain had set her foot in that new possession?

"The King, always ready to avoid causing the least prejudice to the interests of the Most Christian King, his cousin, although knowing from the beginning, that the colony was an unprofitable charge, although Mr. de Ulloa was prevented from taking possession of it, through the want of co-operation of the French troops, on which we had been led to believe that we could rely, and although all the commerce of the colony has not ceased to be in the hands of the French, the King, I say, has declared, that he would assume all the expenses incurred since Ulloa's arrival."

Towards the end of the year 1767, Jean Milhet returned from France, whither, it will be recollected, he had been sent as a delegate by the colonists, in 1765, to remonstrate against the treaty of cession of Louisiana. His long absence had contributed to feed the hopes of his fellow citizens, who supposed that he would not have remained away for so long a time, if he had not seen a fair prospect of success in his mission. But when, on his return, he put to flight all the illusions with which they had deluded themselves, their exasperation reached its climax, and they did not fear to give to Ulloa an open manifestation of all their aversion for the Spanish domination.

Thus closed the year 1767. The 17th and 18th of January, 1768, were the two coldest days that had ever been known in Louisiana. All the orange trees perished, a second time, throughout the colony, as in 1748. In front of New Orleans, the river was frozen, on both sides, to thirty and forty feet from its banks.

The rigor of the season did not divert the attention of the inhabitants from the main calamity which was impending over them, and the thermometer of agitation was daily rising in the colony. There seemed to be a fixed determination, to construe into an offence everything that Ulloa could say or do. His manner of living, his tastes, his habits, his conversations, the most trivial occurrences in his household, were interpreted so as to keep up the excitement; and the estrangement between the people and their new governor had become complete. Ulloa was a man of the most amiable dispositions, but he was of that nervous, excitable temperament, which is said to be the attribute of those who consecrate their days and nights to study. He, who had associated with Newton, with Folkes, La Condamine, Voltaire, and the most distinguished men of the age, he, whose society was courted in the most polite circles of Europe, found himself suddenly thrown into an uncongenial atmosphere, and soon discovered that he was very little appreciated by those whom he had been sent to govern. His desire to please was met with cold repulse; his plans to benefit were not understood; the expression of his determination to correct certain abuses, was tortured into threats of oppression and into an invasion of established rights. Even the superiority of his high intellectual and moral qualifications, unfitted him to be the welcome guest which he otherwise might have been. His sense of rectitude revolted at many things, on which he commented perhaps in terms too severe, and he was thought to be harsh and cruel. Averse to convivialities and to worldly amusements, a man of spare habits, he had little in common, as to tastes and pursuits, with those among whom he had come to live; and as he allowed his indifference to fellowship with them to become visible, and, as in several instances, when surrounded by the magnates of the land, he had been observed to be moody and abstracted, he was reported to be supercilious and haughty. At times, when interrupted in his favorite studies, to listen to some petty grievance or some trivial application, he had received the intruder with some peevishness of manner, or with cutting sarcasm, and hence he was said to be ill tempered and prejudiced. Ulloa could not but be alive to the painfulness of the situation in which he was placed; and the injustice with which he was treated, made him perhaps unjust to others. He had been goaded into contempt for the colony and its inhabitants; and, conscious of his worth, he took very little pains to conceal, that he considered himself as being very much out of his element in Louisiana. Placed amidst a poor and illiterate community of a few thousand souls, in a country hardly redeemed from its primitive character of a wilderness, he had very little space left for the range of his great native and acquired powers of intellect. Therefore, he may well be supposed to have felt the agonies of a mind, used to expansion without limits, then suddenly confined within the narrowest possible space, and to have realized the existence of the fair spirit of the air, which, as we read of in fairy tales, a hostile magician had corked up in a bottle. Hence, he was soured into discontent and lived in retirement waiting for better times.

But to those who frequented his house, as retainers or friends, he showed himself to the best advantage, and excited their warmest admiration. Three times a week, he threw open his saloons, where, about the same visitors, few in number, used to assemble. There was not above a score of the colonists and of the French officers, who ventured to attend on these occasions. They were those who did not fear to abstain from showing hostility to the Spanish Governor, and who had thereby made themselves obnoxious to the majority of the inhabitants, and to their brother officers, who pursued a different course. Thus Aubry, Bellevue, Vaugine, Roche, Populus de St. Protais, Grand-Pré, Grand-Maison, Olivier de Vezin, Reggio, De Lachaise, Dreux, Maxent, and others, had, by their attendance at Ulloa's house, the moral courage to show openly their adhesion to the Spanish government. Foucault, the Intendant Commissary, would occasionally appear, but as it was well known that his sympathies were on the side of the opposition, he came, as it were, in his official capacity only, was received as such with cold formality, and as, under such circumstances, he could not help laboring under some degree of embarrassment, he would soon relieve himself, by never remaining long in an atmosphere, in which he did not feel at ease.

On these evenings, the late Marchioness of Abrado, now the Señora de Ulloa, was the centre of attraction. To great personal beauty she joined a cultivated mind, the accomplishment of musical talent, and the fascination of manner of the high bred lady. On Ulloa's return to Spain, she became an object of admiration at the court of Madrid. But, in Louisiana, she had shared the unpopularity of her husband, and few of the French ladies in the colony had paid her the respectful attentions and civilities, to which she was entitled. The aversion entertained for her husband, her very rank, her wealth, the other advantages which she possessed, and which, probably, were too many things at once to be forgiven and forgotten, had perhaps contributed to produce the feeling of alienation that was exhibited in her regard. This feeling the Señora de Ulloa had made no efforts to overcome, and had even given it more intensity, by appearing provokingly indifferent to the solitude in which she was left by those of her sex. Nay, she unconsciously provoked resentment and passionate abuse, by showing herself in public, attended by several young Indian girls, whom she had brought over with her from Peru, whom she delighted to fondle, as pets or favorites, and whom she treated almost with that kind of familiarity which is used only towards equals. Owing to this circumstance, much blame was thrown upon her in the colony, for *keeping low company*, as it was said, and for associating with *mulatresses*. The haughty smile and the merriment, with which the aristocratic lady received this report, when carried up to her ears, gave still deeper offence to the community.

No man could be more entertaining than Ulloa, in his moments of relaxation. He was sprightly and even playful, and his conversation was a rich mixture of humorous wit and deep learning. As a man who had made himself famous by his travels, he had an inexhaustible fund of observations on the countries and nations, with which he had become familiar; and as one who had left no field of science unexplored, he brought to bear even on the most commonplace topic, such a variety of knowledge, that he clothed with interest what did not seem to admit of any. His favorite position was to stand up at the mantel corner of the fireplace, and there, with his hands behind his back, his eyes sparkling, and his face beaming with animation, he gathered round him and kept, as it were fettered by a spell, a group of admiring listeners. He was a man of middle stature, stooping a little, with pale cheeks, thoughtful brow, limbs thin and spare—in a word—the very prototype of the lover of the midnight lamp.

As a matter of course, all the Spanish functionaries and officers were present on these occasions. Of them the most conspicuous were: Loyola, the Commissary of War and Intendant, Gayarre, the Contador, or Royal Comptroller and Auditor, Navarro, the Treasurer, Piernas, the commander of the two companies of foot that had come with Ulloa, and d'Acosta, the captain of the frigate which had transported the Spanish Governor to the colony, and which had ever since remained in the river. They were men of merit, and by their urbanity of manner and various accomplishments, they contributed their share to the pleasantness of the passing hour.

On the 20th of January, 1768, Aubry wrote to his government: "I am still waiting for the arrival of the Spanish troops, without which it is absolutely impossible that Ulloa should take possession of the colony. In the mean time, the affairs are conducted as much as possible as if it had been effected.

"But I am in one of the most extraordinary positions. I command for the king of France, and, at the same time, I govern the colony as if it belonged to the king of Spain. A French commander is gradually moulding Frenchmen to Spanish domination. The Spanish Governor urges me to issue ordinances, in relation to the police and commerce of the country, which take the people by surprise, considering that they are not used to such novelties. This colony is an instrument which it is necessary to take to pieces and to remodel, so as to make it play to the Spanish tune. The Spanish flag is now waving at the extremities of the province. It is at the Balize, at Missouri, on the bank of the Iberville river, and opposite Natchez. Mr. de Ulloa has just established these four posts, and has distributed among them the ninety soldiers that came with him. This operation was executed peaceably, without any accident, and has produced no change in our posts, which still continue in existence as for the past, so that, in all those which are on the banks of the Mississippi, from the Balize to the Illinois, the French flag is kept up as before.

"It is no pleasant mission to govern a colony, which undergoes so many revolutions, which has not known, for three years, whether it is Spanish or French, and which, until Spain shall take formal possession, is, to speak properly, without a master. When that event shall happen, I shall feel authorized to say to Mr. de Ulloa, that I deliver into his hands a Spanish colony, considering the changes and novelties which I have introduced in concert with him, during its French administration.

"It seems to me that Mr. de Ulloa is frequently too punctilious, and raises difficulties about trifles. We sometimes dispute about things which are clear and just beyond any possible doubt, and about which there would be no discussion, even between two private individuals in a state of poverty." With regard to Ulloa, he was so well pleased with Aubry, that, on his recommendation, the Spanish Government made to that officer a present of three thousand dollars.

Two thirds of the year, 1768, had passed away in apparent quiet. But a secret conspiracy had been kept alive in the town of New Orleans and in the neighboring parishes, to drive away the Spaniards from the colony. The chief conspirators were some of its most influential men, such as: Lafrénière, the king's Attorney-General, Foucault, the Intendant Commissary, Masan, a retired captain of infantry, a wealthy planter, and a knight of St. Louis, Marquis, a captain in the Swiss troops enlisted in the service of France, Noyan, a retired captain of cavalry, and Bienville, a lieutenant in the navy, both, the nephews of Bienville, the founder of the colony, Doucet, a distinguished lawyer, Jean and Joseph Milhet, Caresse, Petit, and Poupet, who were among the principal merchants, Hardy de Boisblanc, a former member of the Superior Council and a planter of note, Villeré, the commander of the German coast.

Lafrénière was a native of Louisiana, and of an obscure family His father, a poor Canadian, who had followed Bienville to Louisiana, had, by dint of industry, acquired some fortune, and had sent his son to be educated in France. A plebeian by birth, Lafrénière had the majestic aspect of a king, so much so, that he had been nicknamed Louis XIV. He was a man of strong passions, expensive tastes, and domineering temper. He was gifted with considerable eloquence, bordering, it is true, on the bombastic, but well calculated to produce an impression on the masses. His ambition was unbounded, and was supported by an indomitable energy. He had those qualifications of mind, soul, and temperament, which, under different circumstances, will, however paradoxical it may appear, make a man feel and act, truly and honestly to himself and to others, either as an intense aristocrat, or as an impetuous demagogue, a devoted tribune of the people—that being, whom Shakspeare calls: "*the tongue of the common mouth.*" This was the man who was the acknowledged leader of the anti Spanish party, and his efforts had been incessant, to pave the way to the contemplated insurrection.

A secret association had been formed, and the chiefs of the conspiracy used to meet, either at Masan's house, or at a house situated out of the precincts of the town, but contiguous to it, which belonged to one Mrs. Pradel, who was the avowed mistress of the Intendant Foucault. This house was surrounded by a large garden, thickly shaded with those magnificent trees, which are the pride of Louisiana. There the conspirators used to resort, at night, one by one, from different directions, and discussed the plans they had prepared.

There, after the dangerous occupation for which they had met was over, they sauntered in the perfumed alleys of roses, myrtles and magnolias of their fair associate in the partnership of conspiracy, and then they ended the evening in merriment and in the enjoyment of a luxurious banquet. This circumstance puts one in mind of the meeting, as related by Alfred de Vigny, of young Cinq-mars and his friends, at the house of the faithless courtezan Marion de Lorme, when that unfortunate favorite of Louis XIII. dared to head a conspiracy against the omnipotent and all-seeing minister, Cardinal Richelieu. But the secret of this conspiracy was better kept than that of the one to which I have alluded, and Aubry and Ulloa were not informed of it, before the 25th of October, when it was too late and all was ready to insure success.

The Germans and Acadians had been long tampered with, and Ulloa having lately sent Maxent, with bags of dollars, to pay these people, for grains and other provisions which the Spanish Government had bought, and of which the payment had been delayed, the conspirators became apprehensive that this circumstance would operate unfavorably for them, on these Germans and Acadians, whom they had persuaded that their claims would never be acknowledged and settled. Therefore, when Maxent stopped at the house of D'Arensbourg, the old Swedish captain, who, it will be remembered, had come to the colony, in 1721, after having distinguished himself at the battle of Pultawa, and who was one of the most respected inhabitants of Louisiana, he was arrested by Verret, under the authority of Villeré, who commanded at the German coast, and all the government money was taken away from him. A capuchin, who was the curate of that settlement, had been one of the most active tools of the conspirators, and, by circu-

GENERAL INSURRECTION. 189

lating every kind of exciting rumors, he had powerfully helped them in inducing the Germans and Acadians to rise against the Spaniards. On the 27th, Foucault convened a meeting of the Superior Council for the next day. During the night, the guns which were at the Tchoupitoulas gate, were spiked, and, the next morning, on the 28th, the Acadians, headed by Noyan, and the Germans by Villeré, entered the town, armed with fowling-pieces, with muskets, and all sorts of weapons. The planters who lived below New Orleans, also forced its gates and joined the other confederates. Marquis had been appointed commander-in-chief of the insurgents, and immediately entered into the duties of his new office. The town became the theatre of fearful alarm and confusion. The Spanish frigate broke the bridge which connected her with the bank of the river, and moved off to cast anchor in deeper water. The rumor that she was going to fire at the town produced the wildest excitement. All the private and public houses closed their doors, and heavy patrols of the insurgents, who were completely masters of New Orleans, paraded through its streets.

Aubry took, with great celerity and energy, all the necessary measures to protect the Spaniards, and to save Ulloa from injury. He had cartridges distributed to his men, who numbered only one hundred and ten, the rest being scattered throughout the colony in its different posts, and had them ready for action. He assembled their officers, and told them that he would die, rather than suffer that a hair should be touched on Ulloa's head, and that he relied on their zeal and fidelity. He sent for Lafrénière, and urged him to desist from an enterprise, which would be his perdition and the ruin of the colony; he told him that he would oppose it with force and arms, and that a great deal of blood would be shed. Seeing that he could not change Lafrénière's resolution, he added: "Well, sir, remember that the chiefs of a conspiracy have always met with a tragical end." He sent also for Foucault, and asked him what side he would take. On Foucault's answering with his usual ambiguity, Aubry told him that he would ruin himself beyond redemption, if he did not oppose so atrocious a rebellion. But he could not prevail on Foucault to pursue any decided course. His appeals to the other leaders were equally fruitless. In the evening, seeing that, to use his own expressions, *all was in a state of combustion*, he waited on Ulloa, and, informing him that he could not answer for his life, requested him to retire with his wife on board of the frigate of his Catholic Majesty. He then accompanied the Spanish Governor to that place of security, and left with him an officer and twenty men.

On the first appearance of danger, Gayarre, Loyola, Navarro, and the other few Spaniards, who were in the town, with some of their French adherents and friends, who had showed themselves true in the hour of trial, had gathered round Ulloa to die with or save him. They had barricaded his house, and put it in such a state of defence, as would have enabled them to stand a siege, and to sell their lives dearly. After Ulloa's retreat to the frigate, they remained in the same position, expecting to be attacked at every moment, and continued in that state of imminent danger and anxious suspense, for three or four days. Occasionally, the people would come rushing on, as it were to storm the fortifications which had been got up on the spur of the moment, and, uttering fierce shouts, would, with wild gestures, heap abuse on the Spaniards and their king, and deafen their ears with loud hurrahs for the King of France. But, on every one of these occasions, some of the chiefs among the insurgents, who seemed determined to keep the people from committing any unnecessary outrage, appeared among them, and by their exhortations, induced them to abstain from deeds of violence, and to act with that magnanimity which the consciousness of vast superiority of force ought to inspire. They assured them that the Spaniards would retire without resistance, and thereby succeeded, every time, in drawing them away from the spot, to which they were but too often recalled by their excited passions. Besides, it was evident, from the most cursory survey, made even by an unmilitary eye, of the preparations visible in what might be called the little stronghold of the Spaniards, that, with the unyielding temper which is the so well known attribute of their race, they had made themselves ready for the most desperate struggle. This, also, contributed perhaps to ward off the threatened blow. The following passage in Aubry's letter to O'Reilly, when rendering an account of these events, shows how great the danger had been: "Several times," said he, "the party of the rebels and that of the Spaniards, which certainly was not the strongest, were near coming to blows. Should that misfortune have happened, your Excellency would now be treading on the ashes of New Orleans."

In compliance with Foucault's convocation, the Superior Council had met at eight o'clock on the morning of the 28th. The members present were: Foucault, Lafrénière, Huchet de Kernion, De Launay, and Laplace, the rest of the council being absent for the alleged cause of sickness. Caresse was then introduced, and presented a petition, signed by about six hundred planters, merchants, and others, demanding the restoration of some liberties and ancient rights, the granting of new privileges, and the expulsion of Ulloa and of the other Spanish officers. This petition, which is said to have been written by Lafrénière and Doucet, was not read, but was referred to Huchet de Kernion and De Launay, with instructions to report on the following day. On the proposition of Lafrénière, who represented that there would not be a full council at the next meeting, on account of sickness among the members, and that it was impossible to delay action on a matter of so much importance, it was determined that supernumerary members of the council be appointed. On the joint recommendation of Foucault and Lafrénière, Messrs. Hardy de Boisblanc, Thomassin, Fleuriau, Bobé, Ducros, and Labarre were elected, and a resolution was passed, inviting them to be present at the meeting of the 29th.

The petition presented to the Superior Council for the expulsion of Ulloa had been signed in a large assembly, which had taken place early on the 28th, and which had been addressed with great vehemence by Lafrénière, Doucet, Jean and Joseph Milhet.

On the 29th, the Superior Council met at nine o'clock in the morning, to take into consideration that petition. To back it, the insurgents, to the number of about one thousand, were assembled on the public square, round a white flag, which they had hoisted up in its centre, and declared that they would exterminate all the Spaniards and their adherents, if the decree of expulsion should not be issued, because they were determined to submit to no other government than that of France. The Superior Council, composed of thirteen members, before deliberating, inquired of Aubry, through its president, whether Ulloa had exhibited to him his powers to take possession of the colony in the name of the King of Spain. Aubry answered that

PROCEEDINGS BEFORE THE COUNCIL. 193

nothing very decisive had ever been shown to him on the subject. Then the Attorney General rose and said :*

" Gentlemen : the first and most interesting point to be examined, is the step taken by all the planters and merchants in concert, who being threatened with slavery, and laboring under grievances which have been enumerated, address your tribunal, and require justice for the violations of the solemn act of cession of this colony.

" Is yours a competent tribunal ? are these complaints just ?

" I shall now proceed to demonstrate the extent of the royal authority vested in the Superior Council. The parliaments and Superior Council are the depositaries of the laws, under the protection of which the people live happy ; they are created and organized to be, from the very nature of their official tenure, the sworn patrons of virtuous citizens ; and they are established for the purpose of executing the ordinances, edicts, and declarations of kings, after they are registered. Such has been the will and pleasure of Louis the well-beloved, our Liege Lord and King, in whose name all your decrees, to the present day, have been issued and carried into execution. The act of cession, the only title of which his Catholic Majesty's commissioner can avail himself, to make his demands *auctoritate et proprietate*, was addressed to the late Mr. D'Abbadie, with orders to cause it to be registered in the Superior Council of the colony, to the end that the different classes of the said colony may be informed of its contents, and may be enabled to have recourse to it upon occasion, that instrument being calculated for no other purpose.

* Note. See all the proceedings in the Appendix.

"Mr. Ulloa's letter, dated from Havana, July 10th, 1765, which expresses his dispositions to do the inhabitants all the services they can desire, was addressed to you, gentlemen, with a request to make it known to the said inhabitants, that in thus acting, he would only discharge his duty and gratify his inclinations. The said letter was, by your decree, after full deliberation, published, set up, and registered, as a pledge to the inhabitants, of happiness and tranquillity. Another letter of the month of October last, written to Mr. Aubry, proves that justice still continues to be administered in the colony, in the name of Louis the well beloved. It results from the solemn act of cession and its accessories, that the planters, merchants and other inhabitants have the most solid basis to stand upon, when they present you with their most humble remonstrances; and that you, Gentlemen, are fully authorized to pronounce thereupon. Let us now proceed to a scrupulous examination of the act of cession, and of the letter written by Ulloa to the Superior Council. I think it likewise incumbent on me to cite, word for word, an extract of the King's letter, which was published, set up, and registered.

"This very solemn act of cession, which gives the title of property to his Catholic Majesty, secures for the inhabitants of the colony the preservation of ancient and known privileges; and the royal word of our sovereign Lord the King promises, and gives us ground to hope for, others, which the calamities of war have prevented him from making his subjects enjoy. The ancient privileges having been suppressed by the authority of his Catholic Majesty's commissioner, property becomes precarious. The act of cession, which was the mere result of good will and friendship, was made with reserves which confirm the liberties and privileges of the inhabitants, and which promise them a life of tranquillity, under the protection and shelter of their canon and civil laws. As property accruing from a cession by free right cannot be claimed and obtained, except on the condition of complying, during the whole possession of said property, with the reserves contained in said act of cession, our sovereign Lord the King hopes and flatters himself that, *in consequence of the friendship and affection shown by his Catholic Majesty, he will be pleased to give such orders to his governor, and to other officers employed in his service in that colony, as may be conducive to the advantage and tranquillity of the inhabitants, and that they shall be ruled, and their fortunes and estates managed according to the laws, forms and customs of said colony.* Can Mr. Ulloa's titles give authority to ordinances and orders, which violate the respect due to the solemn act of cession? The ancient privileges, the tranquillity of the subjects of France, the laws, forms and customs of the colony are rendered sacred by a royal promise, by a registering ordered by the Superior Council and by a publication solemnly decreed and universally known. The sole aim of the letter of our sovereign Lord the King, was to grant to the different classes of the colony a recourse to the act of cession. Therefore, nothing can be better grounded or more legal than the right of remonstrating, which the inhabitants and citizens of the colony have acquired by royal authority.

"Let us proceed to an examination of the letter of Mr. Ulloa, written to the Superior Council of New Orleans, dated the 10th of July 1765. I shall here cite, word for word, the article relative to the Superior Council and the inhabitants:

"*I flatter myself, beforehand, that it will afford me favorable opportunities, to render you all the services that you and the inhabitants of your town may desire—of which I beg you to give them the assurance from me, and to let them know that, in acting thus, I only discharge my duty and gratify my inclinations.*

"Mr. de Ulloa proved thereby the orders which he had received from his Catholic Majesty, conformably to the solemn act of cession, and manifested a sentiment, which is indispensable in any governor, who is desirous of rendering good services to his King in the colonies.

" Without population there can be no commerce, and without commerce, no population. In proportion to the extent of both, is the solidity of thrones; both are fed by liberty and competition, which are the nursing mothers of the State, of which the spirit of monopoly is the tyrant and step-mother. Without liberty, there are but few virtues. Despotism breeds pusillanimity and deepens the abyss of vices. Man is considered as sinning before God, only because he retains his free will. Where is the liberty of our planters, of our merchants and of all our inhabitants? Protection and benevolence have given way to despotism; a single authority would absorb and annihilate every thing. All ranks, without distinction, can no longer, without running the risk of being taxed with guilt, do any thing else but tremble, bow their necks to the yoke, and lick the dust. The Superior Council, bulwark of the tranquillity of virtuous citizens, has supported itself only by the combined force of the probity and disinterestedness of its members, and of the confidence of the people in that tribunal. Without taking possession of the colony, without registering, as was necessary, in the Superior Council, his titles and patents, according to the laws, forms and customs of the colony, and without presentation of the act of cession, Mr. de Ulloa has caused a president, three counsellors and a secretary, nominated for the purpose, to take cognizance of facts, which belonged to the jurisdiction of the Superior Council, and in which French citizens were concerned. Often did discontents and disgusts seem to force you to resign your places, but you have always considered it as a duty of your station of counsellors to the most Christian King, to alleviate and calm the murmurs of the oppressed citizens. The love of your country, and the sense of the justice due to every citizen who applies for it, have nourished your zeal. It has always been rendered with the same exactness; although you never thought proper to make representations on the infractions of the act of cession. You have always feared to give encouragement to a mass of discontented people, threatened with the most dreadful calamities; you have preferred public tranquillity. But now, the whole body of the planters, merchants, and other inhabitants of Louisiana apply to you for justice.

" Let us now proceed to an accurate and scrupulous examination of the grievances, complaints and imputations contained in the representations of the planters, merchants and other inhabitants. What sad and dismal pictures do the said representations bring before your eyes! The scourges of the last war, a suspension to this day of the payment of seven millions of the King's paper money, issued to supply the calls of the service, and received with confidence by the inhabitants of the colony, had obstructed the ease and facility of the circulation, but the activity and industry of the planter and of the French merchant had almost got the better of all difficulties. The most remote corners of the possessions of the Savages had been discovered, the fur trade had been carried to its highest perfection, and the new culture of cotton, joined to that of indigo and tobacco, secured cargoes to those who were engaged in fitting out ships. The commissioner of his Catholic Majesty had promised ten years of free trade—that period being sufficient for every subject of France, attached to his sovereign Lord and King. But the tobacco of this colony being prohibited in Spain, where those of Havana are the only ones allowed, the timber (a considerable branch of the income of the inhabitants) being useless to Spain, which is furnished in this article by its possessions, and the indigo being inferior to that of Guatimala, which supplies more than is requisite to the manufactures of Spain, the returns of the commodities of the inhabitants of this colony to the Peninsula became a ruinous trade, and the inhabitants were delivered up to the most dreadful misery. His Catholic Majesty's commissioner had publicly declared his conviction of the impossibility of this country's trading with Spain; all patronage, favor, and encouragement were formally promised to the inhabitants; the title of protector was decreed to Mr. Ulloa; the hope and the activity necessary to the success of the planter were nourished by the faith and confidence reposed in these assurances of the Spanish governor.

"But by the effect of what undermining and imperceptible fatality, have we seen a house, worth twenty thousand livres, sold for six thousand, and plantations, all on a sudden, lose one half and two thirds of their intrinsic value? Fortunes waste away, and specie is more scarce than ever; confidence is lost, and discouragement becomes general; the plaintive cries of distress are heard on every side; the precious name of subject of France is seen to be eclipsing itself, and the fatal decree concerning the commerce of Louisiana, gives the colony the last fatal stroke which must lead to its total annihilation. The Spanish flag is set up at the Balize, at the Illinois, and other places; no title, no letters patent were presented to the Superior Council; time flies apace; the delays fixed for the liberty of emigration will soon expire, force will tyrannise, we shall be reduced to live in slavery and loaded with chains, or precipitately to forsake establishments transmitted down from the grand-father to the grandson. All the planters, merchants and other inhabitants of Louisiana call upon you, to restore them to their sovereign Lord the King Louis the well beloved; they tender to you their treasures and their blood to live and die French.

"Let us proceed to sum up the charges, grievances and imputations.

"Mr. de Ulloa has caused counsellors, named by himself, to take cognizance of facts, concerning French subjects, which appertained only to the jurisdiction of the Superior Council. The sentences of that new tribunal have been signified to, and put in execution against, Mess. Cadis and Leblanc. Mr. Ulloa has supported the negroes dissatisfied with their masters. He has presented to the Superior Council none of his titles, powers and provisions, as commissioner of his Catholic Majesty; he has not exhibited his copy of the act of cession, in order to have it registered; he has, without the said indispensable formalities, set up the Spanish flag at the Balize, at the Illinois, and other places; he has, without legal authority, vexed, punished and oppressed subjects of France; he has even confined some of them in the frigate of his Catholic Majesty; he has, by his authority alone, usurped the fourth part of the common of the inhabitants of the town, has appropriated it to himself, and has caused it to be fenced in, that his horses might graze there.

"Having maturely weighed all this, I require in behalf of the King:

"That the sentences pronounced by the counsellors nominated for the purpose, and put in execution against Mess. Cadis and Leblanc, subjects of France, be declared encroachments upon the authority of our sovereign Lord the King, and destructive of the respect due to his supreme justice, seated in his Superior Council, in as much as they violate the laws, forms and customs of the colony, confirmed and guarantied by the solemn act of cession.

"That Mr. de Ulloa be declared to have violated our laws, forms and customs, and the orders of his Catholic Majesty in relation to the act of cession, as it appears by his letter, dated from Havana, on the 10th of July, 1765.

"That he be declared usurper of illegal authority, by causing subjects of France to be punished and oppressed, without having previously complied with the laws, forms, and customs, in having his powers, titles and provisions registered by the Superior Council, with the copy of the act of cession.

"That Mr. Ulloa, commissioner of his Catholic Majesty, be enjoined to leave the colony in the frigate in which he came, without delay, to avoid accidents or new clamors, and to go and give an account of his conduct to his Catholic Majesty; and with regard to the different posts established by the said Mr. Ulloa, that he be desired to leave in writing such orders, as he shall think necessary; that he be declared responsible, for all the events which he might have foreseen; and that Mess. Aubry and Foucault be requested and even summoned, in the name of our sovereign Lord the King, to continue to govern and administer the colony as heretofore.

"That all ships, sailing from this colony, shall not be despatched, without passports signed by Mr. Foucault, as intendant commissary of his most Christian Majesty.

" That the taking possession of the colony can neither be proposed nor attempted by any means, without new orders from his most Christian Majesty.

" That Messrs. Loyola, Gayarre, and Navarro be declared guarantees of their signature, on the bonds which they have issued, if they do not produce the orders of his Catholic Majesty, empowering them to issue said bonds and papers; and that a sufficient time be granted them to settle their accounts.

" That the planters, merchants and other inhabitants be empowered to elect deputies, to carry their petitions and supplications to our sovereign Lord the King.

" That it be resolved and determined, that the Superior Council shall make representations to our sovereign Lord the King; that its decree, when ready to be issued, be read, set up, published and registered.

" That collated copies thereof be sent to his Grace the Duke of Praslin, with a letter of the Superior Council, and likewise to all the posts of the colony, to be there read, set up, published and registered."

Then Mess. Huchet De Kernion and Piot De Launay, to whom the petition of the colonists had been referred, having made their report, the whole being duly weighed and deliberated upon, the attorney general having been heard and having retired, the Council proceeded to frame its decree.

Every one of the thirteen members gave his opinion separately, and in writing. Hardy de Boisblanc, during the deliberations, was observed to be one of the most violent advocates of the expulsion of Ulloa. Aubry, who had put his handful of men under arms, and who had been very active in every part of the town, to maintain order as much as possible, and to prevent the outbreaking of popular passion into deeds of blood, presented himself before the Council, and remonstrated against the decree, which, he was informed, they were going to adopt. He called their attention to the consequences of what they were doing, and to the magnitude of the affair, of which they presumed to take cognizance. He told them that they had no jurisdiction over the case on which they were preparing to decide, that Ulloa was the commissioner and representative of a great king, and that they would provoke the resentment of their most Christian and Catholic Majesties, by sending him out of the colony. But seeing, he said, that neither prayers nor threats could produce any impression, except on two or three, who seemed to be moderate, and that the rest allowed themselves to be swayed by the sentiments of Lafrénière, he desisted from his vain attempts.

At 12 o'clock, the Superior Council adjourned, after having, with Foucault's exception, agreed on their decree. It was in conformity with Lafrénière's conclusions, which were all adopted, and almost in the very words he had used. The time allowed Ulloa to quit the colony, was only three days, and he was to depart, either in the frigate of his Catholic Majesty in which he had come, or in whatever other vessel he should think proper. Loyola, Gayarre and Navarro were permitted to remain to settle their accounts, but were made personally responsible for the bonds and papers they had put in circulation, unless they showed their authority to emit them, under the special orders of his Catholic Majesty. In conclusion, the Council said: "We order all our bailiffs and sergeants to perform all the acts and formalities requisite for carrying the present decree into execution; we, at the same time, empower them to do so. We also enjoin the substitute of the King's attorney general to superintend the execution, and to apprize the court, thereof, in due time.

" Given at the Council chamber, on the 29th of October, 1768."

Foucault, who had been, under ground, one of the most ardent firebrands of the insurrection, and who had secretly goaded on the conspirators in every step they had taken, faithful to the plan he had followed, to shelter himself against any future contingencies of danger, to save his responsibility, and to insure his safety, by not breaking into any open and palpable act of rebellion, on the plea that, as the French King's intendant, he was restrained, and forced to a great deal of caution, by his official position, and that, by appearing not to be entirely with his associates, he could afford more real and effective aid to their cause, gave his opinion in writing, as follows :

" The intention of the King, our master, being that the colony should belong, fully and without reserve, to his Catholic Majesty, by virtue of the treaty of cession, my opinion is that none of the Spanish officers who have come here by order of their government, can be legally sent away; that, considering the causes of discontent enumerated in the petition of the citizens, and Ulloa's omission to take possession of the colony with the usual formalities, he, the said Ulloa, should be prohibited from exercising the powers of Governor, in anything relating to the French subjects now in Louisiana, or who may come thereto, hereafter, either as colonists or not; and that every thing appertaining to the commerce carried on by the French and other nations with this colony, be regulated, as it was before his arrival; nevertheless, that all the officers of the Spanish administration should continue their respective functions, in order to provide for the supplies necessary to the town and to the Posts, for the payment of all salaries, and for the expenses of the French troops, which will continue to serve, and of the works which will be deemed proper; this, until the decision of the courts of France and Spain be known, reserving to the delegates of the people the right to address his Catholic Majesty, in the most respectful and lawful manner, in order to obtain the privileges they claim."

Aubry, with his characteristic energy and frankness of behavior, without hesitation or equivocation, protested against the proceedings of the Council in these terms:

"I protest against the decree of the Council which dismisses Don Antonio de Ulloa from this colony. Their most Christian and Catholic Majesties will be offended at the treatment inflicted on a personage of his character; and though I have so small a force subject to my orders, I would, with all my might, oppose his departure, were I not apprehensive of endangering his life, as well as the lives of all the Spaniards in the colony.

"Deliberated at the Council chamber, on the 29th of October, 1768."

At 2 o'clock P. M. the decree of the Superior Council was officially communicated to Ulloa on board of the frigate, and to the assembled insurgents. "The most intense enthusiasm," said the Council in a letter to the French government, "followed this information, when given to the people. Women and children were seen rushing at the post which supported the French flag, and kissing it with passion; the air was rent with thousands of cries of: *Long live the King! Long live Louis the well beloved!* What a glorious moment, sire, for so great a monarch!"

On the adjournment of the Council, its members had

been invited by Foucault to dine at his house. They took their seats at the table, at 2 o'clock, and at five, whilst they were enjoying the last course of the banquet, Noyan and some others entered the room, and, addressing Foucault and Lafrénière, begged them to prevail on the Council to visit the Barracks, where all the planters, merchants and other colonists were assembled. Coffee,* to close the convivial festivity, was immediately called for, and then, at the request of Foucault and Lafrénière, the Council, in a body, with the exception of Messrs. Lalande d'Apremont and Huchet de Kernion, who said that they were sick and retired, proceeded to meet the insurgents, by whom they were welcomed with loud acclamations, and the welkin rang with tumultuous and prolonged cries of: *Long live the King of France! Long live Louis the well beloved!* These cries were responded to and repeated by the Council in a body. From the Barracks, the Council, followed by some citizens of note and consequence, went to Aubry's house. There, both Foucault and Lafrénière addressed him, and requested him to resume the government of the colony in the name of the King of France. Aubry again reproached them with what they had done, and said that they would soon see his prophecies realized.

Some reflections present themselves to the mind, in reviewing Lafrénière's address to the Council. Thus, it is apparent that he had assumed false and untenable grounds, and he must have known them to be such, when he argued in the Council, that the treaty of cession was with conditions and reserves, that the letter of Louis XV. to D'Abbadie was binding on the King of Spain, and that it secured in law to the colonists their

* See the written deposition of Garic, the clerk of the Council, on the trial of Lafrénière and others.

ancient rights and privileges. It is equally evident that it was, by the most forced construction, that he interpreted into an acknowledgment of those rights Ulloa's letter to the Council, which this officer wrote from Havana, giving notice of his coming, and which contained nothing but empty and vague expressions of civility, usual on such occasions. Foucault was therefore right when he said, that the treaty of cession was absolute, that the officers of the King of Spain could not legally be dismissed from the colony, and that, if the colonists were oppressed by those officers, their only course, save the inalienable right of revolution in cases of extreme hardship, was to apply to his Catholic Majesty for redress. But, in his desire to pursue a middle course and to keep on terms with both parties, he fell into a state of contradiction and inconsistency. To invite and to allow Ulloa to pay all the French functionaries and the French troops, and to assume all the expenses of the colony, was to invite and to allow him to be its governor. He could not, except as such, perform what he was requested to do; and the public functionaries, as soon as they accepted the pay of Spain, ceased to be French and became Spanish. The French troops, from the moment that they were supported by the Spanish treasury, had virtually passed into the service of Spain, and owed obedience to the Spanish governor. Thus Aubry, having consented to Ulloa's assuming all the expenses of the colony, acted logically in executing the mandates of that officer, and in behaving only as his lieutenant. It was too late to allege the want of the formality of taking possession and of the vain parade of a public ceremony, when that possession had been effectually taken by the colony's being entirely supplied, in all the wants of its administration and in every thing else, out of the Spanish treasury, with the consent and invitation of all. Ulloa's authority could not be partially admitted; it was impossible not to reject or to recognize it in its integrity. Therefore, Foucault's recommendation to retain Ulloa in the colony, as merely a French paymaster, and to deprive him of all authority as a Spanish governor, seems to be almost ludicrously incoherent. The fact is, that the colonists had achieved a revolution, and had, by force of arms, annulled the treaty of cession made between France and Spain. Foucault forgot that, on such occasions, men must have the courage of acknowledging the paternity of their acts; that, as a revolution cannot be disguised, it had better be proclaimed; and that it is a futile attempt to reconcile with the existing political organization and laws, and to defend in their name, what is frequently their manifest disrupture and violation, and a return to the reserved and natural rights of man.

There is a passage in Lafrénière's address, of which Louisiana may well be proud, and of which she can boast, as spoken by one of her children, in 1768, before the voice of 1776 was heard. "In proportion," said he, "to the extent both of commerce and population, is the solidity of thrones; both are fed by liberty and competition, which are the nursing mothers of the State, of which the spirit of monopoly is the tyrant and stepmother. Without liberty there are but few virtues. Despotism breeds pusillanimity, and deepens the abyss of vices. Man is considered as sinning before God, only because he retains his free will." To appreciate this bold language, it must be remembered that it was officially uttered by the attorney general of an absolute King, and that it was intended to reach the ears of the despotic government of France.

Another passage of Lafrénière's address must be

commented upon in justice to Ulloa. It must be observed that he said: "His Catholic Majesty's commissioner had publicly declared his conviction of the impossibility of this country's trading with Spain. All patronage, favor and encouragement were formally promised to the inhabitants; the title of protector was decreed to Mr. Ulloa; the hope and activity, necessary to the success of the planter, were sustained by the faith and confidence reposed in these assurances of the Spanish governor." This shows what spirit had animated Ulloa on his arrival in Louisiana. His enlightened mind had immediately discovered all the wants of the colony, and it had cost him no effort to be convinced, that it was laboring under fatal commercial restrictions. He had expressed himself to that effect, and had promised his intercession with his government. He had kept his word, and had made remonstrances, which had been disregarded. Instead of inviting, he had deprecated, the commercial decree which had been sent to him from Madrid, which he had been bound to put in force, and which had produced so much discontent. It was therefore with great injustice that, in this instance, he had been charged by the inhabitants with duplicity and wanton tyranny.

But whatever had been his faults, his virtues, the merits and demerits of his deeds, his connection with Louisiana, as governor, had now ceased for ever.

FIFTH LECTURE.

AUBRY'S REFLECTIONS ON THE LATE REVOLUTION—THE SUPERIOR COUNCIL ANNULS HIS PROTEST AGAINST THEIR DECREE—ULLOA'S LETTER TO AUBRY—CIRCUMSTANCES OF ULLOA'S DEPARTURE—MEMORIAL OR MANIFESTO OF THE COLONISTS IN THEIR JUSTIFICATION—THE COUNCIL APPOINTS A COMMITTEE OF INQUIRY IN RELATION TO THE ACCUSATIONS BROUGHT AGAINST ULLOA, AND ON WHICH HIS EXPULSION HAD BEEN BASED—DEPOSITIONS OF THE WITNESSES—THE COUNCIL'S LETTER TO THE DUKE OF PRASLIN—THEIR REPRESENTATIONS TO THE KING—COMPOSITION AND NATURE OF THE NEW TRIBUNAL ESTABLISHED BY ULLOA—FOUCAULT'S LETTER TO THE DUKE OF PRASLIN—AUBRY'S TO THE SAME—ULLOA'S ARRIVAL AT HAVANA—HIS LETTERS TO THE MARQUIS OF GRIMALDI ON THE REVOLUTION AND THE SITUATION OF THE COLONY—PETITION OF THE COLONISTS TO THE COUNCIL, PRAYING FOR THE EXPULSION OF THE SPANISH FRIGATE, THE VOLANTE—THE COUNCIL'S DECREE ON THIS SUBJECT—FOUCAULT'S DESPATCHES TO THE FRENCH GOVERNMENT—HIS TREACHERY—AUBRY'S OPINION OF ULLOA AND OF THE CONSPIRATORS—HIS WISHES AND VIEWS EXPRESSED TO THE FRENCH GOVERNMENT—THE NEWS OF THE REVOLUTION REACHES SPAIN—DELIBERATIONS OF THE COUNCIL OF MINISTERS—SPAIN DETERMINES TO RETAIN POSSESSION OF LOUISIANA—LETTER OF THE MARQUIS OF GRIMALDI, ON THE SUBJECT, TO THE COUNT OF FUENTES, AMBASSADOR OF SPAIN AT THE COURT OF VERSAILLES—GENERAL O'REILLY IS SENT TO LOUISIANA WITH FULL POWERS TO PUT DOWN THE INSURRECTION, AND TO TRY THE REBELS—DOUBTS AND ANXIETIES IN THE COLONY—BEGINNING OF A REACTION AGAINST THE CHIEFS OF THE REVOLUTION.

ON the 30th of October, 1768, Aubry sent to one of the ministers in France a detailed statement of all that had occurred, and said of the Superior Council: "Seeing that I could not oppose what they had resolved upon, and that their minds were made up, I protested against their decree which orders the expulsion, within three days, of him whom his Catholic Majesty had sent to take possession of the colony. I look upon this action as one of the greatest outrages that could be committed. If a dozen individuals, who had contributed not a little to set all on fire, had been spared the country, that event would not have happened. It is my duty to inform your excellency that, although it is the universal wish of the colonists to remain French, and although they protest their fidelity to the King of France, yet every thing is *topsy turvy*. It is desired that I remain governor, and Mr. Foucault, intendant. But violence is the order of the day. Much apparent respect is shown to me, but I am not obeyed. Having no troops at my disposal to enforce my authority, it is reduced to a mere shadow, and my person and the dignity of my office are both degraded."

This despatch was intrusted to De Lapeyrière, a Knight of St. Louis, whom Aubry sent to France, to give all the information that might be wanted in relation to the late revolution. The insurgents lost no time in selecting their delegates, to carry their representations to the foot of the throne. Lesassier was appointed by the Superior Council, Bienville, a Lieutenant in the navy, by the planters, and Milhet by the merchants. Bienville having refused, on the ground that his military commission was incompatible with the mandate for which he had been chosen, St. Lette was put in his place.

With regard to Ulloa, he was preparing to leave the country within the time which had been allotted to him, and he wrote to Aubry, to authorize him to withdraw the Spanish troops from the posts which they occupied, and to send them to Havana. "*He has even been so generous*," said Aubry, "*as to order the Spanish commissary to continue to pay the French troops and their officers.*"

On the 31st of October, the Council met again, and annulled, in the following terms, Aubry's protest:

"Having taken into consideration the protest made by Mr. Aubry, Knight of the royal and military order of St. Louis, governor of this province for his Most Christian Majesty, n relation to the decree of court delivered on the 29th of the present month, against Mr. Ulloa, commissioner of his Catholic Majesty; and this protest being read whilst the audience was holding, and the King's attorney-general being heard thereupon, and the matter thoroughly debated, the Council, without condemning the motives which have caused Mr. Aubry to protest against the decree of court, of the 29th of the present month, has declared and declares the said protest null and void, and orders that the said decree shall have its full force and entire effect, and shall be executed according to its form and tenor.

"Deliberated upon, and given, at the Council Chamber, October, 31, 1768."

On that day, Ulloa wrote to Aubry: "no reproaches can be addressed to me; for, if I had forts constructed, or gave any other commands, it was with your advice and consent, and with the approbation of the King, my master, to whom the colony belongs; and your excellency being the Governor-general of said colony, to whom was directed the edict of his Most Christian Majesty, declaring the cession, the Superior Council, which is nothing but a civil tribunal, has nothing to do with it."

In the evening, Ulloa embarked with all his family in a French vessel, which he had chartered, because he could not, as was alleged, depart in the Spanish frigate, which needed repairs. On the 1st of November, at the dawning of light, a numerous band of colonists, who had spent the preceding night at a wedding, and who were probably laboring under the ordinary effects of a festivity of this kind, appeared on the bank of the river, where the French vessel was moored, and indulged in the singing of patriotic songs and in the uttering of shouts of exultation. One of them, named Petit, cut the ropes which made fast the vessel, and the joyous band had the satisfaction to see her go down the stream. But she stopped at a short distance, and did not sail before the afternoon, in presence of the sergeants and bailiffs of the Council, who reported thereupon to that body. Marquis had ordered fifty men of the militia on board of a boat, to accompany, as far as the mouth of the river, the vessel which was to carry away Ulloa, and had instructed them to garrison the fort at the Balize, with the view to oppose any Spanish force that might come. These men had already embarked, when Aubry commanded them to desist from their enterprise and to land, under pain of being fired at. "*On that occasion*," said he, in one of his despatches, "*I was obeyed for the first time.*"

After the expulsion of Ulloa, the planters and merchants of Louisiana, put forth a memorial or manifesto, in justification of the revolution of the 28th of October, which was published by Braud, the King's printer, with the authorization of Foucault, the intendant commissary. It repeats all that had been said by Lafrénière in his address to the Council, and although containing further allegations and being more developed in its arguments, it seems to have been written by him, and certainly bears the stamp of his style. It begins with expressing the deep regrets of the colonists at being threatened with the loss of so beneficent a master as Louis XV., who is for his subjects, the *image of God on earth, and an incomparable monarch*—the *most august of sovereigns*, under whose cherished sway, it is the wish of the colonists to live and die, and they tender the remnants of their broken fortunes, their blood, their children, and their families, to remain under the paternal rule of Louis *the well beloved*. They also bestow exaggerated praise on the prime minister, Duke of Choiseul, and seem to forget, or not to be aware, that he was the very man who had transferred them away to Spain. Among the other heads of accusation which they bring against Ulloa, they complain of his having granted to five or six persons, the exclusive privilege of trading with the Illinois district, and they also refer to the restrictions on commerce imposed by the famous decree of the 6th of September, 1766. They accuse him of the violation of *fair promises made on his arrival,* of an *antipathy to humanity, and of a natural disposition to do evil deeds.* In support of which, they mention his closing all the passes of the Mississippi, except one, which he chose, precisely because it was the most shallow, the most difficult, and the most perilous; his ordering the pilots not to pass the night on board of any vessel coming to, or going out of the Mississippi, and his causing thereby many accidents and great damages; the sending of honest and respectable citizens to the mines, and other acts of vexation and tyranny; the sequestration of goods; the establishment of a new tribunal, in violation of the rights and jurisdiction appertaining to the Superior Council; his interfering with the importation of Negroes; his ordering a brick-yard to be abandoned, on the ground that it was too close to the fortifications of the town, and because the holes which the Negroes dug, to supply the kiln with earth, became full of putrid water, which he said, corrupted the air, notwithstanding the assertions of physicians to the contrary; his treatment of the Acadians, whom he threatened to sell as slaves; his negociating with an Englishman the setting at liberty of four Germans detained on board of the Spanish frigate, in consideration of the payment of fifteen dollars per head; his haughtiness, his love of money, his sordid avarice; his contempt for the ecclesiastical laws of the colony, his absence from the French churches, and his having Mass said in his own house. They allege that he had the sacrament of marriage conferred under his own roof by his chaplain, on a white man and a black female slave, without the permission of the curate, without the requisite previous publications, without any of the forms or solemnities established by the church, in contempt of the decrees of the Council of Trent, and against the precise directions of the civil and canon laws which governed the colony.

"Is there any thing reprehensible," they said, "in the step to which we have been driven by Mr. de Ulloa's conduct, and by the vexations to which it led? What harm have we done in shaking off a foreign yoke, which was made still more heavy and crushing by the hand which imposed it? What offence have we committed in claiming back our laws, our country, our sovereign, and in consecrating to him our everlasting love? Are such laudable attempts without an example in our history? Have not more than one city in France, such as Cahors and Montauban, and even whole provinces, such as the Guerci, the Rouergue, and Gascony, repeatedly broken with patriotic rage the English yoke, or refused to be fettered by foreign chains? Solemn compacts, treaties of cession, and even positive orders from our kings often attempted in vain to accomplish, what British arms could not achieve, although smiled upon by victory; and that noble resistance to the decrees of our natural born sovereigns, far from kindling their wrath, stirred up the fountain of their paternal attachment, forced them into helping their loving subjects, and thus wrought out their deliverance."

After having given the reasons, why the colony of Louisiana could not be of any advantage to Spain, they proceeded to enumerate those which ought to induce France to retain a possession, that was calculated to indemnify her for the loss of Canada.

"The remaining of this colony in the hands of France," so they argued, "is a better security and guaranty for the provinces of Spain bordering on Louisiana, than the cession made to that crown. The unfavorable impressions already conceived by the Indians against the Spanish nation, and which have prompted them, not only to insult, but also to threaten with great violence the Spanish Captain Rici, who commands at the Illinois, would, in case of war, enlist them in the ranks of any hostile power to Spain. On the contrary, the Indian tribes always side with the French soldiers, without inquiring who their enemy is. This is the true bulwark for Spain. Since she cannot find any advantage in the acquisition of this immense possession, and since it is beyond doubt that, from our limited commerce with her, we could not expect any thing beyond the bare support of our existence, why should the two sovereigns agree to make us miserable, for the sole pleasure of doing it? Such sentiments do not enter the hearts of kings, and it would be a crime to entertain any such supposition. * * * *

"Scrupulous observers of the respect due to crowned heads, and of the mutual considerations of amity which civilized nations ought to cherish, we should feel deeply grieved, if we had lost sight of them in what we have done. There is nothing offensive for the Court of Madrid, in the exposition of our wants and in the assurances of our attachment, which we lay at the feet of our august Sovereign. We dare hope that these demonstrations of our zeal, will contribute to show to all the nations of the earth, how true is the appellation of *well beloved*, which the whole world gives to him, and which no other monarch ever did possess. Perhaps, even in Madrid it will be said: *Happy the prince, our ally, who finds the inviolable attachment of his subjects to his domination and to his glorious person, an obstacle to his treaty of cession!*

' We are aware that the commissioner of Spain took before his departure, and still continues to gather, through his emissaries, certificates from certain individuals residing among us, who are his mercenary clients, seduced by brilliant promises, and who are looking out for proselytes, by persuading the ignorant and frightening the weak. But whatever may be the contents of these certificates, which are not very authentic, they never can deny what is of public notoriety and contradict the voice of the people.   *   *   *   *   *

" It is to his beneficent Majesty that we, the planters, merchants and colonists of Louisiana, address our most humble prayers, that he may immediately resume possession of the colony; and being resolved to live and die under his dear domination, as well as determined to do all that may be required for the prosperity of his arms, the extension of his power, and the glory of his reign, we supplicate him to deign to preserve to us our patriotic name of Frenchmen, our laws and our privileges."

The whole of this long document is interesting, as representing the manners, the sentiments, the passions, feelings, and talents of the time, but it is a confused mixture of truths and errors, and is written in very defective style. It must be remarked, in connexion with it, that, with regard to the monopoly of trade granted by Ulloa in the Illinois district, it had been already established by D'Abbadie in 1764, and that such grants had been so frequent, since the foundation of the colony, that its inhabitants must have been accustomed to

APPOINTMENT OF A COMMITTEE OF INQUIRY. 217

the system, and that it could not be anticipated that they would resent so acutely its continuation, wrong as it certainly was. As to the hyperbolical expressions of inviolable attachment and unshakable devotion for the glorious person of Louis XV., of Louis *the well beloved*, it may be permitted to wonder at the foundations on which rested such sentiments. Such was not the judgment of France herself on this degraded prince, who, without a feeling of remorse or shame in his royal breast, had allowed her to be stript of her magnificent colonies, which extended without interruption from the mouth of the Mississippi to that of the St. Lawrence, and who, instead of using her treasures in carrying on a glorious war, and in defending her immense American domains, lavished them away among vile flatterers, flung them in the lap of ignoble courtezans, and wasted his long and worthless life amidst the orgies of a corrupt court and the impurities of that famous seat of debauchery, called the *Parc aux cerfs* and imagined for his special benefit, without caring probably, and perhaps without knowing, in what part of America Louisiana was situated, and certainly without conceiving that, beyond the Atlantic, there were men who regretted his domination.

The Superior Council had begun with decreeing at once the expulsion of Ulloa, and six days after his departure, they ordered an inquest in relation to the misdeeds of which this officer was accused. It seems that this should have been the first thing to be done. A committee of inquiry was appointed, composed of Huchet de Kernion and Piot de Launay. The witnesses, heard, corroborated some of the assertions made by Lafrénière, in his address to the Superior Council, and those that were set forth in the memorial of the planters and merchants, in justification of the revolution of the 28th of October, and in addition, they certified to these other facts : That Ulloa had caused several children afflicted with leprosy to be seized, and, notwithstanding the supplications of their parents, had the cruelty to send them to the Balize, where none of their wants were supplied; that he had forbidden slaves to be whipped in New Orleans, in order to please his wife, whose humanity was shocked by their cries, so that the inhabitants, much to their prejudice, were obliged to go six miles out of the town to have their slaves punished; that, for his own personal convenience, he had encroached on a street, which he had reduced to a width of sixteen feet, and that he had thought proper to block up one of the gates of the town, still for his own personal gratification.

Among other curious depositions, is that of the reverend Father Dagobert, vicar-general and curate. He swears that the only causes of reproach he has against Ulloa, are the following: that he, Ulloa, had caused the sacrament of marriage to be administered in his own house by his chaplain, without the required, previous publications, and without the usual formalities; and that he, Father Dagobert, has been assured that the persons thus married, were a white man and a black woman. The witness declares that the marriage took place without his consent. He adds, that Ulloa had assumed the right of having a chapel in his own house, that he had mass said in it, for eighteen months, by the chaplain of the frigate, and, furthermore, that there was no decent place for the establishment of said chapel in said house. The deponent affirms that Miss de Larredo, Marchioness of Abrado, having arrived from Peru at the Balize, where Ulloa had gone to await her, the said Ulloa had carried her up in triumph to New Orleans, pretending to have married her at the Balize, where the nuptial benediction had been administered to them by the chaplain of the frigate, but without the permission of the deponent, and without the required publications, said chaplain having, besides, never been authorized to celebrate marriages in the province. Father Dagobert concludes saying, that this marriage has caused much scandal in the town, has alarmed timorous and scrupulous consciences, and that it is believed to be clandestine, on account of the want of compliance with the civil and canon forms and laws.

On the 22d of November, the Superior Council addressed to the Duke of Praslin a letter, in which they begged him to support the representations they sent to be laid at the foot of the throne. In this letter, they recapitulated all the grievances of the colonists against Ulloa, dwelling on the tyranny, eccentricity, and inflexibility of character of that officer, and the excessive indecency of his deportment. They said: "The court could not without a violation of its oath, to support the laws, and without being recreant to the most essential obligations imposed by religion and humanity, refuse to a whole colony, groaning under its miseries, the justice which it claimed, with so much earnestness, against the oppression of that officer. In fulfilling its duty in that respect, the Council certainly prevented the commission of a striking act of despair, which would have tarnished the lustre of the French name. Under the influence of these motives, the Court rendered against that officer a decree, of which a copy is forwarded to your Excellency." To this letter was annexed the document, containing the representations, which were to be laid before the King, in the name of the Council.

In those representations, the Council made the most seductive description of the prosperity of the colony at the time of the cession, a description which it is impossible to look upon as corresponding with facts. But with Ulloa, as they affirmed, came the most disastrous change in the situation of the province. "He arrived at the Balize," they said, "on the 22d of February, 1766; a tragical event deprived him of eleven of his sailors. Rain, thunder, and a storm introduced him to the inhabitants of New Orleans, on the 5th of March, at noon." After mentioning these bad omens, they then recapitulated the grievances which have already been stated, and made to them some additions, for instance: That Ulloa maintained that he was the king of the colony; that he treated with the utmost contempt the Superior Council, whose powers he wished to destroy, and violated all those rights which had been secured by the treaty of cession and the King's letter to D'Abbadie; and that he carried the infraction of the most sacred privileges so far as to create a new council, which had, among other powers, exclusive jurisdiction over all questions connected with the regulations or decrees on exportation, importation, and other commercial matters. The sentences rendered by that tribunal were annexed to the petition, in order that the King might judge of their illegality. The Superior Council further alleged that three Acadian families, having arrived in the colony at their own expense, asked Ulloa for leave to buy land in the vicinity of their relations and friends, in the upper part of the Mississippi river; but that Ulloa, irritated by th cries of their children, by the critical state of a woman which was on the eve of becoming a mother, and by the representations of the men, forbade their remaining in the colony, and had them put on board of an English ship sailing for New England; and that he declared his intention to sell as slaves other Acadians, who had dared to make some humble representations to him; that the subjects of France were threatened with slavery, whilst Negroes were raised by degrees to the dignity of freemen; that he hastened to show his antipathy to the population of the colony, by sending to Havana for a nurse for his child, in order that it might not suck one drop of French blood. "*What pernicious principles are these!*" they exclaimed. "*What barbarous dispositions!*" They further represented that, through the misdeeds of Ulloa, the colony had been thrown into such a state of misery, that half of it was reduced to live on rice and corn; and that, without the wise precautions of Foucault, who had a certain quantity of these articles of food brought down to New Orleans, fathers and mothers would have had, even in the capital, nothing to offer but tears to the plaintive cries of their famished children; that the people became persuaded that Ulloa rejoiced at the success of his attempts to starve them, and that he was determined to reduce the subjects of France to have no other food than the tortilla *; that a general feeling of despair pervaded the colony; that all the colonists, deprived of their ordinary aliments, were condemned to fatten vampires with their life blood, and that, by a malicious and restrictive legislation, they were prevented from acquiring the means of paying their old debts. The Superior Council then proceeded to relate the events which preceded the revolution, those of the revolution itself, and what had followed. They concluded with supplicating the King to retake possession of the colony, and annul the treaty of cession.

"Your Majesty," they said, "will find in all the citizens brave soldiers, who offer to shed their blood and sacrifice their fortunes, to protect the Mexican provinces of Spain and to support your allies, provided they belong

* In Spain, a dish of eggs, and in Mexico, of corn flour, fried in oil or lard, in the round shape of a pie.

only to you, Sire, their most honored Lord and King, Louis the well beloved. O great King, the best of kings, father and protector of your subjects, deign, Sire, to receive into your royal and paternal bosom your devoted children, who have no other desire than that of dying your subjects. It is the wish of this colony. Your Superior Council has thought it their duty to convey the expression of it to Your Majesty. Deign, Sire, to ward off from your subjects new misfortunes. Their hearts are ulcerated, and bleeding from the wounds inflicted by tyranny and despotism. The benefits conferred by the best of kings can alone, Sire, make your people happy. Those who are accustomed to the blessings of a government which is envied by all the other nations, will never be able to subject themselves to the system of exclusiveness and to the despotism which prevail in all the Spanish possessions. Men are born under laws, which become gradually familiar and dear to them, in proportion as from childhood they grow into manhood, when their attachment to them can no longer be destroyed. Men who have reached the meridian of life cannot, of their own free will, remould their character, their heart, their honest and time-honored habits. It can only be accomplished by force. What a modification of their existence does it require! What a struggle, Sire, for citizens who are born the subjects of such a King as Louis the well beloved! Deign again, Sire, listen with favor to the general wish of the colony, and to the most humble representations of your Superior Council."

This address to the King is in a tone of exaggeration which must have weakened the effect it was intended to have. It was not in the temperate language which characterizes truth; but it seemed rather to have been written under the influence of the deepest feelings of anger and hatred. None could believe that *it was the intention of Ulloa to deprive the new subjects of his Catholic Majesty of their ordinary articles of food, and to reduce them to live on nothing but the tortilla.* It was natural to infer that those who could hold it as a heinous crime in Ulloa, to *have given a Spanish nurse to his child*, were too prejudiced or too irritated to see things in their true light, and to make a fair report on what had occurred. There were good grounds for suspecting them of swerving from truth, perhaps involuntarily and unconsciously, in their allegations. The fact is, that there might have been some just reproaches to be addressed to Ulloa, but that his faults were far from being as serious as they were represented to be.

With regard to the new tribunal established by Ulloa, and which was the cause of so many bitter complaints, as usurping the powers of the Superior Council, it was composed of three Spaniards : Loyola, the commissary of war; Don Estevan Antonio Gayarre, the contador or royal comptroller; Don Jose Melchior d'Acosta, the commander of his Catholic Majesty's frigate, and four Frenchmen : Reggio, a retired captain of infantry; Olivier de Vezin, chief surveyor of the colony; De La Chaise, an honorary member of the Superior Council, and Dreux, a captain of militia. It held its sittings in the house of Destréhan, the ex-French treasurer of the colony.

With the Superior Council's address to the King, there went at the same time a letter from Foucault to the Duke of Praslin, in which he justified as well as he could, but in very guarded language, the revolution that had taken place, and in which he said of Ulloa : "Without taking possession of the colony, and even without exhibiting his credentials, he arrogated all powers to himself. He was very harsh and absolute, of extremely difficult access, and refusing to listen to every representation. He showed without the least hesitation or equivocation an implacable hatred for the French nation, and marked every day that he passed here with acts of inhumanity and despotism." He then goes into the details of all his exertions to prevent the expulsion of Ulloa, and declares that it originated in the many causes of irritation and provocation which the people had; he says that he harangued them several times to induce them to remain quiet, and affirms, in direct contradiction of Aubry's declarations in one of his despatches, that, on the breaking out of the insurrection, he joined his efforts to Aubry's, in order to tranquillize the public mind. He concludes with saying that all the colonists hope to resume the privileges and name of Frenchmen, and that, rather than lose these precious advantages, they would quit the colony with their negroes, chattels, goods and all the other property susceptible of being carried away, leaving nothing but a desert to the Spaniards.

Three days later, on the 25th of November, Aubry wrote to the same minister: "I beg you, my Lord, to deign to cast your eye on a letter, which I had the honor to write to you, on the 30th of March, 1767. You will see, in three different passages, that I foresaw the unfortunate event which has occurred. I had informed you that Mr. de Ulloa was not the proper person to govern this colony, notwithstanding his vast intellect, his talents, his learning, his great reputation in all the academies of Europe, and although he is full of honor, of probity, and of zeal for the service of his sovereign. He does not possess the necessary qualifications to command Frenchmen. Instead of endeavoring to gain the hearts (which is absolutely necessary in a change of government,) he has done all that could tend to alienate them. He seemed to despise the first men of the colony, and particularly the members of the Superior Council. By his indiscreet expressions, and by threats which shadowed the forthcoming of a frightful despotism, he caused the Spanish domination to be dreaded, and gave rise to the supposition that he did not like our nation. He has alarmed every body, and, by a deportment as unbecoming as it was surprising in a man of so distinguished a mind, he has not a little contributed to draw down upon himself and his nation the storm which has swept him away.

"In another letter of the 4th of April, 1768, I had the honor to inform you of the deplorable state and of the frightful misery to which this colony is reduced. The uncertainty about the ultimate fate of the French paper currency, the prolonged delays in the payment of the debts of his Catholic Majesty, who has assumed the expenses of the colony, the scarcity of specie, the insolvability of three fourths of the debtors, a diminution in the value of lands and negroes and of every kind of property, amounting to a loss of two thirds, the regret of passing under a foreign domination, which inspires the people with the apprehension of their being unhappy, the Governor's want of capacity to conciliate the affection and esteem of the inhabitants, the news of a decree rendered by his Catholic Majesty, which deprives the colony of its commerce with the Islands and with France —all these motives united, and made still more powerful by the effects of the extreme misery which has prevailed here for so long a time, and which increases daily, have at last goaded the people into desperation, and produced this fatal revolution, which would not have happened, had I had at hand only a body of three hundred men.

*　　*　　*　　*　　*　　*

"It would perhaps be dangerous, at this moment, to impress the culprits with too deep a sense of their offence and of the rigorous punishments to which they expose themselves. The vicinity of the English settlements requires that we should proceed with great caution. Otherwise, it is to be apprehended that despair might drive the insurgents into something still worse.

"I remain at the head of a colony, which has been set topsy turvy by the late revolution, and in the midst of a people who, after looking upon themselves as Spaniards during three years, now detest that nation, and wish not to lose the character of French subjects. With the exception of the officers, whose conduct I cannot but commend, of a handful of old soldiers who have remained faithful, and of a small number of honest people who support me, the rest of the colonists, from the first to the last, wish to preserve the name, character and privileges of Frenchmen."

In another despatch of the same date, Aubry informed the French government that the English had evacuated, in September, the posts of Natchez and Iberville, in conformity with the orders of General Gage, and that they had established their head quarters at St. Augustin, leaving only fifty men at Pensacola and twenty-five at Mobile. Aubry inferred that the object of the English was to concentrate their forces, in consequence of a certain agitation in New England, where had been cast the seeds of that revolution which was to break forth in 1776. "I was waiting only," said he, "for the arrival of the Spanish troops, to deliver up the colony, and to return to France to render an account of my conduct, when a general rebellion of the inhabitants of this province against the Spanish Governor and his nation, which it was not in my power to oppose, and which occurred on the 28th and 29th of October, destroyed in a moment the work of four years, and all the dispositions which I had taken on behalf of the crown of Spain. An audacious petition, insulting to the Spanish nation, rebellious against the King of France, whose orders it set at naught, and signed by six hundred planters and other inhabitants, was presented to demand Ulloa's expulsion," &c., &c.—Such being the light under which a French Governor considered this act of the colonists, it is not astonishing that the Spaniards should have looked upon it as a most heinous offence, and should have punished it accordingly.

Thus was the revolution accomplished. A population, which hardly numbered eighteen hundred men, able to carry arms, and which had in its bosom several thousands of black slaves, whom it was necessary to intimidate into subjection, had rebelled against the will of France, had flung the gauntlet at the Spanish monarchy, and was bearding a powerful nation, whose distinguished trait of character did not consist in the forgiveness of injuries, particularly when her pride was wounded. With regard to France, it was evident that it was vain to rely on her support, since it was the consciousness of her weakness which had compelled her to give up that colony, and to offer it to the King of Spain, who did not care for it. Besides, should France have been disposed to assist the colonists, how could she withdraw the donation she had pressed upon Spain, without indemnifying her for her expenses in the colony, and without punishing the authors of an outrage, to which she had exposed an ally, whose sole object, in accepting the donation of Louisiana, was to be serviceable to the donor! The colonists had long since sent to France intelligent men, as delegates, to urge upon the king their wishes, that the cession of Louisiana be rescinded; and those delegates, on their return, must have informed them of the true state of things, and made it known to them, how fruitless it would be, to endeavor to force France into the resumption of a province, which she considered as a burden, and whose expenses she could no longer meet, on account of the embarrassed situation of her finances. It is therefore impossible not to be astonished at seeing one of these delegates engaged in a conspiracy against the Spaniards, and not to wonder at the temerity of the colonists, in attempting a revolution, of which the direful consequences to them it was but too easy to foresee.

In the mean time, Ulloa had arrived at Havana, and, on the 4th of December, wrote as follows to the Marquis of Grimaldi, one of the ministers in Spain :

"There being a rumor, on the 28th of October, that the insurgents intended to attack my house during the night, and to take possession of all the effects of value which they might find in it, on giving me a receipt for them, in order to enable me to be reimbursed by the treasurers of his Majesty, as rebels generally proceed in a case of insurrection, and having been warned also that they had resolved to do the same with the King's treasury, where they expected to find a capital of more than one hundred thousand dollars, and to attack the frigate of his Majesty, the *Volante*, in which they imagined also that there was money, and, finally, that their intention was to get hold of the papers of the government, and particularly of my correspondence with your Excellency, I retired on board of the frigate, whither I carried along with me all these papers, in order to keep them safe from all danger.

"On the 27th, being made aware of what was brewing, I had taken all the measures which circumstances had permitted, to put the frigate in a state of defence, and to prevent that the King's flag be insulted. No attempt of the kind had been made on the 1st of November, when I embarked with all my household in a French ship for Havana, in conformity with the summons which had been addressed to me.

"On the 16th of November, I went over the bar at the mouth of the river, and arrived yesterday at Havana, after a very painful navigation, the result of a departure so precipitate as not to give me time to provide for any thing.

"I briefly related to the Governor of this place what had happened, and, in the evening of the same day, a council was held to deliberate on what it would be proper to do, in order to afford assistance to the Spanish and French troops in Louisiana. But it was impossible to come to any determination, on account of many difficulties which presented themselves. The day after to-morrow, there will be another council, to ascertain what remains to be done, and what would be most likely to meet the views of his Majesty. The last council was composed of the Governor, of the Marquis of Rubi, lieutenant general, and of Michel de Altariva, intendant of the army.

"My opinion was, that I ought to proceed on my way to Spain, in the first vessel sailing from this port, not only to present your Excellency with a detailed account of what had occurred, and to solve the doubts and difficulties that may arise, but also to furnish your Excellency with the necessary informations to secure the accomplishment of his Majesty's views, either with regard to the principal chiefs of the rebellion, or on other points; for, I am aware that, in such cases, it is very important to know well, not only the nature of the means to be employed, but also the time and the circumstances most opportune for their use. But those gentlemen were of a different opinion, and it seemed to them that it would be more prudent for me, to wait for the orders of his Majesty, to execute what it might please him to decide in this affair, and they thought that the interval of four or five months, which it would require to receive the instructions of his Majesty, would not be detrimental to his service.

"I therefore yielded to their sentiment, although with reluctance, considering that much time would have been gained, had I followed my first impulse, since it would have been as easy for me to go to Spain as to forward a letter."

At the same time, he sent to the Marquis of Grimaldi a despatch containing a relation of the events of the 28th and 29th of October, and the following observations:

"I beg you to recall to your memory a letter, which I wrote to you in March, 1766, a few days after my arrival in New-Orleans, in relation to the character of the inhabitants. What I communicated to you on the subject, was founded on the preliminary informations which Governor Aubry had given to me, and on a letter which I received from Mr. de Kerlerec, in which he gave me an abstract description of the colony, and pitied me much for having been sent to govern such a country, and finally, on what I had experienced myself, during the few days that had elapsed since my coming to this province, as well as on the liberty which the merchants had taken, to present me with a kind of manifesto, containing different articles, on each of which they asked me for a decision, in order that they might frame their measures accordingly. I sent to your Excellency a copy of that memorial, in order that you might know the audacity of the people with whom you would have to deal, who aimed at no less than forcing their sovereign to capitulate with them, and whose expressions, far from being respectful and supplicating, were imperious, insolent and threatening.

" About three months before the outbreak of the revolution, it was known that Mr. de Bienville, the brother of Noyan, and Mr. Masan, the son of the conspirator of that name, had gone secretly to Pensacola, through a canal on the plantation of the latter, which communicated with lake Borgne, without its being ascertained what was the object of their voyage.

" About the same time, a Frenchman, who was a stranger in the colony, and who had come to take possession of certain property belonging to his nephews, then in France and minors, being exasperated at a decree which the Council had rendered against him, under the dictation of Lafrénière, and witnessing my want of power to have done to him such justice as he thought he deserved, assured me that there were traitors in the town, and that those traitors were persons intrusted with high powers, giving me to understand that they were the very persons who, to-day, make a figure at the head of the insurrection.

" When the insurrection began to manifest itself, the persons who were not participators in it, and whose number was pretty considerable, loudly declared what had been the motive of Bienville and Masan's visit to Pensacola, and the conspirators themselves did not hesitate to confess, that these emissaries had gone to solicit the assistance of the English governor general, and to beg him to send troops to support the rebels, after the breaking out of the insurrection. It seems that the Governor's answer was not favorable. For, the said Governor, having reflected maturely on that affair, sent them back, without encouraging their designs.

" It is proper that your Excellency should know that

their plans underwent more than one modification, and that one of them was, as reported, to transform this colony into a republic, under the protection of England; but seeing that they could not obtain from her the assistance which they wished for, they came to the determination to rise without it, and to trample under foot the orders of their sovereign. * *
* * * * * *

"Hence the origin of the conspiracy. It is proper that I should make you acquainted with the interests and the relations of the inhabitants among themselves, in order to give to every one his due.

"The commissary Foucault has always kept up a scandalous connection with a certain widow called Pradel, living with her, even when he resided in a different house, and frequently cohabiting with her on a plantation, which borders on the upper precincts of New-Orleans. About the same time when Bienville and Masan repaired secretly to Pensacola, Madam Pradel went with Foucault to her plantation, the dwelling house of which is contiguous to the town, and there they spent their nights, coming to town only during the day. On the breaking out of the insurrection, it was publicly said that there were in that residence frequent suppers, at which were present Lafrénière, his relations, and the other conspirators, and that, after the convivialities were over, these men passed the rest of the night in the garden, where they had their conferences, so that it is not doubtful but that the blow was struck from that quarter.

"The captain of the German militia, called Villeré, is the brother in law of Lafrénière, and is married to the niece of D'Arensbourg, who commands at the German Coast. The captain of the Tchoupitoulas militia is an individual named Léry, who is Lafrénière's first cousin; thus, the interests of Lafrénière are supported by the three companies of militia, commanded by his cousin, his brother in law and their relations; so that, with mere pretences to induce the militia of the town to rebel, it happens that the whole colony is put in a state of insurrection at the voice of one single man.

" The uncle of Noyan and Bienville had come from Canada to govern Louisiana, and, among the common people he brought over with him, there were four brothers, of the surname of Leroy, who, afterwards, assumed different surnames in Louisiana, one causing himself to be called Lafrénière, the other, Léry, the third, Beaulieu, and the fourth, Chauvin. These four Canadians were of so low an extraction, and had so little education, that they could not write, and had come with an axe on the shoulder to live on their manual labor. The sons of these men are now the chiefs and authors of the rebellion.

" In a letter which I had the honor to write to your Excellency, before the event of the rebellion, I had informed you of the precaution which I had taken to send Mr. Maxent, with fifteen hundred dollars, to pay the Germans for the provisions which had been bought from them, in order to supply the Acadians with food, because the conspirators had availed themselves of the pretext, that this payment would never be made, in order to induce these people to co-operate with them.

" On the day following Maxent's departure, Lafrénière and another individual, named Marquis, sent, early in the morning, Villeré and Verret, in pursuit of Maxent, to arrest him, and to prevent his delivering the money to the Germans, fearing, if they were paid, that the motive which had prompted them to join the rebels, existing no longer, these people might withdraw from the conspiracy, and thus force the conspirators to give up their designs. Maxent arrived at the plantation of D'Arensbourg, for whom I had given him a letter, and when he delivered it to that gentleman, he found him so different from what he expected, that, notwithstanding the very old age of that officer, and the unequivocal proofs, already received, of his fidelity, he discovered in him a man who had entirely yielded to the persuasions of his relations, Villeré and Léry, who had arrayed himself in the defence of liberty, and who had resolved that he should neither be the subject of the King, nor that the colony should belong to his Majesty.

"Maxent was arrested by Verret, as he states in his declaration, at one Cantrelle's house, who is the father in law of another Verret, commanding the Acadians, and where he was exceedingly ill used. The same Verret, whose first name is André, has confirmed Maxent's declaration to Mr. de Sale, lieutenant of foot, who commanded the detachment given to me by the French governor, for the protection of my person and my papers, on the 2d of November, when the vessel in which I had embarked was moored in front of the plantation of Madam D'Aunoy. Consequently it is proved by the detention of the person of Maxent, that a plot had been formed to seduce the province from its fealty to Spain, by preventing the execution of those measures, which prudence had suggested, to remove the pretexts which were intended to be put in use.

"The same André Verret has declared to Mr. de Sale that, with regard to the order to arrest Maxent, he had received it from Villeré, Lafrénière, and Marquis.

"Lafrénière and Foucault have availed themselves of the discontent caused among the merchants by the *commercial decree*. With regard to the Acadians and Germans, they were persuaded to come to town, to be paid what was due to them in reimbursement of their *Canadian bonds.* Accordingly, they came unarmed, with their captains Judice and Verret. It was in town that arms were distributed to them.

" After the success of the rebellion, the Acadians, being discontented at their having been deceived, made reproaches to their chiefs, and complained of their not having been indemnified for their loss of time and for the damage they had incurred in abandoning their labors.

" The Germans were misled by their being made to believe, that they were threatened with tyranny, and by other false assertions, as well as by calumnies against the Spaniards.

" With regard to the great body of the inhabitants, they were driven by force and violence into this scheme of insurrection by the chiefs of the rebels.

" The Germans and the Acadians are nevertheless guilty of ingratitude, because they had received nothing but benefits from the Spaniards. They were enticed away.

" If there was any scarcity of provisions, in 1766, it was the fault of Mr. Foucault alone, who neglected to procure them.

" The names at the bottom of the memorial of the planters, merchants, &c., &c., which I attribute to Lafrénière, were signed on a blank piece of paper, which was subsequently filled up. It bears the stamp of Lafrénière's style, which is easily detected. In that document are to be found those arrogant expressions, that superciliousness and that insolent freedom with which he is in the habit of declaiming against our nation, and of endeavoring to persuade the inhabitants to remain French.

" From the beginning, I had clearly seen that this man would never be a faithful subject of the King, and that he would use all his powers of eloquence to inspire the rest of his countrymen with his sentiments, and your Excellency may remember that I gave you timely information of it, in 1766. At the same time and in the same letters, I informed your Excellency that Lafrénière was considerably in debt—so much so, that the whole of his property could not pay the obligations he had contracted in France. De Noyan, his son in law, Villeré, Milhet, and the principal chiefs of the conspiracy are in the same position.

"It would entirely suit their convenience, that this colony should remain a French possession, that Lafrénière should be the head and the master spirit of the Superior Council, by which means, he, Lafrénière, would be able to defraud his baffled creditors, and to prevent his friends and relations from being ruined by their own creditors, which would be the case, if they were compelled to pay their debts. Lafrénière had entertained the hope that, after the fall of the Spaniards, he would, with the other members of his family, be able to realize large funds, with which he would retire to France. Foucault's object was to keep up the colonial and commercial connection of France with Louisiana, in order that he might retain his office of counselor and commissary, as I have already informed your Excellency.

"It is not the first time that the seditious maxims of Lafrénière have caused troubles. If Mr. de Kerlerec, when he was Governor of this colony, passed over the intrigues and the practices by which this turbulent spirit then agitated the colony, it was because he was obliged to resist, at the same time, both this secret and intestine war and an open one from the English, so that he was not prepared to take efficacious measures to repress such disorders.

"Mr. D'Abbadie, his successor, experienced so much

opposition and so many inconveniences from the same source, that he more than once laid his complaints before the court of France, and represented the risks to which the colony was exposed from the senseless ambition of a subject, who pretended to unite in his person all the powers of the government; and he earnestly insisted on the necessity of removing him from the office of Attorney General, which had been given to him only for a limited time. If the court of France did not comply with his representations, it is because, the cession of Louisiana having been made, it was deemed expedient to leave it to Spain, to act on the reforms which might be thought necessary."

So much for Ulloa's views and self-defence. But his expulsion had not satisfied the insurgents, and, in the month of December, they presented another petition to the Superior Council for the expulsion of the Spanish frigate. It was conceived in these terms:

"Mr. Marquis, late commander of the fourth Swiss company, the chevalier De La Ronde, late lieutenant of foot, Le Breton, late guardsman in the King's household troops, all, syndics* of the planters and colonists of this province, Mess. Caresse and Braquier, syndics of the merchants of New-Orleans, represent: that the frigate which used to serve as a prison to the citizens oppressed by Ulloa, as an asylum to the slaves who rebelled against their masters, and which was but too evident a sign of the expiring freedom of navigation, that this very frigate continues to sport her flag in this harbor, where she seems to domineer; that the posts of Manchac, of Natchez and of the Illinois are still occupied by Spanish garrisons and commanders; that

---

* A Syndic is the chief or headman of a corporation or community, of which he is a member, and with the management of whose affairs he is intrusted.

the officers of his Catholic Majesty are no more disposed to depart, than if this colony was under the rule of Spain, and that, so far, there is no apparent change in the frightful prospect of that foreign domination, which has so much disquieted the inhabitants of this colony; that, with regard to the Spanish frigate, it is not astonishing that her remaining in this port should have caused general discontent, considering that the recollection of the vexations which she exercised in conformity with the orders of Ulloa, both in relation to the freedom of navigation and to that of the citizens, cannot but produce indignation, &c., &c. * * * *

"Said petitioners proceed to represent, that the decree rendered by the court, on the 29th of October last, when it enjoined Mr. Ulloa to embark within three days, either in the frigate, or in such other vessel as he might choose, did also impliedly enjoin the officers of said frigate, to make themselves ready to depart in a few days, and that if Mr. Ulloa was allowed to choose the vessel in which he was to sail, it is only because the court had presumed that the frigate was in want of some repairs to go to sea with security; that even a vague rumor had been spread, that Mr. Ulloa himself, before his departure, had ordered the officers of the frigate to have her promptly repaired, and then to leave the country for Havana, without loss of time; that, in fact, they had taken workmen almost immediately, but that their labors were conducted with excessive slowness; that the careening of that frigate seems to be the work of Penelope; and that there will be no end to it, if their diligence is not stimulated; that, according to the declaration of all the seafaring men of this port, she ought to have been ready a long time since, and that they would undertake to make her seaworthy in fifteen days.

* * * * *

" Said petitioners further represent : That this slow proceeding has no tendency to produce tranquillity and general satisfaction; that devotedly obedient to the orders of his most Christian Majesty, the colonists cherish and revere all that bears such a character; but that they hold in utter detestation all that can perpetuate to their eye the image of the Spanish authority, and the traces of the administration, which Ulloa presented to them under so threatening an aspect, well seconded as he was, by all those to whom he had delegated the slightest particle of the powers he assumed; that the petitioners have lately received sad news, in relation to those who have exercised those illegal powers; that the merchants, Rivard and Bérard, who were going to the Illinois, have been forced to land at the Arkansas, not to hear any longer the insulting language, in which a certain Catalan, named Chouriac, who was sent by the Spaniards to the Illinois, as storekeeper and commissary, expressed himself towards the French nation; that Piernas, the commander of the Spanish troops, when going with said Chouriac to the Illinois district, to assume its government, had met, at the *Ecores à Margot,* a boat which was coming down; that said Piernas and Chouriac stopped her, and pressed out of her two rowers to increase their own crew, by threatening to fire at the boat with their swivel gun if they were not obeyed, and to put in chains the nine men who manned her; that notwithstanding they could spare no one out of their small number, yet they drew lots to ascertain which of them would embark in the Spanish boat, in which they had nothing to expect but ill usage ; that having attempted to stipulate for their wages, the said Chouriac told them that they must go to work for the service of the King without further discussion.

" The petitioners beg leave to state in addition, that

this circumstance recalls to mind another, which is not a less powerful demonstration of the evident tyranny, already exercised by the officers acting under the command of Mr. Ulloa; that these facts are related such as they happened, without the least passion or rancor; and the petitioners ardently wish that the pure spirit of truth which guides their pen, may open the eyes of some bad citizens, if, unfortunately, there should be any among them, whose base and venal souls should still be wavering between the choice of liberty or slavery. Thus the petitioners represent, that Mr. Chamard departed last year in his boat for the Illinois; that having stopped at Natchez, Mr. Piernas, the Spanish commander at that place, addressed one of the passengers on board Chamard's boat, and asked him for provisions, as he feared that he would soon be in need of them; that this passenger answered that some might easily be procured at Pointe Coupée or elsewhere, adding that the boats bound from New Orleans to the Illinois, far from being able to sell their provisions, were obliged to purchase some for their own use at all the posts established on the banks of the river; that Mr. Piernas having retired, the men of the boat thought they had done with him, and that they were pushing from the shore, when suddenly Mr. Piernas had a piece of artillery loaded, to fire at the boat, if she dared to leave the landing, and caused the alarum bell to be tolled, (the ordinary signal to take up arms,) collected his troops, and ordered Mr. de Lavillebeuvre to put himself at their head; that this officer, notwithstanding the strong reluctance which he felt, was obliged to obey, and the provisions had to be delivered up to Piernas; that there never was a specimen of more complete vexation and of better circumstantiated violence; that the natural inference is, that they, the colonists, must be looked upon by the Spaniards as galley slaves ; finally, that the haughty temper and tyrannical pretensions of that self styled officer of his Catholic Majesty cannot but be the cause of unbounded indignation.

" The petitioners further represent, in their aforesaid capacities and character, that it falls within the province of the court to apply the remedy to the evil which they expose, and they do not hesitate to say, that the continuance of these vexations would convert the colony into a desert.

" Therefore they beg the Council to solicit from Mr. Aubry's sense of justice, that he should invite the captain of the Spanish frigate, the *Volante*, to hasten his departure, in the interest of public tranquillity."

The Superior Council, on the conclusions of the attorney general, who supported the petition, rendered a decree in conformity with the prayer of the petitioners.

On the 23d of December, Foucault, continuing the part which he had so long been playing, of secretly instigating insurrection and of openly disclaiming all participation in it—nay—of apparently opposing the measures which he had provoked by underhand suggestions, wrote to his government :

" On the 9th inst. (December, 1768) the syndics of the planters, merchants and inhabitants of this colony handed to me a petition addressed by them, in their official capacity, to the Superior Council, begging that the frigate of the King of Spain, which is moored at the quay of the town, together with the officers and other persons having titles or brevets from his Catholic Majesty, or commissions from Mr. Ulloa, the same having come with him or in other Spanish vessels, be compelled to withdraw from this colony, within the shortest possible delay. I was aware of the vexations which had given rise to this demand, and they were so iniquitous,

that I could not help blaming inwardly captain Piernas, the Spanish commander at Natchez, and Chouriac, whom Ulloa had sent as storekeeper and commissary at the Illinois. But I was at first tempted not to lend a favorable ear to the petition of the colonists, because, in my opinion, the Superior Council could not grant what they prayed for, without going out of the bounds which it had prescribed to itself in its decree of the 29th of October last; and because to dismiss from the colony the vessels and the officers sent to it by his Catholic Majesty, would be an infraction of the orders of our Sovereign, and because it seemed to me that it would be more proper to suspend any of those officers, who should make an abusive use of their authority, and to account for our motives in so doing, &c., &c. * * *
* * * * * * *

" But, for many reasons, I was obliged to convene the Council for the next day. It rendered an interlocutory decree, ordering a judicial investigation of the facts imputed to Piernas and Chouriac, to be reported upon as a basis for further proceedings.

" On the 14th, the Council having met again, to take into consideration the report, which contained the depositions of four witnesses, I gave my opinion in writing, and stated my reasons for strongly opposing any decree of expulsion, either against the frigate, or any Spanish officer. But the Council ordered that its decree of the 29th of October should be carried into full execution, and begged Mr. Aubry to solicit the captain of the frigate to accelerate his departure in the shortest possible delay. It has also begged me to offer to that captain, and if accepted, to furnish him with, any additional number of sailors, workmen, or whatever other things he might deem necessary to have, in order to enable him to quit the colony. I complied with the wishes of the Council on this subject, notwithstanding the reluctance which I felt, but only with regard to the sailors and workmen, because, with regard to provisions and other supplies, I had nothing which I could dispose of in the King's warehouses. I have the honor, my Lord, to transmit to you, herein annexed, copies of the report of the committee of inquiry appointed by the Council, on the charges brought against the Spanish officers, of the opinion which I gave in the Council, and of the decree of that tribunal.

"We shall take the command of the several posts established by Ulloa, in conformity with the request which he addressed to Mr. Aubry, and they shall be occupied by the French, until we receive the orders which we have asked for. We have been for a month in possession of the Post at the Balize. Mr. Aubry and myself have sent Mr. Andry, sub-engineer, to the posts of Iberville and Natchez, in order, jointly with the officers of his Catholic Majesty, who command at these places, to draw and sign the plans and estimates of all the buildings, and make an inventory of all the artillery, provisions, ammunition, merchandise and other effects there to be found, in concert with those commanding officers and the storekeepers; to receive the whole into his custody, and to station at each of these points eight or ten Acadians, in the place of the soldiers, whom it is impossible to send there, on account of the small number of them that are here."

Foucault concludes with saying, that all the Spaniards are withdrawing from the other posts, and that it is agreed with them that, after the event of the 29th of October, the expenses of the colony shall, nevertheless, be supported by the King of Spain, up to the 31st of December next inclusively, and that the account shall be settled accordingly.

This despatch is another proof of the miserable

shuffling, to which Foucault resorted in all those transactions. His plan had been to show himself, in his official acts, as favorable to the insurgents as he possibly could, and to encourage them as far as he could go, without committing himself too much in the eye of the French and Spanish governments. Thus, he had affected to oppose the expulsion of the frigate and of the Spanish officers, and at the same time, he had recommended to suspend from their functions any of these very same officers who might be deemed guilty of an abuse of power. Yet to a man of his intelligence this dilemma must certainly have presented itself: the colony was either a Spanish, or a French province. If French, the colonists had the right, not only to prevent the Spanish officers from exercising their usurped functions, but also to expel them altogether, as intruders and trespassers. On the other hand, if Louisiana was a Spanish possession, and if, as Foucault maintained, the officers of his Catholic Majesty could not be driven away, whence did the colonists derive their authority, save from the right of revolution, to suspend them from their functions, on the plea of abuses of power? Whence the right assumed by Foucault, on behalf of the colonists, to account for so high handed a measure, not to the King of Spain, their new master, but to the late one, the King of France? These inconsistencies evidently proceeded from his desire to steer his bark safely between two opposite shoals.

On the very day when Foucault was writing the preceding despatch, Aubry, whose mind was sufficiently enlightened, and whose judgment was sufficiently calm, to foresee the fatal consequences of what had happened in Louisiana, and therefore whose anxieties were incessantly growing, communicated to the Minister his reflections on the revolution which he had witnessed.

He wrote : " I find myself under the sad necessity of speaking, and of telling all, in spite of my reluctance to do so. The Council behaved badly. The attorney general Lafrénière is one of the principal leaders.

" Mr. de Ulloa committed several faults, but never perpetrated crimes, and, setting aside his rank and his character, did not deserve the treatment which he underwent.

" It is necessary to send here a battalion and a new council. The one, to drive out of the country from ten to twelve firebrands, who rule it as they please, and are the causes of all the harm done ; the other, to administer justice, which is almost entirely set aside.

" Should this revolution produce no change in the arrangements between France and Spain, in relation to this colony, would it not be proper that his Majesty should transmit his orders here as soon as possible, and announce his ultimate and irrevocable will on the cession to Spain, promising pardon and oblivion, save to a few who are guilty, and whom it is absolutely necessary to punish? Besides, it is probable that the guiltiest will take refuge among the English, when they shall learn the arrival of troops.

" It is much to be desired that the officer who may be sent by his Catholic Majesty to take possession of this colony, should have the necessary qualifications. If Mr. de Ulloa had been of a milder and more complaisant disposition, the colony would long ago have become Spanish ; all would have remained quiet, and we should not be in the situation in which we are now. I assure you, my Lord, that, but for me, he would have been sent away two years ago.

" It is desirable that, for some time, vessels should be allowed to come here from France and from the Islands. It is the greatest benefit that his

Catholic Majesty could confer on the inhabitants of Louisiana.

"Should the province remain to France, its inhabitants would be transported with joy. It would be the most agreeable news they could receive, as they generally have French hearts. But I am certain that, at present, they would prefer passing under the English domination than the Spanish, unless his Catholic Majesty should be disposed to grant them some privileges and advantages, to induce them to live under his flag. Ulloa's too great severity has frightened them, and they fear to be governed as despotically as the Mexicans.

"With a million a year, France could keep up here a sufficient force to support the administration of this possession, and to make to the Indians the necessary presents, and she would preserve a colony, where a great attachment is felt for her, and whose commerce may be very advantageous."

It must be observed that Aubry denounced to his government *a dozen of firebrands, who had become the masters of the country, and whom it was absolutely necessary to punish;* and declared *that the honest administration of justice was trampled under foot by the Superior Council.* If such were the sentiments of a Frenchman, whose prejudices and feelings must have been enlisted in favor of his countrymen, if such was the language of the chief of the colony, when addressing his own government, what must have been the impressions of the Spaniards, and is it to be wondered that they subsequently pursued the course which I shall have to describe!

When Ulloa arrived at Havana, he found in that city eight hundred troops, that were preparing to come to New-Orleans, with Urissa, late consul of Spain at Bor-

COUNCIL OF MINISTERS IN SPAIN. 247

deaux, and recently promoted to the office of intendant of Louisiana. Urissa had stopped at Havana to take a million of dollars, which the King of Spain had appropriated to meet the payment of his intended expenses in the new domain which he had just acquired. If the eight hundred men, and particularly, if the million of dollars, a sum which the colonists had never, as yet, seen in coin in Louisiana, had arrived in time, it is likely that there would have been no revolution. But, on being informed of the treatment inflicted on Ulloa, Urissa determined to return to Europe.

The news of the revolution in Louisiana reached Spain in forty days, and a cabinet council was held on the subject, to determine* whether Spain should retain Louisiana, on account of the extreme importance of establishing barriers to the aggrandizements of the English, or leave it in the hands of France. The council was composed of the Duke of Alba, Don Jaime Masones de Lima, Don Juan Gregorio Muniain, Don Miguel de Muzquiz, the Count of Aranda, the baron Don Julian de Arriaga and the Marquis of San Juan de Piedras Albas. It was on the 11th of February, 1769, that the Marquis of Grimaldi submitted to these gentlemen all the documents relative to what had occurred in Louisiana, requesting them to give, individually, their separate opinion in writing. On the 5th of March, the Duke of Alba gave this brief and characteristic opinion. It bears the stamp of the hereditary temper of the men of that haughty and inflexible house.

" I am of opinion that the King ought to retain Louisiana, on account of the extreme importance of the river Mississippi's being the fixed and settled limit of the English possessions.

---

* Sobre si conviene conservar España esta posesion, por la suma importancia de poner limites á los Ingleses, o quedarse por de la Francia.

"That his Majesty should choose a man of intelligence and energy, and send him with the necessary forces to subject those people, and, at the same time, with all the powers to cure such disorders, by striking them at the root.

"That the form of the government in the colony be radically changed, in order to leave no means within the reach of the malice or audacity of those people, to attempt other revolutions.

"That all the members of the Superior Council there existing, and the deputies of the commerce of Bordeaux, be immediately transported to Europe, and also every other person that may be suspected.

"And, taking into consideration that, from the possession of that colony, it does not seem that any other advantage can be derived, than that of determining incontestable limits between the neighboring powers, I am of opinion that it be reduced within very narrow bounds, in order that its administration should cost the King as little as possible.

"But finally, what, to my judgment, appears to be of more importance than all the rest, is that it be seen throughout the world, and particularly in America, that the King knows and is able to repress any attempt whatever, derogatory to the respect due to the royal majesty."*

Don Jaime Masones de Lima, Don Miguel de Muzquiz, and Don Julian de Arriaga gave their opinions on the 21st of March. Don Jaime Masones de Lima said:

"Having examined the documents submitted to my consideration, it seems to me that it would be proper

---

* Lo que enfin importa mas que todo, á mi parecer, es que se vea en el mundo, y en America especialmente, que el Rey sabe y puede reprimir cualquiera intento contrario al respeto que se debe á la Majestad.

to retain possession of that colony, considering that the river Mississippi forms an already established line of demarcation between the possession of the French and of the English. I have only to add that this advantage, which is the only one I can conceive, is not counterbalanced by the inconveniences which I foresee, as being likely to result, in the future, from retaining possession of that colony.

" One of them is, that the colony is entirely inhabited by Frenchmen, who are openly inimical to our government, and who are supported by the partiality of their countrymen in France; that there is no fortified place in it (presidio) and that the quality of the soil does not admit of such works, the want of which would require a larger number of troops, to keep the colonists in subjection. Such being the case, it is proper to consider whether the expenses of retaining that possession, are not liable to exceed the damages which we may suffer from its contraband trade, should it be in other hands.

" The Count of Fuentes, in the letter which was read to the council of ministers, treats this question with sufficient precision and details, and in a manner which did not fail to produce much impression on my mind.

" But I further say that, in case my opinion should not prevail, on the policy of our retaining that colonial possession, and in case, for the reasons given by the Count of Fuentes, and for the inconveniences I have pointed out, his Majesty should be inclined to leave it in the hands of France, then, the better to provide for the future, I recommend a stipulation by which it should be understood, that France shall never cede that province, either to the English or to the colonists themselves, without the consent of Spain, reserving its reversion to us, whenever France shall feel disposed to part with it.

"Having done with the question of his Majesty's retaining possession of the colony, which is the one specially presented to the council, I proceed to express what offers itself to my mind, on the offence committed by its inhabitants against the person of Don Antonio de Ulloa, as this subject is somewhat connected with the other.

"Supposing then that Spain is to retain possession of that colony according to my opinion, I consider that the crime committed by the inhabitants deserves the most severe and rigorous punishment, on account of the circumstances which accompanied its commission. But, however offensive their conduct may have been to the King and to his subjects, it remains not the less an outrage against the Majesty of the most Christian King, because, so far as we are concerned, the colonists having before them no other document than the act of cession made by his most Christian Majesty, and registered by their Superior Council, and until now, Spain having not by any public act taken solemn possession of the province, the correct construction to be put on what has occurred, may be looked upon as problematical among the French, and even among us. But, considering that the colonists declare themselves to be the subjects of his most Christian Majesty, they thus increase their culpability, on account of the notorious insolence with which they disobeyed his orders, as they could not plead their ignorance of the treaty of cession.

"For these reasons, I have come to the conclusion that, whatever be the means that we may employ, to obtain satisfaction for so enormous an offence, it would be proper that we should come to an understanding with France; so that, by procuring her concurrence in the punishment of that offence, we shall avoid that any military operation, to which we might proceed by ourselves, be accused of being unjust, by those who consider the question of possession as doubtful, and who would argue that we enforce our authority, without having previously established our sovereignty, because we never made apparent and publicly known to the colonists, by any act of notoriety, the new obligation of vassalage to which they were subjected, by virtue of the cession made by his most Christian Majesty.

" This is all that my poor abilities venture to suggest to the King, in order that his Majesty may resolve what may be most agreeable to his royal breast, as the determination which he will take, will certainly be the best for the occasion."

So much for the very considerate and courtier-like opinion of Don Jaime Masones de Lima. Now comes Don Juan de Arriaga.

" From the moment, said he, that France offered to cede Louisiana, it seemed opportune to me to take her, not because it might be a profitable possession to us, in a pecuniary point of view, but because of the advantage which we obtain, of securing indisputable limits between us and the English, who never stand in need of some pretext or other, to overstep them, without any open and avowed act of transgression.

" For the same reason, I persist in my former opinion; but I recommend that proper precautions be taken in the establishment of the government of that colony, not only on account of what occurred recently, as on account of the informations we have acquired on the composition of that population, which, as Ulloa says in one of his despatches, is made up of all sorts of people, without fealty, without law and without religion. It is therefore evident that, unless we cut off and remove the most conspicuous and most vitiated portion of that population, and unless we establish for the rest new rules of government, not only with regard to the political, but also the religious organization of that colony, we cannot, with any security, rely on that possession, except it be through force, and with the aid of troops to bring those people to submission; the consequences of which measures would be our going into enormous expenses, and our being in a state of constant suspicion and anxiety.

"The examination of the means to be employed requires the most serious reflection, and calls for the most detailed information from Ulloa, because the points which it is necessary to regulate are numerous. One of the first to be taken into consideration, is the number of troops to be sent there, and the expenses it will put us to, in order to restrict them within what can be supplied out of the royal revenue and treasury of Mexico; and although it is not to be hoped that the commerce of that colony can be of any advantage to his majesty, nevertheless, it is necessary to determine by whom and how it is to be carried on, it being important that there be no failure in that part of it which is relative to the Indians, with whom we must, by all means, keep on terms of amity."

As to the Marquis of San Juan de Piedras Albas, he said:

"I think that it is of extreme importance for Spain, to retain under her domination that part of the colony of Louisiana which was ceded by France, not only because it is a valuable barrier and a means of protection for the provinces of New Spain and the Mexican Gulf, but also for the other reasons which were given verbally in the cabinet council, and which have convinced me in the most effective manner, that, taking into consideration the position of Louisiana, in no other hands than in ours can that colony, for the present and for the future, be as important and useful to Spain; and, under the circumstances in which we are placed, supposing that France persists, as she does beyond a doubt, in her disposition to ratify her voluntary donation to Spain, and is prepared, (considering that she is more particularly interested in resenting the insolent want of respect with which she was disobeyed by her subjects and vassals,) to accomplish what, so far, she has not been able to execute, and to put Spain in quiet and peaceful possession of that domain, I reiterate the opinion which I have already expressed: that Spain must maintain herself in the possession of that province, which was ceded to her in good faith, and which was not formally delivered up to her, on account of the criminal disobedience of its inhabitants."

On the next day, the 22d of March, the Count of Aranda, who had the reputation of being one of the shrewdest and ablest statesmen of Spain, presented a somewhat more elaborate opinion than those of his colleagues. Taken in connexion with the events which have happened on the continent of North America, and which have transformed colonies into empires, it certainly is a curious and remarkable document.

"Considering, he said, the original cause of the acquisition of Louisiana by Spain, and the reasons which were then given for it; and whereas that colony must be looked upon as one of the dependencies of the crown, and as so much territory annexed to our Mexican provinces, I am of opinion that it was wisely done, to accept the donation which France made of her, and that it is indispensable to keep possession of that acquisition, at whatever cost.

"The more or less fertility and extent of Louisiana is not the principal question to be examined. But we ought to judge of the importance of that acquisition, from the fact that it extends our Mexican territories to the bank of the Mississippi, a well known barrier, and a distant one from the population of New-Mexico, and that it furnishes us, through that river, with an indelible line of demarcation between our provinces and those of the English, which have been widened by their acquisition of our domain of Florida; and that it gives the occasion to create, at certain determined points, a chain of posts which, in time of peace, will be the evidences of our territorial rights, and will prevent usurpations and trespasses made under the plea of ignorance. Besides securing the notoriety and the indisputable acknowledgment of our sovereignty, we obtain a precious protection for ourselves, and oppose a serious impediment to the progress of the English, because, in case of a rupture with them, they will have to begin their operations from afar, will be exposed to great losses before having gained much ground, and will not have the advantage to make, in anticipation, their preparations, secretly, in the interior of their possessions, in order to shorten and facilitate their operations, at the breaking out of hostilities.

" In short, under this view, which is full of interest, the insurrection at New-Orleans seems to be an object of the greatest importance, not only for the reasons which have already been expressed, but on account of its consequences.

" Its situation in the Gulf of Mexico, its being already, as it were, an European town by its population, its being inhabited altogether by merchants and traders, and its being converted into a free port, which no doubt would be the case, would attract thither large numbers from Europe; and considering that a republic in Louisiana would be independent from all the European powers, it would then become the interest of all to keep on terms of amity with her, and to support her existence.

"The favorable circumstances in which Louisiana would then be placed, would not only increase her population, but also enlarge her limits, and transform her into a rich, flourishing and free State, in sight of our provinces, which would present the melancholy contrast of exhaustion and of the want of cultivation.*

"From the example under their eyes, the inhabitants of our vast Mexican domains would be led to consider their utter want of commerce, the extortions of their different governors, the little esteem in which they are held, the few offices which they are permitted to fill, and would weigh the great inducement which they would have to hate still more the Spanish domination and to think that they can brave it with more security, when they shall see that a weak province, compared with their extensive and populous country, can make good her position with impunity and secure her prosperity.

"Even if by dint of efforts to meliorate as much as possible the government of the Mexican provinces, and improve the condition of their inhabitants, we should succeed in avoiding the fatal revolution which might break out, how could we prevent the illicit commerce of Louisiana by sea with all the harbors on our coasts, and also by land with Texas and New-Mexico, and through them to old Mexico?

"To think of being agreeable to France by returning to her what she ceded, would be attended by the gravest inconveniences; because, besides that in her hands, the colony, by its situation, would be a possession prejudicial to our commerce, furthermore, on the first emergency, she would avail herself of that pledge,

* A remarkable prophecy!

to cede it to the English, whom it suits exceedingly, and would use it so as to obtain better terms for peace.

"I can easily imagine the costs of fitting out the proper expedition, to retake possession of Louisiana, as well as to keep her for the future, and also the doubts which present themselves, whether, in the progress of time, the profits which might be derived from that colony, would compensate for the immediate expenses to be incurred, or, at least, meet those that would be required annually. But all these reasons, individually and collectively, cannot counterbalance, in my judgment, those which militate on the other side, considering that the keeping of that possession, although expensive, is necessary to preserve our principal dominions.

"Of what importance to us is it, that the French should retain their known limits with regard to the English, when such not being the case on the side of our territories, it will be left to their own pleasure, on their retaking possession of Louisiana, to extend their frontiers at will and to our prejudice? So that, instead of keeping at a distance our neighboring enemy, by retaining Louisiana in our hands, we should admit between him and us another power, and that power might recognize no barriers to his own encroachments upon our possessions. Thus, for the very reason that there are no established limits between Louisiana and Mexico, the present rebels would, if they were permitted to remain so, have a pretext for claiming an arbitrary extension of territory, and, besides the disputes to which it would give rise, it would put us under the necessity of going to the expense of establishing a new *cordon.*

"It seems to me, therefore, that the best policy is to

repossess ourselves of New-Orleans, with sufficient forces to prevent the possibility of any disgrace to the King's arms ; to expel from the colony all those who were the causes of the late troubles, confiscating their property as a punishment for their rebellion ; to order that all those who are innocent, but who may not choose to submit themselves to the new domination, be transported to France, or where they please ; to send some Spanish families to Louisiana, to serve as the main root of the new population which is to rule in that country ; to limit, for the present, that population to the extent which will be sufficient to keep up, there, just enough of cultivation to make of New-Orleans a place capable of offering temporary resources, in cases of need, to the commerce and fleets of his majesty ; and, for the purpose of making known our frontiers as plainly as possible, to establish all along those of the English a chain of posts, at regular intervals of thirty miles, or at the most important points.

"I am also of opinion that we ought not to have in New-Orleans more than one small fort, to keep the people in subjection, and to cause the flag of his Majesty to be respected, in case any insult to it should be attempted by the enemies of the crown. By abstaining from making of that town a place of importance, we shall avoid making it an object of attack ; because, if with that view, an enemy should send there a considerable body of troops, these very forces might ultimately serve to carry on further designs against Mexico, and our other domains in that part of America.

"What is also of importance, is to ingratiate ourselves with those different Indian nations that are on bad terms with the English, because, by fomenting hostilities on the part of these Indians, we shall keep the northern establishments of the English in a state of alarm, and by this means, oblige them to retain there all their forces, because, should they dare to do otherwise, the Indians I have spoken of, being on their shoulders, would immediately devastate their territories by their irruptions."

On the 24th, Don Miguel de Muzquiz delivered his written opinion in these terms :

"I find inconveniences in leaving Louisiana to the French, but still greater ones, and more certain, in its being retained by Spain.

"From the moment that the French made their first settlements in that country, they have been, to the present time, imagining more than one project to approach the provinces of Texas and New-Mexico, and they have not been able to execute their plans, not only on account of the distances to be overcome, but also because they never could gain the good will of the Indians, and because they had to watch the proceedings of their English neighbors. These same obstacles still subsist for the French and preserve us from the threatened danger of their penetrating into Texas and New Mexico.

"The French have long been in possession of that province, where they are accustomed to enjoy a freedom, as to their persons and as to their commerce, which our laws do not admit of; but they are obliged to suffer and tolerate the excesses which are committed by the Indians, and as these savages prefer a state of war to any other, and as they are armed, they can make sudden and fatal attacks.

"The navigation of the Mississippi is common both to the French and to the English, and, although their respective territorial limits are determined, it will be impossible for them to avoid having disputes arising from competition, if there be any commerce carried on, and it is better that the encountering of these difficulties should fall on the French rather than on the Spaniards. The French can easily provide for the preservation of Louisiana and keep the English in check with little expense.

"The Spaniards would have many disagreements* with the French inhabitants of Louisiana and with the Indians, because they would lack the necessary patience to manage these people, and although their submission might be secured by the strong arm of force, yet I do not conceive that the object to be attained is worth the cost.

"It is true that the French will have ingress into the Gulf of Mexico, under the pretext of going to Louisiana, and will be able to carry on a contraband trade, but, besides that it is impossible to prevent this evil, even were Louisiana ours, it does not seem to me that the injuries which we wish to escape from, would be equal to the expenses that the possession of that colony would entail upon us.

"Should we retain Louisiana, we should incur a perpetual and annual expenditure of three hundred thousand dollars, put ourselves under the necessity of increasing the number of our officers, have incessant causes of difficulties with the English, and have to encounter numerous obstacles in the administration of that possession.

"In time of war, we should have to reinforce that province, and the means employed to accomplish this aim, would be so much wanting for the preservation and

* Los Españoles tendrian muchos disgustos con los Franceses que se quedasen, y con los Indios salvajes, porque les faltaria la paciencia que se necesitaria para contemplarlos, y aunque con la fuerza se puede asegurar todo, no concibo que el objeto merezca tanto gasto.

defence of more essential points ; so that, weakened as we are at present, by the necessity of providing for so many scattered posts in America, we should increase our weakness by putting ourselves to the charge of maintaining and defending Louisiana, whilst, leaving her to the French, it is probable that they would protect her against the English better than we can do.

" For these reasons and others to be deduced from them, my opinion is, that it is proper for the crown to abandon Louisiana to the French. It remains to be examined, whether the King can do so, without any forfeit of honor. Ulloa took possession of the government of the colony, only ad interim, so that said act may be considered as merely preparatory to the solemn formality of a final taking of possession, by the officers and troops he was waiting for ; and thus, according to my judgment, the offence is common to the two crowns, and should Louisiana remain in the hands of France, it would become her sense of self dignity, not to suffer to go unpunished those who have disobeyed the orders of her king."

On the 31st (March), Don Juan Gregorio Muniain closed the consultation with the following concise opinion :

" The situation of the colony of New-Orleans which, with its limits, extends itself all along the right bank of the Mississippi, as far as the unknown mountains, many leagues beyond its meeting with the Missouri, secures the following advantages :

" 1°.—It establishes between New-Mexico and the territories ceded to England invariable limits, such as the course of a river which preserves its name from its source to its mouth in the Gulf of Mexico.

" 2°.—By giving to that colony the same uniform

system of government which has been imposed on all our American provinces, and by keeping in active service at the port of New-Orleans a small and light frigate, we shall repress the commercial frauds which are meditated against us from Florida, and put a stop to the contraband trade.

" 3°.—By encouraging the cultivation of wheat, and other grains and plants, we shall promote a trade in flour and vegetables, of extreme utility to Havana, Puerto-Rico and the other Islands.

" 4°.—It seems to me that the expenses attending the preservation and administration of that colony, cannot be greater than those to which we were put in Florida, by the possession of St. Augustin, Pensacola and Apalache, and those which we incur, at present, in maintaining our Presidios in New-Mexico, some of which, if not all, could be suppressed with advantage.

" 5°.—In order to avoid that the English establish themselves without opposition in our territory, by crossing the river Mississippi, it will be necessary to erect some small fortified posts according to the fashion of the country, that will serve as scouts, and will advise the governor of the colony of the least possible change.

" 6°.—Should this colony be ceded to France with all its territorial enlargement, that power might extend itself towards Mexico, and establish with that country an illicit commerce, as the merchants of that nation have already done. Besides, should France be worsted in war by the English, she would have an object of value to offer to them, to obtain an advantageous peace for her establishments in Africa and Asia.

" For these reasons I am of opinion, that it is proper to keep possession of the colony of New Orleans with all its limits."

These deliberations of the statesmen of Spain, in 1769, show, in an interesting manner, the policy which guided her in the formation and prosecution of her colonial system, and give the key to her subsequent administration of Louisiana. But it is impossible to peruse them without a smile, when taken in connexion with those wonderful events, those political, moral, social and national transformations, and those irresistible workings of the human mind, which have since so changed the face of the world, in little more than three quarters of a century. To the eye of philosophy, how illustrative is it of the vanity of man, when, with his puny foresight and blind wisdom, he strains to look into futurity, and, attempting to prepare for its exigencies, builds up his tower of strength, which he fancies of sufficiently enduring materials to meet those anticipated necessities, of which time only has the secret!

It has been seen that only one minister, in the council of Spain, was of opinion that Louisiana ought to be returned to France. Some time after, in the month of May, the Marquis of Grimaldi informed the Count of Fuentes, the Spanish ambassador at the Court of Versailles, of all the proceedings which had taken place at the Court of Madrid, and said:

" The King approved of the conclusions to which had come the council of ministers, not only on account of the reasons by them expressed, but also on considering that, if what had occurred in Louisiana remained unpunished, this bad example might have a fatal influence over our other American possessions, and even over those of the other powers, in which a spirit of sedition and independence has begun to spread, as it appears by what lately happened to the French themselves in the Island of St. Domingo. His Majesty concluded also, that from his being essentially in possession of Louisiana in virtue of a very legitimate title, although it is not completed by the ceremony of taking possession, that colony was to be reputed a province of the crown, and its inhabitants, his subjects; from which it resulted that it appertained to his Majesty alone, to recover that possession, and to punish the temerity of the colonists, and the offence of which they have been guilty towards his government and his people. His Majesty thought also, that it was necessary that it be seen throughout the world, that he knew and was able, without the assistance of any foreign power, to repress the audacity of sedition, and all designs whatever, derogatory to the respect due to his dignity and to his crown. In accordance with these principles, his Majesty has resolved to use force to reduce the rebels to submission, and has ordered that the necessary measures to that effect be taken without delay.

"Don Alexandro O'Reilly, Inspector and Lieutenant general of the royal armies, had already been designated by the King to repair to Havana and to other cities in New-Spain, in order to review the troops and militia, and it seemed to his Majesty that this officer could at the same time be intrusted with the expedition against Louisiana. Consequently, being ordered to hasten his departure, O'Reilly immediately went to Cadix, where he found a frigate which had been prepared for him. He embarked, and he must be, at present, near the Island of Cuba. He has drawn none of his means of operation from Cadix, because it was thought proper to conceal the object of his commission. To that effect, he received an ostensible order, which treated of nothing else than of inspection and general review, but he well knew that he would find at Havana all of which he stood in need. The instruction given to him was, to take at that place the battalions of infantry, the ammunition and the other materials which he might deem necessary, to transport himself to Louisiana, and, after having taken possession of her in the name of his Majesty, to have the heads of the rebellion tried and punished according to law, and then to remove out of the colony all the individuals and families, whose presence might endanger its tranquillity. He was also ordered to provide for the military and police organization of the province, to establish the necessary rules for a correct administration of justice and of the finances, to secure the dependence and the subordination of the inhabitants, and to frame the new form of government—the whole, according to the verbal instructions which had been or might be given to him. He takes along with him persons learned in the law, who will superintend the judicial proceedings, and he has been authorized to have recourse to the force of arms, in case the inhabitants should oblige him to resort to it by their resistance. It seemed proper to invest Don Alexandro O'Reilly with these extensive powers, on account of the distance at which we are from that country. But, as the King, whose character is well known, is always inclined to be mild and clement, he has ordered O'Reilly to be informed that his will is, that a lenient course be pursued in the colony, and that expulsion from it be the only punishment inflicted on those who have deserved a more severe one.

"I could have informed you sooner of all this, but, as you will not have to act in the matter, because the King has assumed to take satisfaction himself for the offence committed by the inhabitants of the colony, we judged that it would be useless to send you, by the ordinary courier, the great mass of papers which would be necessary, to make you acquainted with all that had occurred. I had also thought of transmitting to you, with these documents, the Memorial or Manifesto published by the inhabitants of Louisiana. But I am persuaded that a printed copy of it must have reached you, considering that it has been republished in France, with the decree of the Superior Council. I do not think that I am at liberty to conceal from you, Sir, that, when the King was made aware of the insolent language of that document, he felt greatly indignant, and that his indignation was not less, when he was informed that the authors of that memorial had not only succeeded in making it public, but also had caused to be inserted in different European gazettes, under the head of a *Paris article*, a certain composition in which our government and nation were represented under the blackest colors. The entire freedom with which the delegates from the colony are allowed to remain in Paris has contributed, not a little, to the publication of those insolent declamations, and our enemies may have imagined that these men were not disapproved by the minister of his most Christian Majesty, from the fact that not the slightest demonstration has been made against them. I must however assure you that the King never suspected any thing of the sort, and that, besides, he is convinced that the honor of his government and the credit of his nation can never depend upon the invectives of gazetiers, and of those who are their instigators. But I must tell you frankly, that the delicate feelings of his Majesty would never have allowed him, had he been in the place of his cousin of France, to be satisfied with closing his ears to those who style themselves the delegates of the colony, and that he certainly would have caused to be punished, the audacity of reprinting and republishing in Spain, injurious writings to the government of his most Christian Majesty and to the French nation. His Majesty thought that we must not remain contented with the intimate union which binds the two monarchs and the two ministers, but that we must make it embrace the two nations, and he is certain that writings of this kind will not produce such results. Your Excellency knows very well that the loss of great interests is looked upon in Spain with indifference, but that it is not so with regard to insults and contumelies.

" As soon as we received the said manifesto of the colonists, it was determined that Mr. de Ulloa should answer the fables and the exaggerated accusations which it contains. But before his being informed of this determination, he had anticipated our intentions, and had sent from Cadix the communication hereto annexed. The copy of it which I send you, with the abstract which accompanies it, renders, as it were, useless, all the other papers which I had intended to forward to you. These two documents will demonstrate to you, that the true object of the inhabitants of the colony, and particularly of the heads of the sedition, was to live in the most absolute independence, without laws, without police and without order, and that the King has treated, and intended to treat them, at all future time, with kindness, and to favor them with marks of predilection and with a grant of liberty, far different from those which his other American colonies have been permitted to enjoy, whatever may be their merit, and whatever services they may have rendered to the metropolis.

" You will give an account of the whole of this to the Duke of Choiseul, and you will ask him for a letter or declaration from his Most Christian Majesty, in improbation of the conduct of the inhabitants of Louisiana. You will beg that minister to invite his Most Christian Majesty to declare, that the said inhabitants of the colony, being the subjects of the king his cousin, must throw themselves upon his mercy and live under his laws. The act of cession of the colony, as you will see by a mere reference to the copy, was absolute, and without any obligation whatever on the part of the King. Only, in the letter subsequently written to Mr. D'Abbadie, with regard to the delivering up of the colony to Spain, his Most Christian Majesty insinuated to the King his cousin his expectations, that his Catholic Majesty would maintain the inhabitants in the enjoyment of their privileges. This is what the King was resolved upon, and he had even issued orders accordingly, but said inhabitants have made themselves unworthy of this favor by their rebellion.

"This is all, sir, that I have to request you to attend to, for the present; for although the Gazette of France* ought, as a matter of course, to have disavowed the article inserted in some of the papers of the Low Countries under the head of *Paris News*, it would now be a little too late to do so, and it would not become us to solicit such a thing. We have contented ourselves with writing to Vienna and Holland, to have the remedy applied to the evil."

The old hereditary temper of Spain is condensed in this composition, and particularly in this phrase: "*Your Excellency knows very well that the loss of great interests is looked upon in Spain with indifference, but that it is not so with regard to insults and contumelies.*" As an expression of feelings and sentiments, as an exhibition of cold and solemn majesty, this document is as characteristic, in its way, of the Spanish nation, as the awe inspiring grandeur of that architectural wonder, the well known palace of the Escurial.

While the fate of Louisiana was thus discussed and settled in Spain, that colony had resumed a certain degree of apparent tranquillity, but it is to be questioned

* The official journal.

whether it was not as much the torpor occasioned by fear, as the calm which betokens true repose and a sense of security. Now that the revolution had been accomplished, its results could be measured with more accuracy. Now that the storm was hushed, that the angry waves were smoothed into a liquid plain, it was easy to discover if any thing was left floating on its surface to inspire hope. Now that the excitement of action had given way to the considerate workings of reflection, there was ample leisure to examine the extent and nature of the dangers which had been brooding, and which many thought they saw rising up like black clouds on the verge of the horizon. What would France do? What would Spain resolve? These were questions which anxiety propounded to itself, and could not answer. They were not few, those who already repented of what they had done, and who earnestly struggled to show that they had not participated in the revolution. As it had frequently occurred in similar circumstances, the leaders were beginning to find themselves in a state of isolation, and to be alone pointed out to the anger of the coming avenger. The crowd, among which they had lately stood, now shrank away from them gradually, in obedience to the same instinct which prompts the wayfarer to avoid, when the lightning flashes, the proximity of those tall trees, whose shade he would have courted, had heaven smiled on the green honors of their majestic heads.

SIXTH LECTURE.

REACTION IN THE COLONY AGAINST THE AUTHORS OF THE REVOLUTION—AUBRY'S LETTER ON THIS SUBJECT—FORTITUDE AND PERSEVERANCE OF THE CHIEFS OF THE INSURGENTS—ATTEMPT TO COMPEL THE SPANISH FRIGATE TO DEPART FROM THE COLONY—SECOND DECREE OF THE COUNCIL AGAINST SAID VESSEL—EXPLANATIONS ASKED OF AUBRY BY THE COUNCIL—AUBRY'S HAUGHTY ANSWER—HIS BOLD ATTITUDE AGAINST THE INSURGENTS—THE COLONISTS' ADDRESS TO THE DUKE OF PRASLIN—AUBRY'S LETTER TO THE SAME—THE DELEGATES OF THE COLONISTS TO FRANCE FAIL IN THEIR MISSION—THE DELEGATE ST. LETTE AND THE DUKE OF CHOISEUL—DECREE OF THE FRENCH GOVERNMENT CONVERTING THE PAPER CURRENCY OF THE COLONY INTO BONDS BEARING INTEREST—FOUCAULT'S TREACHERY TO HIS CONFEDERATES—HE DENOUNCES THEM IN A DISPATCH TO THE FRENCH GOVERNMENT—THIRD DEMONSTRATION AGAINST THE FRIGATE—IT IS COUNTERACTED BY AUBRY—THE FRIGATE DEPARTS VOLUNTARILY—WHAT OCCURRED ON THE OCCASION—INCREASE OF THE REACTION—THE COLONISTS ATTEMPT TO GAIN THE FAVOR AND PROTECTION OF GAYARRE, LOYOLA, AND NAVARRO—DESPERATE RESOLUTIONS OF THE LEADERS OF THE REVOLUTION—THEIR FRUITLESS ATTEMPTS TO THROW THEMSELVES INTO THE ARMS OF ENGLAND—THEY PROPOSE TO EXPEL AUBRY AND THE FRENCH TROOPS—THEIR PLAN OF A REPUBLIC—PROJECTED ESTABLISHMENT OF A BANK— THE LEADERS ARE ABANDONED BY THE PEOPLE—ARRIVAL OF O'REILLY AT THE BALIZE WITH SPANISH TROOPS—VAIN EFFORTS AT RESISTANCE—LAFRÉNIÈRE AND HIS ASSOCIATES INFORM AUBRY THAT THEY SUBMIT TO THE SPANIARDS—O'REILLY'S BIOGRAPHY—HE SENDS BOULIGNY AS A MESSENGER TO AUBRY—HIS RECEPTION BY LOYOLA, GAYARRE, AND NAVARRO—THEY WAIT ON AUBRY AT MIDNIGHT—AUBRY'S DEPORTMENT ON THAT OCCASION—AUBRY'S SPEECH TO THE PEOPLE ON THE PUBLIC SQUARE—LAFRÉNIÈRE, MILHET, AND MARQUIS GO TO THE BALIZE AND PRESENT THEIR HOMAGE TO O'REILLY—LAFRÉNIÈRE AND MARQUIS' SPEECHES—O'REILLY'S ANSWER—AUBRY GOES DOWN THE RIVER TO PRESENT HIS RESPECTS TO O'REILLY— AUBRY'S PROCLAMATION—ARRIVAL OF O'REILLY AT NEW ORLEANS—POSSESSION OF THE COLONY TAKEN ON THE 18TH OF AUGUST, 1769—AUBRY'S DISPATCH TO HIS GOVERNMENT ON THIS EVENT—O'REILLY GIVES A FESTIVAL IN HONOR OF AUBRY AND THE FRENCH AUTHORITIES—O'REILLY'S LETTER OF INQUIRY TO AUBRY—AUBRY'S ANSWER—ARREST OF THE CHIEF CONSPIRATORS—O'REILLY'S SPEECH TO THEM—THEY ARE IMPRISONED TO STAND THEIR TRIAL FOR REBELLION—VILLERÉ'S DEATH—TRADITION OF THE BLOODY SHIRT—O'REILLY'S PROCLAMATION GRANTING FULL PARDON TO ALL, EXCEPT TO A FEW LEADERS—SOLEMN OATH OF ALLEGIANCE TAKEN OR TO BE TAKEN BY ALL THE INHABITANTS OF LOUISIANA—FOUCAULT'S ARREST—HE EXCEPTS TO THE JURISDICTION OF THE SPANISH TRIBUNAL—HIS PLEA IS ADMITTED—HE IS TRANSPORTED TO FRANCE, AND SHUT UP IN THE BASTILE—ARREST OF BRAUD, THE KING'S PRINTER—HIS PLEA IN SELF JUSTIFICATION—HIS DEFENCE IS FOUND GOOD, AND HE IS SET AT LIBERTY—AUBRY'S SERVILITY TO, AND

ENTHUSIASM FOR, O'REILLY—AUBRY'S LETTER TO THE FRENCH GOVERNMENT, IN WHICH HE EXTOLS EVERY ACT OF O'REILLY—O'REILLY'S OPINION OF FOUCAULT—AUBRY'S SPEECH TO O'REILLY, IN HIS OWN NAME, AND IN THAT OF THE WHOLE BODY OF FRENCH OFFICERS.

The year 1768 had closed in gloom for the colonists, and no sunshine had opened the career of its successor. A lowering cloud seemed to have settled over the whole colony, and the doubts which existed on the course to be pursued by Spain and France, were thought to be worse than the saddest realities. The chiefs of the insurgents were evidently losing ground, and the Spanish officers, Loyola, Gayarre, and Navarro began to meet with more smiles than frowns, and to discover a very perceptible disposition to court their favor. Governor Aubry himself appears to have been actuated by this feeling, when, on the 15th of February, 1769, he spontaneously wrote this letter to the captain general of the island of Cuba:

"I hope that Mr. Ulloa does me justice, and that he has testified to my good conduct; for, no one ever loved and venerated the Spanish nation more than I do. This revolution disgraces the French of Louisiana. Although it has not as yet spent its fury and its frenzied course, yet it seems to me that some of the most obstinate among the insurgents, begin to look into the future with some uneasiness, and even fear; and if, in these circumstances, we were favored with the arrival of a battalion and the receipt of some money, coupled with assurances that all that has occurred shall be forgotten or forgiven, tranquillity would soon be restored, after the infliction of the just punishments which they deserve, on a small number of seditious persons, who have usurped all powers in this colony and who have done all the harm."

Nevertheless, those chiefs of the insurrection, to

whom Aubry was alluding, and who had already lost some of their influence, struggled against the impending perils of their situation with no faltering courage. They tried to embolden their confederates, by showing them that they persisted in their original designs, and that their faith in their ultimate success was not shaken. Thus, the Spanish frigate, against which a decree of expulsion had been issued, on the 14th of December, 1768, having ever since remained motionless in the river, in defiance of the decree, the conspirators convened a meeting of the Superior Council, on the 20th of February, 1769. The Council asked Aubry to explain why its decree had not been executed. Aubry haughtily answered that the captain of the Spanish frigate would depart at the precise time only which had been prescribed to him by Ulloa, and that, if any attempt was made to hasten that departure, he, Aubry, would oppose it by force. Accordingly, he equipped four hundred men, Spanish and French, to back his word, and to show that he was determined to be true to his declaration. This demonstration he thought himself called upon to make, on account of the issuing of a decree by the Superior Council, in confirmation of its former order of expulsion against the frigate.

It will be observed that Aubry, who had been so powerless at the breaking out of the revolution, on the 28th of October, had now a respectable force in hand to oppose the conspirators, and assumed a much bolder attitude. These were unmistakable signs of the reaction which had taken place.

But the colonists who had remained faithful to the cause of the revolution, sent, on the 20th of March, another petition to the Duke of Praslin, in which they sued for his support near the king, and repeated about the same arguments and the same language which they had used in their former addresses. Similar applications had been made to every prince of the blood, and almost to every person supposed to exercise some influence at court.

When this address reached the minister Duke of Praslin, he, almost at the same time, received a despatch, of the 1st of April, from Aubry, in which this officer informed him that the people being overwhelmed by the misery to which they were reduced, were murmuring against the chiefs of the insurrection, whose party was rapidly thinning away.

In the mean time, the new deputies, whom the colonists had sent to France, succeeded no better than their predecessors. Bienville, on whose support they might have relied, so far as it went, had ceased to exist, and the minister Duke of Choiseul, who had advised the cession, was still in office. St. Lette, one of the deputies, had, in early life, attracted the friendly regard of that nobleman, and a sort of intimacy had sprung up between them. The Duke welcomed with open arms the friend of his youthful days, and prevented his return to Louisiana, by giving him a lucrative employment in the East Indies. But he received with marked displeasure St. Lette's colleagues, and treated them as troublesome intruders. He told them that it was too late for the King of France to undo what he had done; and that the King of Spain had given the necessary orders to take possession of the province. Nothing now remained for the deputies to do, but to hasten back and to inform their fellow citizens of their irrevocable doom.

These deputies had also been instructed to solicit from the French government some final settlement, concerning the notes which it had emitted, and which formed the currency of the country. The King of

FOUCAULT'S TREACHERY. 273

France took into consideration their representations on the subject, and ordered that these notes be brought back to the French treasury in Louisiana, before the 1st of September, 1769, in order to be converted into bonds bearing an interest of five per cent. until complete payment. It will be recollected that Ulloa had offered, in 1766, to take up this paper at the rate of depreciation, (75 per cent.,)—which had been fixed by the French government itself, and to pay for its value in dollars. The colonists had refused, on the ground that the King of France would, in the end, redeem that paper currency at par. Thus, as it is seen, their hopes were not realized, and the conversion which had been resorted to, being looked upon as an expedient of doubtful character, which promised little for the future, if appreciated with the experience of the past, was not calculated to restore any degree of ease to the affairs of the colony.

Foucault, who had taken so active a part in the conspiracy, although in his official acts and his language in public, he had endeavored so to equivocate as to be able to side, when the time should come, with the victorious party, and to claim the merit of having always belonged to its flag, having studied the signs of the horizon, and ascertained from which quarter the wind was likely to blow, trimmed his sails accordingly. The cloak which had concealed the conspirator was partially laid aside, not to show the true character beneath its folds, but to allow the head of the informer to peer out, and watch the opportunity for open denunciation. Thus, on the 21st of March, he had written to the French cabinet at Versailles, to justify himself for having convened the Council, which had expelled Ulloa, and he had given it out as an excuse, that he had yielded to force only, as he had not at his

18

disposal over one hundred and fifty men, to oppose the one thousand rebels who threatened the Spaniards. He also declared that, if there were any truth in the rumors whispered about, the Syndics or headmen, who had been selected by the different classes of the inhabitants, to watch over their interests, had sadly misused the powers delegated to them; that the number of persons demanding the complete expulsion of the Spaniards had considerably diminished, and furthermore, that many were opposed to it, because they feared losing, in that case, what was due to them for the Spanish obligations they held in their hands.

The cautious phraseology in which the whole of Foucault's despatch is written, may be offered as a model of composition to such artful villains. "Were it possible for me," said he, "to feel the public pulse on these matters, I should perhaps verify that these rumors are well founded. Should this be the fact, I would then, jointly with Mr. Aubry, pursue such a course as would be sufficient to overawe certain individuals, who take themselves to be very important beings. They are, after all, but pretty bad fellows, who, being loaded with debt, seem striving, with eager emulation, to avail themselves of the overthrow of the colony, in order to retain with impunity the funds which have been advanced to them, and who are indifferent about the country they may live in, considering that they are not bound to Louisiana by the actual possession of any real estate. I think that, were it not for them, I should no longer stand witness to the most indecent and audacious deportment. There would no longer be any reason to fear the execution of the detestable project, which is said to have been formed, of burning New-Orleans, on the first news of the arrival of the Spanish troops, if it be still decreed that Louisiana must belong to his

Catholic Majesty. Mr. D'Acosta, the captain of the frigate, would be at liberty to prepare himself quietly to regulate his departure, according to the orders given to him by Ulloa, and the other Spaniards might do the same. The officers of the Spanish administration would no longer be exposed to a forced departure, without having time to settle their accounts, and the anarchy and confusion which have taken the place of the small amount of good order that prevailed in this colony, would soon disappear. But, being under the apprehension, when trying to avoid one evil, of falling into another equally great, I have taken the resolution to be silent and inactive, whilst waiting for the orders of the two courts of France and Spain. Without caring, however, for the discontent produced by all my acts of opposition to the enterprises of these turbulent spirits against the Spaniards, I will use the most practicable means, to contrive that the officers of the Spanish administration remain here until the receipt of those orders."

It is no very far stretch of the imagination to suppose that, on the very day when this letter was written, in which the fathers of the insurrection to which Foucault had stood sponsor, were denounced as *bankrupts, thieves, detestable incendiaries, and the like,* this same man entertained at supper, as usual, at the country seat of his paramour, Madam Pradel, those *turbulent spirits and would be important beings* whom he had denounced to the French government, and who, of course, could be no other than his friends and confederates, Lafrénière, Villeré, Noyan, Masan, &c.—whom he had goaded on to shake off the hated Spanish yoke, and with whose destinies he seemed to have linked his fortunes. There are few conspiracies and perilous enterprises, in which such men as Foucault are not to be detected. They are the alloy, the baser metal which appears to be necessary to the composition of the great human coinage. Experience teaches, and the study of historical records demonstrates, that, within the shadow of every man of noble thoughts and deeds, there always lie some evil spirits, crouching in ambush, and watching for every opportunity to prey on the object of their envy and hatred. It must be admitted that, in the drama in which he was engaged, Foucault acted his part, with a consistency of infamy, and a cool, systematic regularity of treachery, which must obtain for him much credit with congenial minds. It is but tardy justice, consolatory, it is true, as all acts of justice are, that such a felon should be dragged before the tribunal of posterity, and hung up on the gibbet of atonement.

Notwithstanding the disheartening prospect they had before them, some of the conspirators persisted in their designs, and attempted to make another demonstration against the Spanish frigate, by inducing the Germans to come to town for that purpose. But Aubry sent to the German Coast several officers, whose presence and exhortations prevented the outbreak which was intended. "Mr. de Lafrénière," wrote Aubry, "has much contributed to restore tranquillity. This, to be just to him, must be said in his favor, whatever may have been his previous errors." Great indeed must have been the reaction, when Lafrénière came forth to advocate acquiescence!

But the captain of the frigate, in order to do away with all pretexts for further disturbances, resolved to sail on the 20th of April. On that day, all the officers of that vessel waited in a body on Governor Aubry, and thanked him for the protection and the many favors they had received at his hands. On their returning to the frigate, they met on the bank of the river a large concourse of people, who had assembled to witness their

DEPARTURE OF THE FRIGATE. 277

departure. The crowd was silent, and gave no sign of hostility. On the contrary, some among them addressed words of sympathy, of personal respect and of friendly greeting to the officers, as they passed along. As soon as Captain D'Acosta stepped on the deck of the *Volante*, men were seen running up the masts, and she began to unfurl her broad sails to the strong breeze which courted them to its embrace. Soon after, the three Spanish dignitaries, Loyola, Gayarre and Navarro, who had accompanied D'Acosta on board, were seen descending into their boat, and rapidly approaching the bank of the river. On their landing, the crowd opened before them with respect, and as these gentlemen trod through this human avenue, on their way to their residences, they bowed, right and left, with some degree of stately formality. No outward signs showed what they may have felt, at being thus left alone in the midst of a hostile population. In the steady look with which they met the public gaze, there was no fear, no anger, no defiance, but only an expression of cold indifference, although perhaps a close observer might have detected the suppressed scrutinizing glance, which strove to study on the surrounding faces the secret feelings of the hearts.

In the mean time, the frigate had begun to move on the water, and, as she gracefully glided by, Captain D'Acosta, standing up on the quarter deck, raised his hand to his hat, took it off, and bowed to the crowd with, as some affected to believe, all the pride of mock humility. At this very moment, the frigate poured out her broadsides, in a salute to the town, and emerging from the cloud of smoke, with all her colors gaily sporting in the wind, was seen, in a few minutes, turning round that point, on the opposite side of the river, where now stands the town of Algiers. Thus the last satisfaction which the colonists had desired, had been granted to them; yet it was evident that no feeling of exultation existed among the assemblage, that stood gazing at the turbid waters of the Mississippi, for some time after the frigate had disappeared. No shouts of joy or triumph had been uttered; silence was on the lips, and anxiety in the hearts of all. They seemed to be in an atmosphere of gloom; and that undefined feeling which proceeds from the vague anticipation of coming danger, pervaded the whole multitude. At last, they dispersed in small detached groups, whispering to each other, and bearing stamped on their brows the thoughts that worked in their brains.

The revolutionary tide was indeed ebbing fast away, and leaving stranded on the shore, those it had borne onward to momentary success. The conspirators had hoped at first, that, on their showing a strong aversion to a foreign domination, and on their expelling the Spanish Governor, they might have induced both the French and Spanish governments, to consider as null the treaty of cession—the more so, that Spain did not seem to set any value on the donation which had been presented to her. When this hope had been frustrated, they attempted to throw themselves into the arms of England, by sending emissaries to the governor of Pensacola, with whom they were to enter into arrangements. But the reception which they met in that quarter, convinced them that they were to look elsewhere for support. England, besides the breach of faith of which she would have been guilty, and besides giving the bad example of encouraging the rebellion of colonies, was not then disposed to renew the long wars she had waged against France and Spain, merely for the then paltry consideration of the acquisition of Louisiana.

Reduced to the last stage of despair, the Hotspurs among the insurgents proposed to expel Aubry, and the few French troops that were in the colony, to proclaim New-Orleans a free port, and to form a republic, where the oppressed and the needy among all the nations of the earth, would find a refuge and a home. The chief of the republic was to be styled *Protector*, and to be assisted by a council of forty men elected by the people, either for life, or for a certain number of years. A bank, on the plan of that of Amsterdam or of Venice, was to be created, and to furnish the commonwealth with the currency of which it would stand in need. The Swiss captain Marquis had originated this scheme of a republic; and he violently and openly recommended its adoption —so much so, that it became a subject of discussion, for and against, in printed and in manuscript documents, which were circulated through the colony, and some of which are really of a curious character.

If the plan of Marquis could have been executed, and a Lord Protector elected, it is probable that Lafrénière would have become the Cromwell of Louisiana. There is no doubt but that the colonists would have eagerly adopted this form of government, had it been possible at the time; for it must be recollected that, from the earliest existence of the colony, almost all its governors had uniformly complained of the republican spirit which they had observed in the inhabitants. It would seem as if the European emigrants, on their arriving in Louisiana, had so imbibed the conception and the love of independence from the roaming life of the aborigines, from the sight of the boundless forests, from the immensity of the domain which invited conquest, that they waxed impatient of the yoke imposed upon them by a distant power. But the colonists, on maturer and cooler reflection, became convinced that France, Spain and England, for reasons too obvious to be enumerated, would never permit their rebellion to terminate successfully into the establishment of a republic in Louisiana. They therefore abandoned the idea as quixotic; but they, nevertheless, bequeathed to their posterity the right of claiming for Louisiana the merit of having been the first European colony that entertained the design of proclaiming her independence. The stoutest hearts, however, and the noblest minds cannot achieve impossibilities. The thought of a republic had been but a rosy colored bubble of the imagination, or rather a flitting rainbow, spanning the firmament of a dream, and encouraging hopes but to have them extinguished in the night of the gathering storm. So was it with the majority of the colonists, who, in the wreck of their fortunes, having in vain looked round for any means of salvation, now abandoned themselves to the course of events, and were constrained passively to wait for what fate would ultimately decide.

Rumors were rife in the colony, as to the preparations which Spain was making, to take possession of Louisiana, and to punish the insult which had been offered to her. Nothing positive, however, could be ascertained, and the very vagueness of the information received, added to the anxieties of the public mind. Those who had played the most conspicuous part in the conspiracy were advised to fly; but this could be more easily proposed than executed. It would have been impossible for them to sell their property, on account of the extreme penury to which the province was reduced; and if there had been men able to purchase, they would have hesitated to invest their money in so insecure a manner; for, these sales might perhaps have been set aside, on the ground that they were not made in good faith, but, in collusion, only to protect traitors, and to defraud the Spanish treasury of what confiscation would have brought into its coffers. The leaders of the insurrection, therefore, recoiled from the idea of breaking the ties which bound them to Louisiana, where some of them were born, and where the rest had passed the greater portion of their lives; and they turned away from the dire prospect of dragging, in poverty, with their families, the miserable existence of exiles in foreign lands. Besides, many among them flattered themselves that a prompt and entire submission on their part, coupled with assurances of repentance, would secure pardon and safety.

In proportion as all ideas of resistance were gradually abandoned, and as the schemes of the authors of the revolution were successively demonstrated to be impracticable, Loyola, Gayarre, and Navarro, had seen the circle of their friends increasing, and their own importance rising in the colony. It was supposed that, from their having gone through all the phases of the revolution, and from their official position, they might exercise great influence on the determination, which the Spanish government might subsequently take, and it is very natural that a propitiation of their favor should have been sought by those who trembled for their lives, or for the safety of the objects they loved. These three Spanish officers were men capable of sympathizing with the deep anxieties which they saw, and they became painfully affected by the direct and indirect appeals, which were repeatedly made to their feelings. Not knowing what their government intended to do, and careful not to commit themselves to any course of action in their official capacity, they were obliged to act with a considerable degree of caution, imposed upon them by the peculiar circumstances under which they were placed, and they had to confine themselves to mere assurances, as to their personal feelings and wishes, and as to the expectations to be formed from the well-known clemency, which was a distinguished feature in the character of Charles III.

Thus matters stood, when, on the morning of the 24th of July, 1769, the whole town of New Orleans was thrown into violent commotion, by the news that a formidable Spanish fleet had made its appearance at the Balize, that General O'Reilly was the officer whom the court of Madrid had appointed to take possession of Louisiana, and that he brought with him such large forces, that any attempt at resistance would be preposterous. Marquis, however, stuck a white cockade in his hat, and appeared on the public square, where he made ineffectual efforts to persuade the people to oppose the landing of the Spaniards. Only one hundred men joined him, and set up the white cockade of France. Petit made his appearance with a pair of pistols in his hands, spoke with the most passionate violence against the Spaniards, whom, he said, the colonists were bound to fight to the last, and declared himself ready to blow out the brains of every coward that would not co-operate in that holy war. But they both soon retired, when they found out that their words met with no sympathizing echo, and that theirs was the voice in the wilderness.

Seeing the hopelessness of their condition, the leaders of the insurgents became greatly alarmed, on being convinced that they could not even make a *show* of resistance, so as perhaps to secure favorable terms of capitulation; and, being humbled by the desperate state to which they were reduced, presented themselves before Aubry, to ask for his advice and protection. They were evidently thrown into dismay, by the magnitude of the armament which had been fitted out against them, and put under the direction of one of the most skilful generals of Europe. Aubry did all he could to cheer and encourage them; he expressed the belief that General O'Reilly could not possibly come with the intention of carrying terror and desolation through the land, and he observed that, no blood having been spilt, it was to be hoped that the colonists, if they submitted promptly, would not in vain trust to the good heart and clemency of his Catholic Majesty. He also promised that he would make them acquainted with O'Reilly's intentions, as soon as he should be informed of them. In the mean time, he ordered them to remain quiet, and they took the engagement to obey his instructions. Then, without loss of time, Aubry despatched an officer to the German Coast, to tranquillize its inhabitants, and to command them, in the name of the King, not to stir, under the penalty of being punished as rebels.

The Spanish general, whose arrival was soon to be expected, was born in Ireland,[*] about the year 1735. He was a Catholic, and following the example of many of his countrymen who belonged to that creed, and who, on that account, labored under many disabilities in their native country, he sought to better his fortunes by enlisting in the armies of one of the continental powers. For this purpose, Alexander O'Reilly went to Spain, when very young, and entered the service of the Spanish nation, by joining a body of Irishmen known under the name of the *Hibernia regiment.* In the war to which gave rise the pretensions of the different princes of Europe to the Austrian succession, on the death of the emperor Charles VI., who left no other lineal descendant than Maria Theresa, O'Reilly served with distinction in Italy, and received a wound which lamed him for the remnant of his days. In 1757, he obtained permission to enter the Austrian army, and, under the orders of his countryman, Field-marshal de

[*] Biographie universelle de Michaud.

Lascy, he made two campaigns against the Prussians. In 1759, he volunteered in the armies of France, and distinguished himself so much, that the Marshal Duke of Broglie warmly recommended him to the King of Spain, when he returned to that country. This recommendation procured for O'Reilly the grade of Lieutenant-colonel, and, as such, he served in Portugal with the Spaniards, against the Portuguese assisted by the English. This war was not glorious for Spain; but O'Reilly obtained great reputation at the head of a body of light troops, which had been intrusted to his command. Even at that time, he was reputed one of the best officers in the Spanish armies. Hence he soon rose to the rank of Brigadier-General, and the post of drilling adjutant was created for him. It was in the discharge of these functions, that he taught the Spanish troops the German manœuvres and tactics. On the conclusion of the peace treaty signed at Fontainebleau, in 1762, which restored Havana to Spain, he was raised to the rank of Major-General, and sent to that city, where he was to be the second in command. He re-established the fortifications of the island of Cuba, and particularly of Havana, which had been ruined by the English, and returned to Spain, where he was appointed Inspector-General of the king's infantry; and Charles III. paid him the compliment of honoring with his presence the operations of a manœuvring camp, of which he gave him the command. He was next sent to New Orleans, in 1769, where I shall have to relate in details the part which he acted. In 1765, General O'Reilly, by his presence of mind, the rapidity of his movements, and his cool intrepidity, had had the good luck to save the King's life in the famous Madrid insurrection, which forced the sovereign to fly to Aranjuez. From that time, he continued to rise in the favor of a monarch, who was well known for the persevering and extraordinary gratitude which he always cherished for all services rendered to his person. Although O'Reilly, as a foreigner, had excited antipathies and jealousies, which threw many impediments in his way, yet his merits could not but be acknowledged, and it was admitted that the Spanish armies were indebted to him for many useful reforms and marked improvements. He was made a Count, and his breast glittered with military decorations.

In 1774, he was given the command of the great expedition, which Spain undertook against Algiers, and which was composed of forty ships of the line, three hundred and fifty transports, and thirty thousand men; but this immense convoy did not arrive in time; and O'Reilly not receiving, when wanted, the flat boats which had been prepared to facilitate a simultaneous landing of the whole of his forces, and after having waited fifteen days, in daily danger of running his vessels aground, was obliged to resort to a partial landing of his troops, and put out a body of ten thousand men, commanded by the Marquis of La Romana. This corps had been ordered so to establish itself on the shore, as to protect the landing of the rest of the army. But La Romana, carried away by his own impetuosity and by that of his men, pursued the vanguard of the enemy to a point in the interior, where he had to contend with very superior numbers, intrenched behind fig trees and hedges of nopals. The Spanish troops fought with undaunted courage, and lost four thousand men, with their chief La Romana. During that time, the rest of the army was landing; but this first check had demoralized the troops; the reluctance which they had to serve under a foreigner, was fast ripening into a spirit of sedition; it was maliciously circulated that O'Reilly had sacrificed La Romana, of whom he was said to be jealous; and he discovered that he no longer had at his command the proper elements to secure success. Under these circumstances, he found it necessary to return to his ships, and he went back to Spain with much grief at the frustration of his hopes. His only consolation was, that the plan of attack he had conceived, was approved by all the judges of military art, and that the bravery he had displayed was much admired. His enemies themselves admitted, that he had shown himself wherever there was most danger, during the engagement with the Algerines, that he had exposed his person with the utmost recklessness, and that the horse he mounted had received two wounds. The unfortunate result of this expedition lowered him, however, in the estimation of the Spanish nation; but the King remained true to him and put him at the head of a military school, lately established. He was afterwards appointed Commander-general of the province of Andalusia and governor of Cadix, where he exhibited all the talents of a great administrator. But, at the death of Charles III., in December, 1788, he fell into complete disfavor, and lived in absolute retirement in the province of Catalonia. His name had, nevertheless, retained considerable influence in the Spanish armies; and, after the death of General Ricardos, in 1794, he was thought to be the most skilful general to be opposed to the French. He was therefore appointed to the command of the army of the East Pyrenees, and he was on his way to his destination, when he died suddenly at an advanced age. His descendants now reside in the island of Cuba. "General O'Reilly," says Michaud in his biographical sketch of that officer, "had always been an object of malignant envy, and had many enemies, whom the flexibility of his temper and the soft influence of his conciliating manners could not reconcile to his advancement, in a nation proverbially proud and suspicious of foreigners."

It was, as I said, on the morning of the 24th of July, that the inhabitants of New Orleans were informed of the arrival of O'Reilly at the Balize. In the evening, there came the intelligence that a Spanish officer, bearing despatches from O'Reilly to Aubry, was ascending the river. There was, on that night, no thought of sleep for the greater part of the population, and they were seen clustering in groups in the streets, or hurrying from house to house. At about ten o'clock, Loyola, Gayarre, and Navarro, preceded by torches and followed by their subordinates, friends, and adherents, were observed traversing the town, and moving towards the landing place. At eleven, the Spanish envoy, whose name was Francisco Bouligny, arrived in front of the public square, and, leaping ashore, was greeted by his countrymen, to whom he was a token of speedy relief. Passing through the large and anxious crowd that had gathered round them in silence, the Spanish officers went to the house of the French governor, who had retired to bed. He was immediately waked up, according to the instructions which he had left, and he received with much affability O'Reilly's messenger, who delivered to him the letter of which he had charge. Aubry read it twice over, but, on his not being able fully to understand its meaning, Bouligny proposed to translate it, and his offer was accepted. In this letter O'Reilly informed Aubry of the object of his mission, and requested the French governor to take all the necessary measures, to facilitate the transfer of Louisiana from France to Spain, and the execution of the designs of their respective sovereigns. "Tell General O'Reilly," said Aubry to Bouligny in answer to this despatch, "that I am ready at any time to deliver up this province to his Excellency, and that should the colonists make the slightest opposition to it, I am determined to join my forces to his, to punish the insolence of the rebels."

On the 25th, Bouligny, Gayarre, Navarro, and Loyola dined at Aubry's, with the highest among the civil authorities and the most influential among the French officers and colonists. The past seemed to have been forgotten, the dinner was very gay, and towards its close, Aubry addressing Bouligny and looking round the table, expressed to him, with marked emphasis, his satisfaction that the people *had at last listened to the counsels of prudence, and had taken the only resolution which could save the colony from complete destruction.* In the evening, Bouligny and the other Spanish officers promenaded through the streets of the town, and were greeted everywhere with cordiality, and even with apparent demonstrations of joy. On the next day, the 26th, at nine of the morning, Aubry addressed in these words the people, whom he had summoned to meet on the public square: "I have to announce to you that Mr. D' O'Reilly is now in the river, at the head of several regiments that have come with him from Spain. He is sent to take possession of Louisiana, in the name of the King of Spain, by virtue of the sacred orders of their most Christian and Catholic Majesties, and he will present me with his credentials, at our first meeting. You can judge of the degree of irritation which the King of Spain must feel, from his sending to this distant country a General of such great distinction. It is therefore prudent for you to open your eyes on your past conduct, and to prevent your own ruin and that of your native or adopted country. You must be aware that nothing short of a prompt and entire submission, can now ward off the misfortunes with which you are threatened. I think that, in these delicate circumstances, I can assume the responsibility to assure you that, if you offer no resistance, General O'Reilly will treat you favorably, and that you will not be deceived in having full reliance on the clemency and tenderness of disposition of his Catholic Majesty. I order you, at the same time, in the name of the King, to abstain from resorting to any meeting and to forbear from taking up arms, except in obedience to an express order from me, under the penalty of being treated as rebels, who disobey his Majesty's commands." He then dissolved the assembly, and returned to his house.

A short time after, Lafrénière called on Governor Aubry, and informed him that, having full confidence in the generosity and magnanimity of General O'Reilly, he, Marquis, and Milhet had resolved, provided that Aubry favored them with a letter to his Excellency, to go down the river, in order to present their homages to the Spanish general, to give him the assurance, in the name of the people, of their complete submission, and to entreat him to intercede for them near his Catholic Majesty, whose clemency they implored. Aubry eagerly accepted this proposition, encouraged Lafrénière in his resolution, and told him that it was the only rational one he could take. On that day, the Spanish officers dined again at Aubry's, with some of the former chief conspirators, and then Bouligny departed with Lafrénière, Marquis, Milhet, the harbor master, and the oldest commissioned captain in the French troops, whom Aubry sent, the one, to pilot O'Reilly's vessels through the pass at the Balize, and the other to compliment his Excellency, as is customary on such occasions.

After forty hours' navigation, Don Francisco Bouligny reached the Balize, and presented Lafrénière and his companions to O'Reilly, who received them in state, on the deck of the flag ship, which was crowded with a host of officers, who had come from the other vessels to witness the scene. Lafrénière was to be the spokesman of his party, but, when introduced to the presence of O'Reilly, he felt one of those sudden emotions, from which the boldest heart is not free, on occasions of peculiar solemnity, and his powers of speech failed him for a moment; but encouraged, however, by the benignant expression which he observed in O'Reilly's face, he soon rallied, and, in a somewhat faltering voice, delivered the following address, which O'Reilly ordered Bouligny to take down: "Excellency, Mr. Marquis, an ex-captain of a Swiss company, Mr. Milhet, a lieutenant of militia and a merchant, and I, Lafrénière, a planter, and the King's attorney general, have been chosen as delegates by the inhabitants of Louisiana, and requested to come and assure your Excellency of their submission to the orders of their Catholic and most Christian Majesties, and of their veneration for the virtues and military talents which have raised you to the eminent dignities with which you are clothed. We are instructed to express to you the profound respect of the colony for his Catholic Majesty, and its love for his most Christian Majesty, and for all the august house of Bourbon. The colony never had the intention to be wanting in the profound respect which it cherishes for the great monarch whom you represent. The harshness of Mr. Ulloa's temper, and the subversion of the privileges guarantied by the act of cession, were the only causes of the revolution which took place in the colony. We beg your Excellency not to consider Louisiana as a conquered country. The orders of which you are the earer, are sufficient to put you in possession of this province, and they make a greater impression on our hearts, than the arms which you carry with you. The French are docile, and accustomed to a mild government. On your arrival, you will find every one disposed to yield obedience to the orders of the two majesties. The colony claims from your benevolence the grant of privileges, and from your equity, the allowance of sufficient delays for those who may choose to emigrate."

Don Alexandro O'Reilly* listened to this address, without interrupting the orator, and with the grave and imposing aspect, said an eye-witness, which his rank and dignity required. He then answered: " Gentlemen, it is impossible to judge of facts and events, without having previously obtained a sufficient knowledge of their causes. On my arrival in your town, I shall take special care to become acquainted with the whole truth, to form right conclusions, and to examine the reasons alleged for your justification. You may rest assured that no one can be better disposed than I am, to render good services to the colonists, and that my doing the least injury to any one would be to me a matter of deep regret.† I shall be the first to furnish you with all the means I may possibly dispose of, to enable you to tranquillize the people; and you may assure them of the good dispositions with which I am animated, and which are natural to my character. I see with pleasure the resolution which you have taken. Had it not been so, you may well be persuaded that I would have caused the flag of my king to be respected, and that, to accomplish it, I would have allowed no consideration to arrest me in my course. Such was my resolution, and I would

---

* Don Alexandro O'Reilly escuchó esta arenga sin interrumpirla, con la seriedad y señorio correspondiente á su caracter.

† Yo seré el primero en facilitar á los medios para que tranquilizen á todo el pueblo, asegurando le de las buenas disposiciones en que me hallo llevado de mi caracter.

have ascended the river as high as the Illinois, if necessary. Men, when in a state of frenzy, do not reflect, and cannot see the consequences of their actions. If it were not so, how could a handful of people, like you, have imagined themselves capable of resisting one of the most powerful sovereigns of Europe? How could you think that the most Christian King, bound to the king my master, by the ties of blood and by those of the closest friendship, could ever have assisted you, and lent a willing ear to the clamors of a seditious people?"

Here, Marquis interrupted the General, to object to the application of the word *seditious*, and to give some reasons in explanation of the course pursued by the colonists. The General answered with gentle condescension: "Be at ease;* I have already told you, gentlemen, that I will listen with pleasure to your arguments, when the time shall come. God be praised, I am free from all prejudices, and I am aware that things, which from afar may look as if they were clothed with the dark hue of guilt, may, at a shorter distance, appear decked in the white robes of innocence."

The General detained them to dine with him, treated them with the most delicate politeness, with the utmost suavity of manner, and sent them back, says Bouligny, one of the persons present at the interview, *full of admiration for his talents, and with good hopes that their past faults should be forgotten.*

O'Reilly, in order to have proper quarters prepared for his troops, sent back Bouligny to New Orleans, with two other officers named Karbonary and Bordenave.

On the 15th of August, Aubry went down the river, to

---

* El General le respondió con dulzura—Ya he dicho a Vs, Señores, que á un tiempo escucharé con gusto las razones de Vs. A Dios gracias, estoy libre de preocupaciones, y no ignoro que muchas veces las cosas que parecen negras desde lejos, suelen verse blancas, quando uno se aprocsima.

offer his respects to O'Reilly, who was on his way up, and to come to an understanding with him, as to the manner and time of taking possession of the colony. On consultation, they fixed the 18th for that ceremony. On the 16th, Aubry returned to New Orleans, and issued a proclamation, enjoining the inhabitants of the town and the most respectable among those of the neighboring country, to be at the *august ceremony, and to be ready to present themselves to his Excellency, Don Alexandro O'Reilly, in order to assure him of their entire submission and of their inviolable fidelity to his Catholic Majesty.* On the 17th, in the morning, the whole Spanish fleet, numbering twenty-four sails, appeared in front of New Orleans. Immediately all the necessary preparations were made for landing, and flying bridges were dropped from the vessels to the bank of the river. On the 18th, early in the day, the French governor, with a numerous train of officers, came to compliment the new governor, who went ashore in company with his visiters, and proceeded with them to the house which was destined for him. But before 12 o'clock, O'Reilly returned to his fleet, in order to prepare for the landing of the whole of his forces.

At 5 o'clock, in the afternoon, a gun fired by the flag ship gave the signal for the landing of the Spaniards. The French troops and the militia of the colony, with Aubry at their head, were already drawn up in a line, parallel to the river, and in front of the ships, in that part of the public square which is nearest to the church. On the signal being heard, the Spanish troops were seen pouring out of the fleet in solid columns, and moving, with admirable precision, to the points which had been designated to them. These troops, numbering 2600 men, were among the choicest of Spain, and had been picked by O'Reilly himself. With colors flying, and with the rapidity of motion of the most practised veterans, they marched on, battalions after battalions, exciting the admiration and the awe of the population by their martial aspect and their brilliant equipments. The heavy infantry drew themselves up in perpendiculars, on the right and left wings of the French, thus forming three sides of a square. Then came a heavy train of artillery of fifty guns, the light infantry, and the companies of mountain riflemen, (fusileros de montañas,) with the cavalry, which was composed of forty dragoons, and fifty mounted militia men from Havana. All these corps occupied the fourth side of the square near the river, and in front of the French, who were drawn up near the cathedral. All the vessels were dressed in their colors, and their riggings were alive with the Spanish sailors in their holiday apparel. On a sudden, they gave five long and loud shouts of: *Viva el Rey—Long live the King*, to which the troops, on the square, responded in a similar manner. All the bells of the town pealed merrily; a simultaneous discharge from the guns of the twenty-four Spanish vessels enveloped the river in smoke; with emulous rapidity, the fifty guns that were on the square roared out their salute, making the ground tremble as if convulsed with an earthquake; and all along the dark lines of the Spanish infantry, flashed a sheet of fire, as the weaker voice of musketry, also shouting in jubilation, attempted to vie with the thunder of artillery. All this pomp and circumstance of war announced that General O'Reilly was landing.

He soon appeared in the square, where he was received with all the honors due to a captain general, drums beating, banners waving, and all sorts of musical instruments straining their brazen throats, and by their wild and soul stirring sounds, causing the heart to leap and the blood to run electrically through the hot veins.

He was preceded by splendidly accoutred men, who bore heavy silver maces; and the whole of his retinue, which was of the most imposing character, was well calculated to strike the imagination of the people. With a slightly halting gait he advanced towards the French governor, who, with the members of the Council and all the men of note in the colony, stood near a mast which supported the flag of France. Immediately behind O'Reilly followed the officers of the colonial administration of Louisiana, Don Joseph Loyola, the commissary of war and intendant; Don Estevan Gayarre, the contador, or royal comptroller; and Martin Navarro, the treasurer, who were to be restored to their respective functions, which had been interrupted by the revolution. "Sir," said O'Reilly to Aubry, "I have already communicated to you the orders and the credentials with which I am provided, to take possession of this colony, in the name of his Catholic Majesty, and, also, the instructions of his most Christian Majesty, that it be delivered up to me. I beg you to read them aloud to the people." Aubry complied with this request, and then, addressing the colonists by whom he was surrounded, said : " Gentlemen, you have just heard the sacred orders of their most Christian and Catholic Majesties, in relation to the province of Louisiana, which is irrevocably ceded to the crown of Spain. From this moment, you are the subjects of his Catholic Majesty, and by virtue of the orders of the King, my master, I absolve you from your oath of fidelity and obedience to his most Christian Majesty." Then turning to O'Reilly, Aubry handed to him the keys of the gates of the town. The banner of France sunk from the head of the mast where it waved, and was replaced by that of Spain.*

* Los Franceses, dirigidos por su Gobernador, dieron cinco veces : Viva el

Following the example and the orders of Aubry, the French shouted five times : " *Viva el Rey !*" *Long live the King !*—which was repeated three times by the Spanish troops, who recommenced their firing in unison with the fleet.

Then O'Reilly, followed by the principal Spanish officers, and accompanied by Aubry and his retinue, proceeded to the cathedral, where he was received at the threshold by the clergy, with all the honors of the Pallium † and with the other usual solemnities.‡ The curate, or Vicar General, in the name and on behalf of the people, addressed to the General a pathetic harangue, coupled with the most caressing protestations of fidelity on his part. The General answered with concise eloquence, declaring his readiness to protect religion, to cause the ministers of the sanctuary to be respected, to support the authority of the King and the honor of his arms, to devote himself to the public good, and to do justice to all. He then entered the church, where a Te Deum was sung, during which the troops and the fleet renewed their discharges in tokens of rejoicing.

When the pious ceremony was over, O'Reilly and Aubry returned to the public square, where all the Spanish troops filed off before the governors, *in the most redoubtable order and equipage*, says Aubry in one of his despatches, and, after having saluted them, retired to their respective quarters.

In a despatch in which, some time after the taking possession of the country by the Spaniards, he rendered to one of the French ministers an account of the events

---

Rey! Nuestra tropa lo ejecutó trés veces con una descarga graneada, y al mismo tiempo que la salva de la fregata comandante.

† A sort of canopy, under which the Chase of the Eucharist is carried in processions.

‡ El cura ó Vicario principal hizo á S. E. una arenga muy patética en nombre del pueblo, y con las mas tiernas protestas de fidelidad.

which had preceded, and of the results which had followed, O'Reilly's arrival in Louisiana, Aubry says: " In circumstances so deplorable, without troops, without money, without resources, without assistance, having against me the Superior Council and the great majority of the inhabitants, I thought that, in order not to ruin this colony, it was necessary to act with the utmost reserve. I concluded that it was my duty to endeavor, to the best of my abilities, to prevent the effusion of French and Spanish blood, and to preserve this unfortunate country in its integrity, until it be possible to cause its population to respect the orders of their Catholic and most Christian Majesties, determined, however, as I was, to perish with the few officers and soldiers who had remained under my orders, when the fury and violence of the rebels should drive me to the last extremities, and put me under the indispensable necessity of meeting them in battle.

" At the very moment when all seemed to be lost, Providence took compassion of our calamities, and when we were near being submerged by the storm, sent us a liberator, who, by his mere presence and by his wisdom, has, in an instant, reestablished order and tranquillity in a country, which, for a long time past, was in an indescribable state of disorder and confusion.

" After having experienced the most terrible alarms and afflictions, in governing a colony, which I several times saw on the very brink of ruin and destruction, it has been my good luck, by the grace of God, to deliver it up in its integrity into the hands of a General, to whose presence, wisdom and firmness it is now indebted for its tranquillity. Listening with the greatest kindness to those who have any business to transact with him, he fills with hope and satisfaction all the inhabitants, who, after so many disturbances and disorders, see at last the restoration of peace and justice in the country. The thanks which the General was pleased to address to me at the head of my troops, and in presence of the whole people, and the approbation which he expressed of my conduct during all these past unfortunate occurrences, are to me a sure pledge of its obtaining also the sanction of your Excellency."

On the 19th, the day following the ceremony of taking possession, O'Reilly gave, with great pomp, a dinner to the French governor, the Spanish and French authorities, and all the persons of distinction in the colony. In the mean time, with his customary habits of activity, he had not allowed these festivities of the preceding and of the present day, to interfere with the business which he had on hand, and he had proceeded in secret to take the depositions of witnesses, as to what had occurred in the colony, and to peruse all the papers and documents which could give the desired informations on the subject. On the very day he thus entertained Aubry and some of the chiefs of the revolution, he addressed to that officer the following letter: "Sir, as you witnessed all that occurred in this colony, when Don Antonio de Ulloa, appointed governor of the same by his Catholic Majesty, was expelled from it, I beg you to enlighten me on the subject, to make me acquainted with all these events and their true causes, and to furnish me with the names of the persons who induced the people to commit the offence of presenting themselves with arms in their hands, to enforce the violent expulsion of Don Antonio de Ulloa, and to renew the same excesses against all the Spanish officers and troops in the colony.

". As Governor of this colony for his most Christian Majesty, and as the commander of the French troops, you recognized Don Antonio de Ulloa as the person designated by his Catholic Majesty to take, in his royal name, full possession and command of this colony. Consequently, you gave to Ulloa possession of the Balize and of other posts, and the complete cession was deferred, only at the solicitation of Ulloa himself, until the arrival of the Spanish force which he expected, a proof of confidence on your part, which was due to the close union existing between the two crowns.

"It is expedient that you have the kindness to communicate to me, as soon as possible, all that you may know in relation to said revolution, without omitting to quote, literally, all the orders, protests, and public or secret documents, to which you may have had recourse, in order to reduce to, and to keep within, the bounds of duty, the chiefs and agents of the conspiracy.

"It is very essential that I should know who is the person who wrote, printed and circulated the document having for its title: *Decree of the Council, dated October,* 1768, and under what authority this was done. I desire the same information with regard to the other document entitled: *Memorial of the inhabitants of Louisiana on the event of the* 29th *October*, 1768, because all the articles of said documents claim my special attention. I shall put entire faith in your informations, and I again beg you not to omit any circumstance relative to men and things, in what concerns said revolution."

On the 20th, without losing sight of the object of his investigations, O'Reilly went to pay a formal visit to the French governor, with the whole body of Spanish officers.* On that very day, Aubry answered the communication which he had received from O'Reilly, on the preceding one. Aubry's letter is a very long document, in which he designates all the chiefs of the revolution, and relates minutely their respective shares in that

---

* Sin abandonar dicho cuidado, fué à visitar al gobernador frances con todo el cuerpo de oficiales nuestros.

event. No attorney general could have drawn a more precise and more fatal indictment. He concludes in these words: "I will communicate to your Excellency all the decrees, memorials, and other pieces of iniquity which were fabricated in those times of disturbances and disorders. I will deliver into your hands all the protests which I made against such injustices. My conduct shall be laid bare before the most equitable and the most enlightened of judges. His approbation, which I dare flatter myself to deserve, will be the greatest honor and the handsomest reward which I can ever receive." This communication, which is a model of humility and servility, does not redound to the credit of Aubry. Far from interceding in favor of his unfortunate fellow citizens, far from endeavouring to palliate their guilt, which he could have done without deviating from truth, he arraigns them with bitter asperity, and, certainly, is answerable, to a considerable degree, for the shedding of the blood of those he had accused with such violence. If he had contented himself with this brief answer: "The King of France, my master, appointed me governor of this colony, and I cannot believe that the King of Spain wishes to convert me into a common informer," he, perhaps, would have stood higher in the estimation of O'Reilly himself, and, undoubtedly at least, in that of posterity.

On receiving Aubry's communication, O'Reilly's mind was immediately made up. On the next day, the 21st, he communicated to Aubry, at eight o'clock in the morning, the orders of his catholic majesty to arrest and bring to trial, in accordance with the laws, the chiefs of the revolution. Aubry, in one of his despatches, says that he never suspected before that O'Reilly had been invested with any such powers. The Spanish Governor, without loss of time, whilst Aubry was with him, drew

ARREST OF THE INSURGENT LEADERS. 301

to his house, under different pretexts, nine of the leaders of the late insurrection, and had three others, of an inferior rank, arrested in the town hall. They were Nicolas Chauvin de Lafrénière, Jean Baptiste de Noyan, Joseph Villeré, Pierre Caresse, Pierre Marquis, Joseph Milhet, Jean Milhet, Joseph Petit, Balthasar de Masan, Julien Jerome Doucet, Pierre Poupet, and Hardy de Boisblanc. When they were all in his presence, and Aubry standing by, he thus addressed them : " Gentlemen, the Spanish nation is respected and venerated all over the globe. Louisiana seems to be the only country which is not aware of it, and which is deficient in the respect due to that nation. His Catholic Majesty is much displeased at the violence which was lately exercised in this province, and at the offence which was committed against his governor, his officers and his troops. He has been irritated by the writings which have been printed, and which revile his government and the Spanish nation. He orders me to have arrested and tried, according to the laws of the kingdom, the authors of these excesses and of all these deeds of violence."

After having read to them the orders of his Catholic Majesty, which prescribed to him the course he was pursuing, he added : " Gentlemen, I regret to say, that you are accused of being the authors of the late insurrection. I therefore arrest you in the King's name. My earnest wish is, that you may prove your innocence, and that I may soon set you free again. Here are your judges (pointing to some officers who were in the room). They are as equitable as they are learned, and they will listen to your defence.* The only part which I shall take in the trial will be, to favor you as much as I may

* Dijó que S. E. no tomaria otra parte en esta causa (cuyos jueces estaban alli presentes, y les hizò ver), que la que fuese conducente á favorecerlos, y que deseaba que todos pudiesen justificar, plenamente su conducta.

be permitted. In the mean time, all your property, according to the custom of Spain, with regard to prisoners of state, shall be sequestered. But you may rest assured that you shall be treated as well as possible, in the places where you shall be respectively confined. As to your wives and children, be persuaded that I shall grant them all the assistance of which they may stand in need. In relation to the sequestration of your estates and effects, a faithful inventory shall be made of them, and I invite each of you now to appoint whom he pleases, to be present on his behalf, at that inventory, and every person so appointed by you shall also countersign the inventory of your papers."

He paused for an answer; and the unfortunate prisoners, after they had somewhat recovered from the first shock they had felt at such a proceeding, gave, according to O'Reilly's invitation, the names of those who were to represent them, and a list of those names was made on the spot. "Now, gentlemen," resumed O'Reilly, "please to deliver up your swords." Whilst this scene was acting, the whole house had been surrounded by troops, and the rooms had been filling up with grenadiers. One of O'Reilly's aids received the swords of the prisoners, and some officers of grenadiers courteously taking, one the right and the other the left arm of every prisoner, placed them between two companies of grenadiers, and thus, arm in arm, conducted them to their places of confinement, where they were all separated from each other. Some were put in the frigate in which O'Reilly had come, some in two of the other vessels, and the rest in a well-guarded house. It was ordered that they should be interrogated, that their depositions be taken down in writing, and that they be allowed all the conveniences they might want, provided they be not permitted to communicate with each other, nor with any body else. On rendering an account of this event to the French Ministry, Aubry said: "I have the honor to forward to you a list of the small number of those whom the General was indispensably obliged to have arrested. This proves his generosity and the kindness of his heart, considering that there are many others whose criminal conduct would have justified their being treated in the same manner."

With regard to Villeré, it seems that he had been the only one who had prepared to fly with his family and negroes, when he had heard of the arrival of the Spaniards. His plan was to retire to Manchac, under the protection of the English flag. But, either being deceived, as some say, by a letter from Aubry, who pledged himself for his safety, or believing, when he was informed of the kind reception made to his associates in the late revolution, that it was not the intention of the Spanish Government to act with rigor, he gave up his original design and came to town from the German coast, to present himself to the General and ascertain the true state of things. He was one of those who were confined in the frigate. Being of an exceedingly violent temper, this sudden blasting of his hopes threw him,* as the Spanish official report says, into such a fit of frenzy, that he died raving mad, on the day of his arrest. Bossu, in his work on Louisiana, gives a different version, but he is so fanciful in all his relations of pretended facts, that he is hardly to be believed. Judge Martin, in his history of Louisiana, gives a third version, and says: " He (Villeré) was immediately conveyed on board of a frigate that lay at the levee. On hearing of this, his lady, a grand-daughter of De Lachaise, the former commissary general and *ordonnateur*, hastened to the city. As her boat approached the frigate it was hailed and

* Murió al 1° dia de su prision, de terror y enojo, y antes perdió el juicio.

ordered away. She made herself known, and solicited admission to her husband, but was answered she could not see him, as the captain was on shore and had left orders that no communication should be allowed with the prisoner. Villeré recognized his wife's voice, and insisted on being permitted to see her. On this being refused, a struggle ensued, in which he fell, pierced by the bayonets of his guards. His bloody shirt thrown into the boat announced to the lady that she had ceased to be a wife; and a sailor cut the rope that fastened the boat to the frigate." This atrocity of the bloody shirt is not probable. It is not mentioned in the official French despatches, which I have seen, and rests only on popular tradition, which delights in tales of similar exaggeration. It has, no doubt, been preserved and handed down, on account of the dramatic effect which it produces, and which has made it acceptable to the imagination.

It is impossible to describe the terror which the arrest of these men and the death of Villeré scattered far and wide. They were so much identified with the whole population, their personal friends were so numerous, their family connections so extensive, that the misfortune which had befallen them could not but produce a general desolation. Besides, every one trembled for his own life, or for the safety of others, and many, in secret, began to make immediate preparations to fly to the English. In New Orleans, the doors of the majority of the houses were closed, and the inhabitants deserted the streets, which resounded only with the heavy tramp of the patrolling Spaniards. On the 22d of August, the day following the arrest of Lafrénière and his companions, O'Reilly, in order to dissipate the fears which agitated the population, had this proclamation posted up at the public square and at the corner of every street:

"IN THE NAME OF THE KING,

"We, Alexander O'Reilly, Commander of Benfayan, in the order of Alcantara, Major General and Inspector General of the armies of his Catholic Majesty, Captain General and Governor of the Province of Louisiana, in virtue of his Catholic Majesty's orders, and of the powers with which we are invested, declare to all the inhabitants of the Province of Louisiana, that, whatever just cause past events may have given his Majesty, to make them feel his indignation, yet his Majesty's intention is, to listen only to the inspirations of his royal clemency, because he is persuaded that the inhabitants of Louisiana would not have committed the offence of which they are guilty, if they had not been seduced by the intrigues of some ambitious, fanatic, and evil-minded men, who had the temerity to make a criminal use of the ignorance and excessive credulity of their fellow-citizens. These men alone will answer for their crimes, and will be judged in accordance with the laws.

"So generous an act on the part of his Majesty must be a pledge to him that his new subjects will endeavor, every day of their lives, to deserve, by their fidelity, zeal and obedience, the pardon and protection which he grants them from this moment." This proclamation made more than one breast breathe freely, and diminished, to some degree, the feeling of terror which had been produced by the events of the preceding day.

On the 23d, O'Reilly issued a proclamation, inviting the inhabitants of the town and its vicinity to appear before him, at his house, on the 26th, at seven o'clock in the morning, to take their solemn oath of vassalage and fealty to the new sovereign. Those of the inhabitants who resided in distant settlements were informed that, on certain days to be fixed hereafter, and before certain officers to be appointed for this special purpose, they would have to appear in their turn, and to go through the same ceremony. O'Reilly also wrote to Aubry a letter, in which he told him, that he had perused the original of the document entitled: "*Memorial of the planters, merchants, and other inhabitants of Louisiana, on the event of the* 29*th of October*, 1768, which was found in the possession of the printer Braud, with an order signed by the Commissary Foucault, authorizing the publication; that he considered this document as a libel injurious in the highest degree to the authority of the King, and derogatory to the respect due to his royal person; that it was defamatory of the Spanish nation; and that Foucault's crime being fully proved by his signature, there could remain no doubt but that he was one of the chiefs of the late insurrection, and one of the principal authors of the excesses committed against Don Antonio de Ulloa and the government of his Catholic Majesty, wherefore he begged Governor Aubry to have Foucault arrested with the greatest precaution and promptitude, in order that the most unfaithful and criminal conduct of that officer being investigated, both he, O'Reilly, and Aubry, should be able to lay before their respective sovereigns full copies of the proceedings of the trial to which he would be submitted. This request took Aubry by surprise; but he complied with it readily, although he says: *that it caused him a great deal of grief.* He sent Major de Grand-maison, Captain de Lamazelière, and Adjutant Major Aubert, to arrest Foucault, in the name of the King of France, in the house where this Commissary resided, and which was to be his prison. There, with the approbation of O'Reilly, he was guarded by a French detachment and two officers, whom Aubry made personally responsible for the safe keeping of the prisoner. As a measure of precaution, Foucault's guard was to be changed every day. Grand-Maison, assisted by Lamazelière and Aubert, and in the presence of Bobé, the Marine Comptroller, put the seals on Foucault's papers. Bobé was appointed by Aubry to fulfil the functions of Foucault. " I told him," says Aubry to the French Government, " that I would hold him answerable for all the harm that he might do, although I think that he is incapable of doing wrong, because he is an honest man, and has always blamed the conduct of his superior." (Foucault.

On the 25th, O'Reilly was engaged in issuing several provisional decrees, in relation to securing immediately the faithful and prompt administration of justice, and chose from among the inhabitants, those who were reputed the most intelligent and honest, to call them to the discharge of those judicial functions, which the good of the country required.

On the 26th, the ceremony of taking the oath of allegiance was performed, as it had been prescribed. It began with the clergy, to whom precedence was allowed, and so on, through all the classes of the population. " This ceremony," wrote Aubry, "was conducted with much order and dignity. I presented to the General every corps, company, or corporation, according to its rank. The General explained to them, in a loud voice, all the obligations to which they would be subjected by their oath; he told them that they were fully and entirely free to take, or not to take it; that those who should not be disposed to assume such an engagement, were the masters of their own decision, and that he would give them all the time and all the ·necessary facilities to arrange their affairs, and to retire to their country. Almost all the inhabitants took the oath with zeal, and I dare assert that they will, henceforth, be as faithful subjects to his Catholic Majesty, as they were to the most Christian King. After the ceremony was over, I approached the Spanish Governor with the whole body of the French officers, and I told him that we deemed it a compliment and an honor, to serve under the orders of so distinguished a general as he was; that we were ready to shed our blood for the service of the King of Spain, just as willingly as for the King of France; and that, in so doing, we would merely execute the will of the King, our master, which was all that we wished. He was completely satisfied with this demonstration, and answered us in the most obliging manner."

On the 27th, the Acadians and Germans who, although they had made all possible haste to reach New Orleans on the 26th, had not been able to accomplish their object, were admitted to take their oath of allegiance, and were immediately sent back to their rural occupations.

On the 28th, the Spanish troops were engaged in landing from the fleet all the ammunition, provisions, and other materials and effects, of which it had brought an ample supply. On that day, by the order of Aubry, Major de Grand-maison, with Captains Lamazelière and Trudeau, assisted by the notary Garic, and in the presence of Bobé, the marine comptroller, proceeded to raise the seals which had been affixed in Foucault's house, and to inventory all the papers relative to his office, and which were to be handed to Bobé, his successor. "I had also ordered the same officer," wrote Aubry, "to require of Foucault a declaration under oath, of all the moveable and immoveable property he owned in the colony. It appears from his own showing that he owns little or nothing, and has a heavy amount of debts, both in France and in this colony."

Although the preceding operations had given much occupation to General O'Reilly, he did not neglect to inform himself minutely of all the wants of the colony. He despatched messengers to all the distant settlements, to convey official intelligence of his arrival, and of his having taken formal possession of the province, and to authorize their commanders, to receive the oath of allegiance of all the inhabitants residing within their jurisdiction. He requested them also to make known to him what they desired, to supply the necessities of their respective posts.

"His intention," wrote Aubry, " is to introduce no innovations, but those which may be absolutely necessary. He will maintain and cause to be executed all the wise and useful regulations which the government, on account of its weakness, had not been able to enforce for several years back. He will keep in force the Black Code, which, he thinks, contains excellent provisions, not only with regard to the discipline which it establishes among the negroes, but also in relation to the moderation which it prescribes to masters, in the treatment of their slaves. This has infinitely pleased the inhabitants. I have the honor to transmit to you the ordinance, which he has issued on this subject.

"Finally, after so many disturbances and disorders, which had so long desolated this colony, it is surprising that the mere presence of one individual should, in so short a time, have restored good order, peace and tranquillity. Had it been the good fortune of this province that General O'Reilly had arrived sooner, it would never have seen all the calamities from which it has suffered. With the exception of a small number of families, which are in a state of consternation, on account of what has so justly befallen some of their members, who have been arrested, all the rest of the colonists are quiet and satisfied. They are grateful to his Catholic Majesty for having sent them a governor, who listens with kindness to those who have any business with him, and who, although respected and feared, is not the less loved for his generosity, his magnanimity, and his equity, of which all of us feel the effects. He will make the happiness of this colony."

On the 5th of October, Aubry, at the request of O'Reilly, proceeded to the interrogation of Foucault, who declined answering, on the ground that whatever he had done, was in his official capacity of commissary of the King of France and in his name, that to his government alone he was answerable, and that, as he had not seen any order of arrest issued against him by his most Christian Majesty, he protested against the decrees of which he was the object, and excepted to the jurisdiction of any Spanish tribunal, for acts which he had done officially, in the name of the King of France, and on his behalf. Several attempts were made to induce him to undergo an examination, but he remained obstinately silent on those occasions. He merely said that he was willing to stand his trial in France, and he repeatedly asked to be sent thither. Upon consideration, it was thought proper to comply with his request, and, on the 14th of October, he was embarked for France, where, on his arrival, he was thrown into the Bastile.

Speaking of Foucault, in a letter written to the Marquis of Grimaldi, O'Reilly says: "He is a conceited and narrow minded man, who has cheated a host of people here, as it is demonstrated by the amount of debts which he leaves." Indeed it appears from Foucault's own statement of his affairs, that his debts exceeded his worldly goods by twenty-seven thousand dollars, which was a pretty considerable sum at that epoch. The schedule of his debts proves that he had even possessed the art of duping those, whose destruction or expulsion from the colony he had aimed at; for the Spanish Contador, Don Estevan Gayarre, is put down for $780, on the list of his private creditors.

Braud had also been arrested, for having printed the memorial of the planters, merchants, &c. of Louisiana on the event of the 29th of October, 1768. But he pleaded in justification that, as the King's printer, he was bound, by the tenure of his office, to print all that was sent to him by the King's commissary, and he showed Foucault's signature, at the bottom of the manuscript which he had published. This defence was admitted as good, and he was set free.

This was the prelude to the great trial which was soon to begin, and which, ending with the shedding of the blood of men who were loved and respected, whatever their faults may have been, left a deep and indelible impression in the annals of the colony.

SEVENTH LECTURE.

A State Trial in 1769, and one in 1851—Indictment and Arguments presented by the Attorney-General Don Felix del Rey against Lafrénière and the other conspirators—Their Defence—Reflections on the right which the Colonists had to resist the Cession—Quotations from Vattel's law of nations—Judgment against the accused—Some of them are sentenced to the Gallows, and others to Imprisonment—Vain efforts to obtain a Respite from O'Reilly—O'Reilly disposed to connive at the Flight of Noyan, who refuses to avail himself of this favorable circumstance—Want of a White Hangman in the colony—Anecdote of the Black, Jeannot, to whom these functions were tendered—For want of a White Man, as Public Executioner, the accused, who were sentenced to be Hung, are Shot—The Memorial of the Planters, Merchants, and other inhabitants of Louisiana on the event of the 29th of October, 1768, is burnt on the public square—The son of Masan goes to Spain, and throws himself at the feet of the King—He obtains the Pardon of his Father and of the other Prisoners—Aubry, on his Return to France, is Shipwrecked and Lost—Anecdotes of the slaves Artus and Cupido—Their heroic Answer to O'Reilly—O'Reilly's Despatch to Grimaldi, in relation to the Trial, the Judgment and its Execution—Aubry's Letter on the same subject—Reflections on the course pursued by O'Reilly—An Anecdote of Cardinal Richelieu and De Thou, applied to O'Reilly—Sequestration and Confiscation of the Property of the Culprits—Costs of the Trial—Inventory of said Property—Description of the Furniture of the wealthiest houses in Louisiana, 1769—Spartan Simplicity—Description of the Dwellings, Manners, and Customs of the Colonists at the time—Census of the Colony—Its Commerce, Agriculture, and Finances—Final Reflections.

If twelve among the most distinguished citizens of Louisiana were now brought to trial for high treason, as they were in 1769, it would require no effort of the imagination to conceive and portray the scenes, that would be the natural consequences of such an event. What an excitement there would be through the broad length and breadth of the land! What an array of friends, family connexions, wealth, talent, and social influence, rushing to the rescue! What passionate discussions in every place of public resort, and in the sanctuary of every man's household! Could that queen of the mind, to whom none so high as not to do her reverence, and none so low as to be beyond the reach of her care and power, could the press remain impassive, when subjected to the thousand currents of electricity that would play upon her! Would she not, like a mirror, be compelled to reflect the passions of the multitude around, and be exposed, under the pressure of the moment, to be broken and divided into fragments, representing perhaps the antagonistical images of prosecution and defence? Would she not, on one side, echo the hue and cry of hatred or prejudice, and, on the other, would she not repeat the pathetic or argumentative language of justification? Or, if soaring above the fields of contention, she rose up to the pure atmosphere of impartiality, would she not, like the eagle, look down with eager impatience at her quarry, and could she suppress the shrill cry of exultation, at sight of the rich food prepared for her craving appetite? But, whatever might be the scenes acted and the persons in play, it would be on the broad theatre of the most unlimited freedom, in the cheering and illuminating light of the glorious sun of publicity, and under the scrutinizing eye of the whole civilized world.

Now comes the day of trial. Look at that vast room, where stands the seat of judgment. All the doors are open, and within and without the palace of justice are to be seen the serried ranks of an eager crowd. From far and wide, perhaps from the most distant parts of the great American confederacy, men and women have come to share in the emotions of the famous trial which occupies the attention of all, and the preliminaries of which have, for months past, with our modern means of conveying intelligence, been made as familiar to the dweller in the remotest village of Maine, as to the immediate neighbors of the accused. The sheriff has proclaimed the court to be in session; the judge, a man sprung from the loins of the people, and appointed by the people to expound and apply the laws which they themselves have framed, is on the bench; the accused have made their appearance at the bar, and are ready to meet the award of their country. Near them, for their protection and defence, stand some of the most learned and eloquent advocates that ever adorned their profession,—some who, for their national reputation, have been invited from north and south, from east and west, to assist the talent and genius of the State,—some, whose will rules senates, and directs the destinies of one of the most powerful nations of the earth—whose thunders of eloquence rise not only over the boundless plains, over the huge range of mountains, and along the innumerable rivers and lakes of the whole continent of America, but also ride the Atlantic wave, and reach, with undiminished power and majesty, the old European shore. By the side of those whom the law threatens with her uplifted sword, are such champions, interposing their shields, and ready to do battle for presumed innocence; and what is perhaps more cheering and more gladdening to the hearts of the accused, is the presence of their fathers, mothers, brothers, sisters, and other relations, with numerous friends, who throng the hall, and whose eyes speak the sympathies of their souls, and whose sorrow-stricken countenances are calculated to make such an impression on the theoretically immoveable judges!

It is beautiful to see the fortifications and outposts which the law has thrown around the life of the meanest citizen of our country, and which must be carried before it can be forfeited. First, a Grand Jury of his fellow-citizens is to determine whether there are sufficient grounds to put him on his trial; then it is his sacred privilege to be tried by his peers, by a petty jury of the vicinage, drawn by lot. He is furnished in time, to be duly examined and considered by him, with a list of the jury, and with a copy of the indictment found against him; he has the right of peremptory challenge, and of challenge for cause. These are some of the advantages secured to him, and of which a more minute enumeration would be out of place. In such a case as the one I have mentioned, it would probably take many a day to empanel a jury, on account of the difficulty of finding men, who, from the public or private reports, and from the very nature of our institutions, would not, in spite of themselves as it were, have formed an opinion on the guilt or innocence of the accused. Yet the jury is sworn at last! The Attorney General has stated the grounds on which rests the prosecution, and the witnesses for the State are brought to the stand to substantiate them, and are put face to face with the accused. Then come the skirmishes and partial actions between the belligerents, on incidental matters of debate. The examination and cross-examination of witnesses is conducted with the most exquisite skill; the questions of evidence are minutely sifted and elaborately argued; every inch of ground is disputed with unwavering energy. When the witnesses for the defence are presented in their turn, the same keen encounter of wits, of science, of dialectics and of elocution is reacted. During all the while, faithful reports of the proceedings have been conveyed to the expecting millions, through the daily columns of the press. After many days of manœuvrings and counter manœuvrings, and a display of judicial tactics, infinite in variety, the evidence on both sides is closed, and the field of argument is open. Now comes the sublimest of all spectacles—the struggle of intellect against intellect, clad in the gorgeous armor of eloquence. It sheds no blood, but only the divine effulgence of mind, brought into sparkling collision with mind, in the sacred discharge of duty. It is the battle of spirits of the air, of archangels fighting, as the bard saw them, with heavenly weapons. But the storm is over, and all the artillery of argument, of logic, of passion and of art has exhausted its missiles. Now is heard the clear and unimpassioned voice of the judge addressing the jury; he analyses the evidence, he sums up the arguments, he confutes sophistry, he expounds the law, and recommends its impartial application. The verdict of the jury closes the solemn scene.

In 1769, far different proceedings took place, the judges descended into the cells of the accused, and forced them to answer minutely all the questions they deemed proper to propound. The prisoners never saw the witnesses who were brought against them, and never knew who they were. These witnesses were examined in secret; and, with the same secrecy, the rest of the evidence was taken and weighed. It must be said, however, that, with regard to the facts on which the trial was to turn, they were abundantly and clearly proved. Indeed they had been of so public a nature that they could not be denied. Therefore, the accused, themselves, admitted most of them to be true, and confessed the respective parts they had acted in the last insurrection. But they rested their defence on the following grounds: The King of Spain, they said, had never taken possession of Louisiana, and Ulloa, who alleged that he was commissioned to that effect, having never shown his powers and credentials, the colonists were not bound to receive him as the representative of his Catholic

A STATE TRIAL. 317

Majesty, but had the right to consider him as an intruder and an impostor, and to dismiss him from the Province as they did. Not only had the Spaniards never been in possession of Louisiana, but also the colonists had never taken the oath of allegiance to the King of Spain. Therefore, the Province not having become Spanish, it followed that it remained French. Aubry had never ceased to be its governor, and the colonists had not been released from their oath of fealty to the King of France. If the Province had become Spanish, how could Aubry still continue to govern it in the name of the French King? How could justice be administered by the same royal authority? On the other side, if it had remained French, what right had Ulloa, on his introducing himself to French subjects, to be believed, on his word, to be the representative of the Majesty of Spain? What right had he, without exhibiting any credentials, either from Louis XV., or from Charles III., to assume any powers in the colony? And when he did so, was it not the duty of the colonists for their protection, in vindication of their dignity, and in conformity with what was due to their legitimate sovereign of France, to eject the foreign trespasser? But, admitting that the taking possession of the colony by the Spaniards, or that something tantamount to it, had been effected, or that said formal ceremony of taking possession was not absolutely necessary to establish in Louisiana the Spanish domination, yet it could not be pretended that the French laws had ever been repealed, and therefore, they, the accused, were to be tried and judged according to the principles, forms and usages of French jurisprudence, and by those French tribunals and authorities that were competent to take cognizance of their pretended offences, at the time they were alleged to have been committed. Thus, they protested against the application of the Spanish laws to their case, when these laws had never been extended over the colony.

The Licenciate Don Felix del Rey, a practitioner before the Royal Courts of St. Domingo and Mexico, who had been appointed the prosecuting Attorney-General on behalf of the King, against the authors of the insurrection of the 28th of October, 1768, presented to the Court, on the 20th of October, 1769, (all Spanish judicial proceedings being in writing,) a long document, in which he reviewed, with great ability, all the evidence that had been introduced, together with the laws applicable to the case; and he came to the conclusion that the accused had committed the crime of rebellion, wherefore he begged that they be condemned, each and severally, according to their respective degree of guilt, to undergo the penalty they had deserved. He commented with severity on the acts of the prisoners, and particularly on those of Lafrénière and Villeré. The latter being dead, was represented before the court by what was called " An Attorney to his memory," *un avocat à sa mémoire.*

" Lafrénière," said Don Felix del Rey, " who was clothed with the character of the King's attorney general, did not only advise the presentation to the Superior Council of the petition of the planters, merchants, and other colonists of Louisiana, but also maintained with obstinacy that the Council was competent to act upon it, whilst he knew that its real object was, to resist the orders of their most Christian and Catholic Majesties, in relation to the cession and possession of the colony and to many other points which it enumerated, when they could be decided only by the two kings, and were entirely beyond the contracted sphere of the Council. This conduct, on the part of Lafrénière, is that of an unfaithful officer, and makes him guilty of a crime of the gravest and most inexcusable nature, when, at the same time, it proves facts which he has denied. Thus, although being the King's attorney general, and therefore the person who is supposed to be the organ of the throne, who ought to vindicate the royal authority and jurisdiction, who, by the very tenure of his office, is in duty bound, and more so than any body else, to labor efficaciously to carry into execution the decrees of the King his master, and who ought to have been the most zealous of all in maintaining public tranquillity, yet he, Lafrénière, far from having been the real interpreter of the King's sentiments in the Council, far from having defended the authority and jurisdiction of his master, caused this same authority and jurisdiction to be usurped by the Council, by his attributing to said Council the power of taking cognizance of a matter far beyond its competency, and enabling that body to counteract the will of the King, and the reasons of State which had induced his most Christian Majesty to make the cession of Louisiana. On the contrary, his plain duty was, instead of supporting this usurpation of the rights of his Majesty, to maintain, with firmness, that the subject submitted to the Council did not come within its jurisdiction, and ought to be referred to the two kings.

"Such proceedings leave no room to doubt, that the accused did all he could, to secure the success of the conspiracy; and, in order to be convinced of it, it is only necessary to cast a glance at the conclusions of his address to the Council, which breathe hatred and indignation, and in which he is not satisfied with approving and affirming all the allegations of the petition of the colonists, but also permits himself to indulge in the most violent expressions, in order to influence the members of the Council, and to insure the success of the rebellion.

" Such was the deportment of Lafrénière, who thus abused his office of attorney general, and showed himself the chief instigator of the conspiracy, whilst, in conformity with the obligations of his official character, far from being on the side of sedition, he ought to have been more careful than ever, to discharge the duties of a faithful and obedient subject, as did Aubry on that occasion, who sought, with the greatest zeal and activity, to check the conspiracy, to tranquillize the inhabitants, and to keep them in due submission. Had Lafrénière followed such an example of loyalty, I have no doubt but that it would have been possible, to recall the public mind to its usual calm, because he was the most considerable personage in the Council, the one who, on account of his office, exercised the most powerful influence over the people, and because he was the head of a numerous family. Had he joined Aubry, and had he, like this officer, protested, as he ought to have done, against the pretensions of the Council and its decree, the rebels would have been obliged to change their sentiments, and the members of the Council would have been constrained to do the like. What, above all, gives a darker hue to Lafrénière's guilt, is that, at the very moment when he was driving his fellow citizens into rebellion, he, in his capacity of attorney general, was receiving his salary from the King of Spain's treasury.

" With regard to Villeré, who was a man of atrocious dispositions, and remarkable for his pride and violence, he was, undoubtedly, one of the most conspicuous movers in the conspiracy, and signalized himself by deeds of the most striking character. He it was who stirred up to rebellion the Germans, of whom he was the commander; he it was who made them sign the petition requesting the expulsion of Ulloa and of all the other Spaniards. He it was who led them to New Orleans,

PRESENTMENT OF THE ATTORNEY-GENERAL. 321

to incorporate them with the other rebels, and to strengthen the insurrection, as every body must be aware, since, on that day, he was at their head and commanded them. These facts are proved, in every particular, by the depositions of witnesses, which are on record. It is he who had the temerity to order the arrest of Maxent at the German Coast, and to take possession of the money which was destined to the Germans by Ulloa, for the payment of the grains which had been bought from them."

In relation to Petit, who was of a very diminutive size, Don Felix del Rey indulged in a vein of caustic humor, and said, in the sneering language of contempt : " It has been proved that he participated in all that was done by the conspirators, and that, several days before the insurrection, he had declared, with great parade of his importance, that : *ere long, the people would be rid of that devil, Ulloa, because he, Petit, had taken all the necessary measures to drive him off.* On the day of the insurrection, he appeared among the rebels, giving orders, and assuming to be one of the leaders and chief actors, so much so, that he had the insolence to cast off, with his own hands, when Ulloa was expelled, the line which made fast to the shore the vessel in which that officer had embarked, because he felt impatient at the tardiness of the sailors in executing that operation. It was also proved that, on his being informed of the arrival of his Excellency, General O'Reilly, at the Balize, he said : *that there ought to be a general turn out against the Spaniards, and that he would blow out the brains of the coward who should act differently.* These are the most atrocious offences which could be committed by a personage of so much insignificance. Notwithstanding his fury and the gigantic proportions of his pretensions, it was not possible for him to do more. Thus, considering only what

21

he did, there is no reason to doubt, however, that he was one of the most obstinately violent actors among the rebels, and that he would have taken his share in offences still more serious, if his intellectual capacity and the contexture of his physical organization had furnished him with better means of conception and execution."

Don Felix del Rey thus reviewed all that had been proved against every one of the accused, and presented it to the court under its most striking colors. After having related all the events of the revolution, and analysed all the evidence on record, he proceeded to an examination of the laws which he thought applicable to the case. "Although," said he, "according to the strict letter of the law, the crime of high treason or rebellion embraces equally all those who have any share in its enormities, yet our sovereign, the most clement of kings, willing, in order to preserve the people against greater misfortunes, that punishment be inflicted only on a few, with the view of making it an example to others, has ordered by his royal schedule (H.) annexed to the record, that only the chief authors of the revolution and their principal accomplices be brought to trial, and punished in accordance with the degree of their guilt. There is no doubt but that the fact of conspiring, in a seditious manner, against the State, renders the chief authors of this crime and their accomplices equally guilty, although it may not have had for its main object the royal Majesty itself, because, if it be not directed against the person of the prince, it is nevertheless, by its nature, and in its very essence, an act of high treason, and, consequently, it must be followed, on conviction, by the application of the pain of death and by the confiscation of property.

"I do not intend to descend into the abyss of that

multitude of laws, which I might summon to the support of the conclusions to which I have come. I shall content myself with establishing my position on the unshakable foundation of a few laws which bear directly on this case, and which are decisive against the accused. The first law which I shall quote, is that which declares: *that any seditious or factious individual who shall cause an insurrection, and, under the pretext or semblance of defending his liberty or rights, shall take up arms, and excite others to do the same, shall be punished with death, as being guilty of high treason.* This law is clear in itself, and its exact application to this case is equally evident, considering that the accused induced the inhabitants of this province to take up arms, in order to support against Don Antonio de Ulloa the rights which they had set forth in their petition to the Council. It is said in another law that: *if any one produces disturbances or revolts in the kingdom, by causing cities to confederate, or people to assemble in arms, against the peace and dignity of the King or kingdom, he shall be punished with death, and be deprived of all that he may possess.* Another law comes in support of this one, and declares: *that those who shall cause such disturbances shall be traitors, and be punished with death and the loss of their property.* The same declaration is repeated in another law of the *Recopilacion*. In a word, there is no lack of laws, defining with precision, and punishing with uniform severity, the offence to which our attention is called.

"In the present case, it is evident that the accused are seditious men, who conspired against the kingdom, by endeavoring to wrest this colony from the Spanish domination. They also outraged the Spanish legislation, government and nation by the most insulting and opprobrious language, and by their demonstrations of hatred against his Majesty; and this last law which I have quoted, speaks also of this crime. Through their hatred of the king and kingdom, they took up arms under the pretext of defending their liberty and their rights, as they unanimously confess, and finally, they caused a prejudice to the kingdom, in destroying by their rebellion, what the government and treasure of Spain had done, for several years past, in order to increase and improve the resources of this colony. Besides, their conspiracy was the cause of the expenses of fitting out the considerable expedition, which became necessary to reduce them to submission and confirm the possession of his Catholic Majesty; so that, by applying the letter and spirit of the aforesaid laws, it is apparent that the accused are guilty, and deserve to lose their lives and their property. There is also another law, which subjects them to the same penalties, by declaring : *That he who labors by deed or word to induce any people, or any provinces, under the domination of the King, to rise against his Majesty, is a traitor.* The application of this law is so striking that it requires no comment, as it is proved that the accused caused the insurrection of the Germans and Acadians, who were living in quiet submission to his Majesty."

"Such are the laws according to which his Majesty ordered, in his royal Schedule, that those found guilty in this affair be punished; and these laws are consistent with the laws of nations, and particularly with the jurisprudence of every monarchy. The fact is, that there is not perhaps a nation, by which laws of the same nature have not been enacted, and are not put in force against those, who, seditiously and tumultuously, conspire against the State, since the only means of securing the preservation and tranquillity of a kingdom, is to make use of this kind of punishment against those who have the audacity to raise disturbances; and it is impossible to question the legitimate application of these same laws to the crime committed in Louisiana against his Majesty of Spain, when it is taken into consideration, that, on the breaking out of the insurrection of the 28th of October, the sovereignty of the King over Louisiana was established, as much by the possession taken by Don Antonio de Ulloa in the name of his Catholic Majesty, as by the right which the King had acquired over that colony, by virtue of the act of cession made by his most Christian Majesty, which was published in the colony by the order of said Majesty."

"It is idle, on the part of the accused, to say that, Ulloa having never shown his credentials, and having never taken possession of Louisiana, they never were under the domination of Spain, and, therefore, cannot be guilty of the crime of rebellion against her. It is true that the vain pageantry of pulling down the French flag and of raising the standard of Spain, was not exhibited on the public square at New Orleans. But did not Aubry, the representative of the King of France, receive Ulloa as the representative of the King of Spain? Was he not acknowledged as such by the militia, by all the ecclesiastical, military and political corps of the colony? Was not immediate and complete possession of the colony tendered to Ulloa, and even pressed upon him with persevering earnestness? Was it not declined by him on account of an unforeseen circumstance—the refusal of the French troops to serve the King of Spain according to the promise and engagement of their sovereign, and because Ulloa found himself without sufficient forces to occupy all the posts? But did he not take possession of the Balize and of all the posts which are the keys of the province? It is true that the flag of France continued to wave alongside of that of Spain, but it was as the flag of an ally, whose assistance was necessary, and not because the province remained French. Aubry himself retained his authority, only at the request of Ulloa, and, therefore, was only the Spanish governor's delegate—and a mere agent and trustee for the crown of Spain—exercising powers ad interim, on the invitation, with the consent, and for the benefit of his Catholic Majesty."

"Ulloa never was in possession of Louisiana! Then, by what right was the Spanish flag floating from the Balize to the Illinois? How came all the expenses of the colony to be paid out of the Spanish treasury from March 1766 to October 1768, when the insurrection broke loose? How came Aubry to promulgate decrees issued by Ulloa? How came the Superior Council to register them? Was not the financial, commercial and military administration of the colony entirely under the direction of Ulloa? Who granted passports to the merchants? Was it not Ulloa? To whom did the commanders at the several posts apply to be continued in office? Was it not to Ulloa? Was it not with his consent and approbation that Noyan was at the head of the Acadians, and Villeré in the command of the Germans? Whence did the chief conspirator, Lafrénière, derive his salary as Attorney General? Was it not from the Spanish treasury? Was he not in the pay of Spain when he turned upon her? Was it not treason? Who supplied the needy Acadians and Germans with their necessities? Who drove away famine by furnishing the colonists with the provisions they required? Who paid the Clergy? Who repaired the churches? Who gave permission to the planters to export their crops, and to purchase the negroes whom their agricultural pursuits demanded? Was it not Ulloa? And the members of the Council themselves, did they not frequently submit to his approbation the judgments which they had rendered? How came his authority to be thus recognized in the sanctuary of justice? If Ulloa, in the opinion of the colonists, was not clothed with legitimate authority, how came they, during two years, to be daily invoking that authority, and plying him with constant applications for the grant of protection, of privileges and of favors, and for the redress of wrongs? And, after having thus acted, how can they be so graceless as to turn round, and contradict themselves, by saying that he never had any authority? How is it that no vessel was allowed to sail from France to Louisiana, unless she had a passport granted by the Spanish authorities residing in that kingdom? Is it not clear, then, that Louisiana was a Spanish province in the eye of France? And if so for France, how could it be otherwise for the colonists? All these facts, which I have enumerated, are proved beyond doubt or cavil. Do they not constitute possession? And could they have come to pass, had there not been previous and effectual possession, to all intents and purposes? This ground of defence is, therefore, not tenable.

"As to the plea of the want of credentials, and of their not having been duly registered in the archives of the province, why did not the colonists raise that objection, at the threshold, and refuse entrance to Ulloa into their territory, unless he exhibited the authority under which he pretended to act? But, after having so long dispensed with the production of these credentials, after having recognized him as the representative of the King of Spain, after having allowed him, during two years, to exercise all the powers that he did, can they be permitted to argue, from the circumstance of Ulloa's having refused to exhibit his credentials and to have them registered, that they were not bound to obey him as the authorized ministerial embodiment of Spain in the colony, and, therefore, that they did not and could not commit rebellion against our gracious sovereign? If this plea could ever have been good, they have precluded themselves from its use by their own acts, and it is now too late to present it to this court as a shield to rebellious traitors. These acts demonstrate that Ulloa had taken possession of the colony, and that the King of Spain was exercising therein all the powers of sovereignty, when the insurrection of 1768 took place."

"But, admitting, for the sake of argument, that Ulloa never took possession of Louisiana, is it to be inferred from this fact, that the province remained French? Certainly not. The treaty of cession made it a Spanish domain, from the moment it was signed and approved by all the parties. The proof of it is to be found in the French king's letter to D'Abbadie, in which this officer was informed, that it was his Majesty's intention to abdicate all his rights in and to the colony, from the very moment of the cession. Another proof is, that, in this very same document, his most Christian Majesty designates the colonists of Louisiana as the *new subjects of his Catholic Majesty ;* and a third proof is, that France gave effectual information to her officers in the colony, that, from the day of Ulloa's arrival at New Orleans, she would cease to be responsible for the expenses of the colonial administration. Clearly, then, the colony was no longer French. What was it, what could it be, if not Spanish? It is indeed ludicrous to maintain the contrary."

"But, say the accused: we had not taken the oath of allegiance to the King of Spain, and, therefore, we cannot be guilty of the crime of rebellion and high treason against him. This is the weakest kind of sophistry, and its refutation is easy. If the accused were not the subjects of his Catholic Majesty, they were, at least, residents in his domain; and it is a legal doctrine, well settled, long ago, that those who are domiciliated in a foreign country, or who are mere travellers therein, although they are aliens and the subjects of another power, and have not taken the oath of allegiance to the sovereign of the country, in which they happen to be, are bound, during their residence in it, either perpetual or temporary, to be true and obedient to that sovereign, in return for the protection and security which is extended over them; and that they may be as much guilty of rebellion and high treason against him as his natural born subjects. It has even been determined that foreign ambassadors were obliged to abstain from doing anything derogatory to the respect due to the sovereign in whose court they were sent to reside, and could be dismissed for any act done in violation of his rights, of his royal dignity and of the laws of his kingdom; and, if certain immunities on that ground have been granted to them, it is a matter of national courtesy and not of right, and should ambassadors proceed to any overt acts of violence against the sovereign, they would be liable to be punished according to the laws of the land."

" My preceding observations are sufficient to remove all the doubts which may have been raised by the allegations of the accused: that Ulloa had not taken possession of the colony, at the time when the crimes with which they are charged were alleged to have been committed; that they had not sworn fealty to the King of Spain; and that they had remained bound by their oath to the King of France, until they were absolved from it by the solemn ceremony which took place, shortly after General O'Reilly's arrival."

" The true statement of the case may be summed up in a very few words. After the treaty of cession, Louisiana had, for more than two years, been a Spanish province in the eyes of the world, and the colonists themselves, during all that time, had quietly submitted to the Spanish rule, when some factious, perverse and ambitious individuals, not satisfied with Ulloa's administration, and regretting the loss of their former importance, seduced the rest of the people under false pretexts and by circulating the most infamous calumnies, and availed themselves of the irritation produced by a commercial decree unpalatable to the merchants of New-Orleans, to bring on the insurrection of the 29th of October 1768, under the delusive hope that they would thus disgust Spain with the new acquisition which had been tendered to her, and force France to take them back unto her bosom, in order to prevent their throwing themselves into the arms of England. The laws applicable to these criminal acts have been quoted and commented upon; the facts of the case are so authentically proved, the defence of the accused is so futile, and the laws, whose majesty is to be vindicated, speak a language so positive, so commanding and so clear, that what remains for me to do, is only to require, in the King's name, the judgment of the Court."

Don Felix del Rey took no notice of that part of the defence which rested on the ground, that the French laws having never been repealed, and the Spanish laws having never been put in force, the accused were to be tried and judged according to the principles, forms and usages of French jurisprudence, and by those French authorities and tribunals that were competent to take cognizance of their pretended offences, at the time they were alleged to have been committed. It was thought, no doubt, that the King had finally predecided this point, by sending a tribunal, ready formed, from Spain, with all the necessary instructions and powers, to try the authors of the insurrection of 1768. It was not for the members of this tribunal to set aside those instructions, on the ground of their illegality, and to question the authority with which, for a special purpose, they had been clothed by the sovereign, and to listen to arguments against their jurisdiction. This was a matter for the consideration of him from whom their powers originated. But, if Don Felix del Rey had not considered it useless to enter into the discussion of this plea, set up by the accused, he might have answered: That a distinction must be made between the civil and political laws, those which regulate the relations of citizens among themselves, and those which are established for the protection and security of the State. When a territory is acquired by a nation, the civil laws which existed there at the time, must undoubtedly continue in vigor, until they are abrogated, or modified by the new sovereign. But with regard to the political and fundamental laws, as they are inherent to the sovereignty, they follow, ipso facto, its extension wherever it is carried, and are in force, at the very moment when that sovereignty is established. Thus, when in 1803, Gov. Claiborne took possession of Louisiana in the name of the United States of America, the civil laws of that province were not altered by this fact. But suppose the inhabitants of the country, as they did in 1768, had taken up arms, and violently resisted and expelled Governor Claiborne. This would have constituted the crime of rebellion or high treason against the United States. Would the trials, which would have been the inevitable consequences of such deeds of violence, have been conducted according to the forms, rules, customs and laws of France, or Spain, or in conformity with the laws of the United States, as applicable to such cases? Clearly, in accordance with the last, which, almost as a component part of the flag of the United States, would have followed it into the province, and have been in force by the mere fact of possession, without requiring any special promulgation; and all outrages, such as acts of rebellion or high treason, against the collective sovereignty of the United States, would have been repressed, tried and punished according to the laws of these States, and by the tribunals of their own creation, and not according to the laws and by the tribunals established for the protection of the sovereignties of Spain and France. This distinction between civil and political laws is essentially required by their very nature. Thus it seems that the plea set up by the accused in 1769, and on which I do not think it out of place to venture these few remarks, although Don Felix del Rey deemed it unworthy of notice, did not, in reality, rest on any solid foundation.

Be it as it may, it is certain that, if the colonists, instead of having accepted for two years the Spanish domination, had resisted it in the beginning, on the ground that they were no herd of cattle, and could not be transferred away without their consent, they would have presented a more plausible justification, by relying on the following passage of Vattel's law of nations.*

"If the nation has conferred the full sovereignty to its conductor, if it has intrusted to him the care, and, without reserve, given him the right, of treating and contracting with other States, it is considered as having invested him with all the powers necessary to make a valid contract. The prince is then the organ of the nation; what he does is considered as the act of the nation itself; and though he is not the owner of the public property, his alienations of it are valid, as being duly authorized."

* Vattel's Laws of Nations, Chap. xxi. Of the alienation of the public property, or the domain, and that of a part of a State.

"The question becomes more distinct, when it relates, not to the alienation of some parts of the public property, but to the dismemberment of the nation or State itself—the cession of a town or a province that constitutes a part of it. This question, however, admits of a sound decision on the same principles. A nation ought to preserve itself—it ought to preserve all its members—it cannot abandon them; and it is under an engagement to support them in their rank as members of the nation. It has not, then, a right to traffic with their rank and liberty, on account of any advantages it may expect to derive from such a negotiation. They have joined the society for the purpose of being members of it—they submit to the authority of the State, for the purpose of promoting in concert their common welfare and safety, and not of being at its disposal, like a farm or a herd of cattle. But the nation may lawfully abandon them in a case of extreme necessity; and she has the right to cut them off from the body, if the public safety requires it. When, therefore, in such a case, the State gives up a town or a province to a neighbour, or to a powerful enemy, the cession ought to remain valid as to the State, since she has a right to make it; nor can she any longer lay claim to the town or province thus 'alienated, since she has relinquished every right she could have over them."

" But the province or town thus abandoned and dismembered from the State, is not obliged to receive the new master whom the State attempts to set over it. Being separated from the society of which it was a member, it resumes all its original rights; and if it be capable of defending its liberty against the prince who would subject it to his authority, it may lawfully resist him. Francis I. having engaged, by the treaty of Madrid, to cede the Duchy of Burgundy to the emperor Charles

V., the states of that province declared, ' *That, having never been subject but to the crown of France, they would die subject to it; and that, if the King abandoned them, they would take up arms and endeavor to set themselves at liberty, rather than pass into a new state of subjection.*' It is true, subjects are seldom able to make resistance on such occasions; and, in general, their wisest plan will be to submit to their new master, and endeavor to obtain the best terms they can."

This, indeed, would have been the wisest course which the colonists, weak as they were, could have pursued, and it is much to be regretted that they did not do so. Blood would not have been uselessly shed, in an enterprise in which success was materially impossible.

On the 24th of October, the Court found the prisoners guilty, and O'Reilly, as its president, pronounced and signed the judgment, which read thus:

"In the criminal trial instituted by the order of the King, our Sovereign, to discover and punish the chiefs and authors of the conspiracy which broke out in this colony, on the 29th of October of the last year, (1768,) against its Governor Don Antonio de Ulloa, all the grounds of the accusation having been substantially investigated, according to the due forms of law, between the parties,—on one side, the Licentiate Don Felix del Rey, a practising advocate before the royal courts of St. Domingo and Mexico, here acting in his capacity of Attorney General appointed by me for the King, according to the royal authority vested in me,—and on the other, Nicholas Chauvin de Lafrénière, ex-Attorney General for the King of France, and the senior member of the Superior Council, Jean Baptiste Noyan, his son-in-law, Pierre Caresse, Pierre Marquis, Joseph Milhet, an attorney to the memory of Joseph Villeré, on account of this culprit's demise in prison, Joseph Petit, Balthasar

THE JUDGMENT. 335

Masan, Julien Jerome Doucet, Pierre Hardy de Boisblanc, Jean Milhet and Pierre Poupet, accused of having participated in the aforesaid crime and in the subsequent seditions which broke out against the Spanish government and nation; having perused the information, depositions and other documents inserted in the procès verbal of this case; having compared the confessions of the accused with the papers found in the possession of some of them, and by them acknowledged as theirs; the accused being heard in their defence, and the charges brought against them being accompanied with their respective proofs; having heard the conclusions of the Attorney-General in his bill of indictment; all being examined and considered, either in point of fact or of law, in a case replete with circumstances so grave and so extraordinary; and taking into consideration all that results from said trial, to which I refer, I have to declare and I declare, that the aforesaid Attorney General has completely proved what he had to prove, and that the accused have not proved and established the allegations set up in their defence; that they have made out no exception which frees them from the crime imputed to them, and still less saves them from the penalties which, according to our laws, they have incurred for their respective shares in the excesses which have been enumerated by the Attorney General Don Felix del Rey; so that, from the present, I have to condemn and I do condemn the aforesaid Nicolas Chauvin de Lafrénière, Jean Baptiste Noyan, Pierre Caresse, Pierre Marquis and Joseph Milhet, as being the chiefs and principal movers of the aforesaid conspiracy, to the ordinary pain of the gallows, which they have deserved by the infamy of their conduct, and ipso jure, by their participation in so horrible a crime, and to be led to the place of execution, mounted on asses, and each one with a rope round his neck, to be then and there hung until death ensue, and to remain suspended to the gallows until further orders; it being hereby given to be understood that any one having the temerity of carrying away their bodies without leave, or of contravening, in whole or in part, the execution of this very same sentence, shall suffer death. And, as it results also from said trial, and from the declarations of the aforesaid Attorney General, that the late Joseph Villeré stands convicted, likewise, of having been one of the most obstinate promoters of the aforesaid conspiracy, I condemn, in the same manner, his memory to be held and reputed for ever infamous; and, doing equal justice to the other accused, after having taken into consideration the enormity of their crime, as proved by the trial, I condemn the aforesaid Petit to perpetual imprisonment in such a castle or fortress as it may please his Majesty to designate; the aforesaid Balthasar Masan and Julien Jerome Doucet, to ten years' imprisonment; and Pierre Hardy de Boisblanc, Jean Milhet and Pierre Poupet to six years' imprisonment; with the understanding that none of them shall ever be permitted to live in any one of the dominions of his Catholic Majesty, reserving to myself the care to have every one of these sentences provisionally executed, and to cause to be gathered up together and burnt by the hand of the common hangman, all the printed copies of the document entitled 'Memorial of the planters, merchants, and other inhabitants of Louisiana on the event of the 29th of October, 1768,' and that all other publications relative to said conspiracy be dealt with in the same manner; and I have further to decree, and I do decree, in conformity with the same laws, that the property of every one of the accused be confiscated to the profit of the King's treasury; and judging definitively, I pronounce this judgment, with the advice of Doctor

Don Manuel Jose de Urrutia, Auditor of war and of the navy, for the harbor and city of Havana, and the special assessor named by me, for this cause, under the royal authority; and his fees, as well as those of the officers employed in this trial, shall be paid out of the confiscated property, in the manner prescribed by law."

  Signed,   Alexander O'Reilly.
  Countersigned, Manuel Jose de Urrutia.

When this sentence was known, the effects which it produced can easily be conceived. The most strenuous efforts were made, to obtain from O'Reilly that its execution be suspended until an appeal be made to the royal clemency of Charles III. With the same gentleness of manner which characterized all his acts, but with the marked expression of unshakable determination, he replied: "That the Court had given its decision, and that it was final; that he had merely presided over the Court, but that, according to his plighted faith and well-known assurances, he had acted no other part in the trial than that of taking care that the accused be as favorably treated as possible; that he had strictly and honorably kept his word; that he could do no more; that he had instructions which he could not disregard, and which he had communicated to Aubry, to the accused and to their friends; that those instructions ordered him to proceed to an immediate execution of the sentence of the Court, whatever it might be, and that he would do so, in conformity with his duty, however painful it might be to his feelings." Some of those French ladies whose husbands, fathers or brothers had remained faithful to the Spanish cause, thought that, owing to this circumstance, they might, perhaps, exercise some influence over General O'Reilly; and, finding their way to him, they made a passionate appeal in favor of the condemned—such an appeal as the female heart alone can inspire. There were more than one Lady Margaret and one Miss Edith Bellenden, who, with frames trembling with anxiety, poured out their souls in supplications to O'Reilly. Like Graham of Claverhouse, whose character bore considerable affinity to his own, he resisted their intercessions with the most exquisite politeness, but with an inexorable temper, although he was, at that time, hardly more than thirty-four years old, therefore in the prime of life, and still at that age when the soul of man is not yet to be supposed steeled against the tears of woman and the soft emotions of pity and generosity. It is said that some of the Spanish officers, and particularly Loyola, Gayarre and Navarro, acting under the influence of their own feelings, and the promptings of those friends, whom, during a residence of nearly three years in the colony, they had made to themselves among the French population, advised O'Reilly to assume the responsibility of suspending the execution of the Court's judgment, until further orders be received from Spain; but all their applications remained fruitless, and it was soon ascertained that the doom of the accused was sealed. The sentence had been rendered on the 24th of October, and it became known that those who were condemned to death, would be executed on the next day.

If tradition is to be believed, O'Reilly, although inflexible in appearance, was secretly moved to compassion in favor of Noyan, the son-in-law of Lafrénière. This gentleman had lately been married, and his youth, his inexperience and other circumstances, pleaded as strongly in his favor as the numerous friends who left no means untried to save him. Certain words which dropped from the General's mouth gave it to be understood that the escape of this prisoner would be connived at. But Noyan, on being informed of it, heroically refused to avail himself of this favorable circumstance, and said that he would live or die with his associates.

Dumont, who wrote a work on Louisiana in 1753, relates that, when the Province was under the administration of the great India Company, it was found out that, in a civilized government, it was necessary that the office of hangman be regularly and permanently filled up; and that this office was tendered, with all its privileges and perquisites, to a slave of the company, named Jeannot. The grant of his freedom was to be the reward of his acceptance. But Jeannot was a high-spirited black, and peremptorily refused the favor. Yet, when he saw that the French were determined to force him to act in that capacity, he appeared to consent at last, and only begged that he might be permitted to go to his cot. There, seizing a hatchet, he struck off his right arm; then returning to the place where he was waited for to act as hangman, he showed to the assembled multitude the impossibility in which he was, to perform the functions assigned to him. The French were struck with admiration, and Jeannot was appointed overseer of all the negroes belonging to the company. Since that time a negro had always acted as hangman in the colony.

But it was thought that it would be too great an outrage against the feelings of the community, and, at the same time, a very impolitic act, considering the peculiar elements of the population of Louisiana, to have some of its most distinguished citizens hung by a negro. It was therefore necessary to find out a white man, who might be willing to discharge these functions. None, however, although a high reward was offered, presented himself to claim it. Consequently, the Attorney General, Don Felix del Rey, laid before O'Reilly, on the morning of the 25th, a petition in which he informed him of this fact, and begged him, on account of the impossibility of executing the original sentence of the Court, to have the prisoners shot, but without removing the infamy which would have resulted from their suffering death on the gallows. O'Reilly assented to this request, and Francisco Xavier Rodriguez, the clerk of the Court, drew a process verbal of the execution, which took place in his presence, at three o'clock in the afternoon. It appears by this process verbal that Nicolas Chauvin de Lafrénière, Pierre Marquis, Joseph Milhet, Jean Baptiste Noyan and Pierre Caresse, being taken out of prison, and with their arms well pinioned, were conducted, under a heavy escort of grenadiers, to the place of execution, which was occupied by a large body of Spanish troops forming a square. The prisoners being introduced into the middle of this square, Rodriguez, the clerk of the Court, read to them their sentence in Spanish, and it was then repeated to them in French by Henry Garderat, assisted by two other interpreters, Jean Baptiste Garic, and the Lieutenant of artillery, Juan Kely, who had all been specially appointed by O'Reilly to act as interpreters on the trial. Then a copy of the sentence was delivered into the hands of the public crier, who went round, and read it to all the troops and to the people, in a loud and intelligible voice. After these preliminaries were over, the last act of the drama was performed, and the well directed fire of a platoon of grenadiers ended the lives of those unfortunate men. It is said that they met their fate with unshaken fortitude.

On the next day, the 26th of October, the same Rodriguez caused to be burnt, on the public square, all the copies of the "Memorial of the Planters, merchants and other inhabitants of Louisiana," which had been discovered and gathered up together.

Masan and his companions were immediately transported to Havana, and imprisoned in fort Moro. It may be as well to state now that the son of Masan went to Madrid, threw himself at the feet of the King, and begged that his father be pardoned, or that he be permitted to take that father's place. The prayer of this generous young man, which was warmly supported by the French ambassador, touched the King, who granted a full pardon, not only to Masan, but also to Doucet, Boisblanc, Milhet, Poupet and Petit. None of them returned to Louisiana, and it is believed that they went to reside at the Cap Français in St. Domingo.

Aubry left Louisiana for Bordeaux in the brigantine called the *Père de Famille*. This vessel had entered the river Garonne, when she met a heavy storm and went down, near the Tower of Cordouan, with all on board, save the captain, a physician, a sergeant and two sailors, who succeeded in reaching the land in safety. The King, in order to show how much he appreciated the services of Aubry, granted a pension to the brother and to the sister of that officer. Aubry, before his departure from Louisiana, had been offered a high grade in the Spanish army, as a token of satisfaction at the liberal course which he had pursued towards that nation in the colony, but he refused, on the ground that he intended to devote the remnant of his days to the service of his native country. Some there were who thought that those whom they loved so dearly, had unjustly suffered, mostly in consequence of the imprudent denunciations of that officer and of his servility to O'Reilly and the Spaniards. By them his melancholy end was looked upon as an act of the retributive justice of Heaven.

It is related that, among the confiscated slaves of Lafrénière, there was one named Artus, who had the reputation of being an admirable cook. O'Reilly sent for Artus, and said to him : "You are now the King of Spain's property. Until you are sold, you shall be my cook." "You had better change your mind," answered the negro. "I would poison him who ordered my master to be killed." It is also reported that one of Caresse's slaves, whose name was Cupidon, and who was an excellent house servant, refused peremptorily to perform these functions for O'Reilly, because, as he boldly said, " he would not serve his master's assassin." O'Reilly seemed to appreciate the noble sentiment which actuated these faithful slaves, and dismissed them, without resenting the determination which they had both so fearlessly expressed. If these anecdotes are true, they show that negroes are capable of heroic attachment for those that hold them in bondage, and that O'Reilly was not a man of an unamiable disposition.

The bloody execution which took place in Louisiana caused a good deal of excitement in France, and it seems that the French government instructed its agents in Spain, to ascertain what effect it had produced on the Spaniards themselves. I have under my eye a letter written to one of the French ministers by a Mr. Depuyabre, a French agent at Cadix, in answer to the inquiries which had been addressed to him, and in which he says : " All the relations of that event, which were sent from Louisiana to Havana, agree in blaming the rigor with which General O'Reilly punished the most distinguished citizens of Louisiana. The Spaniards here, and others, whatever nation they belonged to, have expressed their detestation of such an act. You know better than any body else what were the orders of which O'Reilly was the bearer, and you can thereby judge whether that officer kept himself, or not, within the sphere of his powers."

It must be recollected that the Marquis of Grimaldi, on the departure of O'Reilly from Spain for Louisiana, had sent to the Count of Fuentes, the Spanish ambassador at the Court of Versailles, a despatch which was intended to be laid before the French ministry, and in which he had said: "It seemed proper to invest Don Alexandro O'Reilly with these extensive powers, on account of the distance at which we are from that country. But, as the King, whose character is well known, is always inclined to be mild and clement, he has ordered O'Reilly to be informed that his will was, that a lenient course be pursued in the colony, and that expulsion from it be the only punishment inflicted on those who have deserved a more severe one."

It would seem, from this document, that O'Reilly should have contented himself with having expelled from the colony those who had deserved a severer punishment —for instance the pain of death. But were the instructions shown to the Court of France and those really given to O'Reilly of the same nature? That is the question. If O'Reilly received the instructions which are mentioned in the despatch of the Marquis of Grimaldi, would he have dared to disobey them, and would he, when such strong appeals were made to him to save the lives of Lafrénière and his companions, have had the unblushing effrontery, on refusing that boon, to plead the orders of the King, and thus, falsely, to throw upon his sovereign the odium of a measure, which was contrary to the expressed will of that very sovereign? Had he assumed this responsibility, on account of some unforeseen circumstances or reasons, would he not have accounted for those circumstances or reasons in his despatches to his government? But, far from using the language of apology or exculpation, for having acted with severity, in violation of his positive instructions, he, on the contrary, applauds himself for the extreme lenity of the course he pursued. This is demonstrated by the despatch which he sent to the Marquis of Grimaldi, to give an account of the closing of the trial and of the execution of the sentence of the Court:

"The trial which began here," said he, "against the twelve chiefs, movers and accomplices of the insurrection which took place in this province, is at an end. Six of them, having deserved death, were sentenced to be hung; but one of these culprits having died in prison, five only were executed, and, as there is no executioner here, they were shot on the 25th of this month (October), at three o'clock of the afternoon. The six others were sentenced to be imprisoned in one of the King's castles, that is, one for life, two for ten years and three for six years, and the property of the twelve was confiscated."

"The six who were sentenced to be imprisoned will be sent to day to one of the forts at Havana. I transmit to the Captain General of that place a copy of the judgment, in order that he may proceed to carry it into execution."

"The property of these prisoners had been sequestrated, from the beginning of their trial. I have just given the necessary orders for the liquidation of said property in accordance with the laws, in order that what belongs to the widows and other creditors may be given to them, and the balance be delivered up into the King's treasury."

"This judgment wipes off entirely the insult made to the dignity and authority of the king in this province, and checks the effects of the bad example which had been given to the subjects of his Majesty. Every body acknowledges the necessity, the justice, and the clemency of this judgment, which sets up an example ever to be remembered. What renders it still more efficacious, is the diligence with which this affair was conducted, and the incontestable nature of the evidence on which this judgment was founded.

"I will treat, for the future, with marked gentleness, all those who signed the representations addressed to the Council, and it will be a great consolation to the public, to know that I shall leave in this colony no painful recollection of that audacious outrage. I will conciliate and tranquillize the public mind by all the means in my power, and nothing will be more conducive to this end, than to let the people know, that all past occurrences shall be forgotten, and that every one shall receive from the government the protection and favor which he may deserve."

This candid exposition which O'Reilly made of his sentiments proves, that he thought himself entitled to much credit for the lenity of his acts. *Everybody*, says he with exultation, *acknowledges the necessity, the justice and the clemency of this judgment, which sets an example ever to be remembered.* And it must not be forgotten that Governor Aubry, writing to his own government, takes the same view of the course of action adopted by O'Reilly. *I have the honor*, said he to the French minister, *of sending a list of the small number of those whom the general was indispensably obliged to have arrested. This proves his generosity and the kindness of his heart, considering that there are many others, whose criminal conduct would have justified their being treated in the same manner.*

To judge fairly of the feelings and ideas of these men, we must transport ourselves back to the days in which they lived, we must adopt the turn of mind which education, habits and associations had given them, and we must become impregnated with the political, social and moral atmosphere in which they had been born. In this age, the treatment which was inflicted on Lafrénière and his companions may be looked upon as tinged with cruelty, if appreciated with our modern feelings of humanity, and with those notions of right and wrong, which now prevail throughout the civilized world. In 1851, Lafrénière and his accomplices would not, probably, have been condemned to an ignominious death, for doing what they did in 1768. They had resisted the exercise of powers which they thought oppressive to them, and which were wielded by an officer, whom they believed to be clothed with dubious authority; they had resorted to every means, even violence, not to be severed from that kingdom, to which the colony was indebted for its birth. But they had shed no blood; and when experience demonstrated to them that their schemes of being re-annexed to France, or to set up for themselves under an independent government, were visionary; when O'Reilly arrived with such forces as it would have been madness to cope with, they tendered, at once, their full and entire submission to the government of Spain. It must be recollected, however, that a century ago, the slightest attempt against royal authority was considered as one of the most heinous crimes that could be committed, and was punished with a severity, which now would not be tolerated by public opinion; and that offences which then were deemed to deserve death, would not now be the cause even of putting a man on his trial. It is not astonishing therefore that both Aubry and O'Reilly should have honestly thought that, to pick out of the rebellious colonists twelve leaders only, six of whom should be shot, and six imprisoned for a greater or lesser period of time, and to grant a full and unconditional pardon to the rest, was an extremely merciful act. Besides, there is no doubt but that O'Reilly was moved by considerations of policy. As Spain did not intend to keep up a large military force in Louisiana, it was necessary to produce such an impression on its inhabitants, as to prevent the repetition of what had occurred; and above all, it was expedient to set a salutary example before the other colonies, to deter them from similar enterprises, and to show, in the language used by the Duke of Alba, in the written opinion on the affairs of Louisiana which he presented to the king as a member of his cabinet: *that the king knew and was able to repress any attempt whatever, derogatory to the respect due to the royal authority.*

Some there are who accuse O'Reilly of treachery and duplicity, on account of the interpretation which they put on the marked civilities which he proffered to the leaders of the insurrection, when they were introduced to him, and on the exceedingly courteous language which he addressed to them. They believe that these men had a right to infer from O'Reilly's deportment, that their past deeds were forgotten, and that they would not be brought to trial; it is said that O'Reilly lulled them into security, in order to keep them within his reach, and to prevent them from seeking their safety in flight, until he should be ready to arrest, at the same time, all the chiefs of the late revolution whom he had singled out. These suppositions derive some strength, it is true, from the opinion expressed by Bouligny, himself a Spanish officer, who was present at the interview between the delegates of the colonists and O'Reilly, at the Balize, and who said: *that the general sent them back with good hopes that their past faults should be forgotten.* It is not astonishing, therefore, that Lafrénière, Marquis and Milhet should have shared with Bouligny such flattering impressions. The secret intentions of deceit attributed to O'Reilly may have been true, but still, in justice to him, it must be remarked that the extreme courtesy of his language and of his deportment is not sufficient, of itself, to warrant the conclusion that it was dictated by duplicity. It was, on the like occasions, the natural tone of the high bred gentlemen of the time, although it may sound to us as smacking of dissimulation, or affectation. Numerous other instances might be cited of the wrong interpretations to be given to the actions and language of the men of past ages, if, as I have already observed, we judge of them according to the criterion of our present usages and customs. I will, in illustration of my assertion, select one instance only, which is striking.

The Cardinal of Richelieu had been, for many years, presiding, as prime minister, over the destinies of France, and had defeated more than one conspiracy against his life and power, formed by the highest nobility, by the mother, and the brother of the king, who hated the state of insignificance to which that master mind had reduced them, and often by the king himself, who used to become their secret accomplice, when in one of his fits of disgust at the thraldom in which he was kept by his proud and domineering minister. Now that the cardinal was broken down by disease and fast approaching his grave, his enemies again lost patience, and gathered under the leadership of young Cinq-Mars, who had become the favorite of the weak king. Hardly had the conspiracy been set on foot, when the wily cardinal had become acquainted with all its workings. Determined to strike a last blow, which would be so crushing that it would, for the future, put an end to such enterprises, he appeared to be wrapped up in fancied security, waiting patiently, for two years, with the self-confidence of genius, until the fruit of his revenge be ripe, before he plucked it. Only on the eve of the breaking out of the conspiracy was it, that, although in a dying condition, he came out in his strength of mind, if not of body, and with one single thrust of his crippled foot, demolished instantaneously the structure which had been so laboriously erected

ANECDOTE OF CARDINAL RICHELIEU.

against him. He terrified the king out of his little wits, brought down almost to his knees the king's vile brother, Gaston D'Orleans, to ask pardon for his share in the conspiracy, and annihilated all those of his enemies whom he thought worthy of his notice. Cinq-Mars and De Thou were those he had particularly singled out for his vengeance. De Thou, being in prison at Tarascon, where the infirm cardinal had himself transported, was ordered to the presence of his mortal enemy, to be by him interrogated. The manner in which they met is remarkable. Let it be remembered that both were aware of the relative positions in which they stood to each other. The Cardinal had made up his mind to have De Thou's head cut off; De Thou knew it, and the Cardinal was conscious that his intentions were no secret for the prisoner. Therefore there could be no attempt, and there could be no wish, to deceive each other. Yet, see how they behave when face to face. The Cardinal, who was in bed and propped up by cushions, when De Thou was ushered into the room by the guards, greeted him with a gentle salute, and, inviting him to be seated by the bed on which he, the Cardinal, was reposing, said, with the utmost suavity of manner: "Sir, I beg you to excuse me for having given you the trouble of coming here." "My Lord," answered De Thou, "I consider the invitation as a favor and an honor." The rest of the interview was in the same style. Was it deceit, irony, affectation or dissimulation? Neither the one nor the other. It was the customary tone of exquisite politeness familiar to two men, who were equally mindful of their respective rank and character, and whose minds were so framed, that they never lost sight, for one moment, of the old adage: *that a gentleman is worth another.* Times have changed, and the highest in the land, were he brought before a Justice of the Peace, not for a matter of life and death, but on a charge of petty trespass, would probably be interrogated in a more commanding tone. But is it to be inferred that, on the occasion I have related, Cardinal Armand Du Plessis, Duke of Richelieu, and the real king of France, acted with hypocrisy towards De Thou?

The inventories made of the property of the twelve gentlemen, whom the decree of the Spanish tribunal had convicted of rebellion, afford interesting proofs of the Spartan simplicity which existed in the colony. Thus the furniture of the bedroom of Madam Villeré, who was the wife of one of the most distinguished citizens of Louisiana, and the grand-daughter of De Lachaise, who came to the colony, in 1723, as ordaining commissary, was described as consisting of a cypress bedstead, three feet wide by six in length, with a mattress of corn shucks and one of feathers on the top, a bolster of corn shucks, and a coarse cotton counterpane or quilt, manufactured probably by the lady herself, or by her servants; six chairs of cypress wood, with straw bottoms; some candlesticks with common wax, the candles made in the country, &c., &c. The rest of the house was not more splendidly furnished, and the house itself, as described in the inventory, must have looked very much like one of those modest and unpainted little wood structures which are, to this day, to be seen in many parts of the banks of the river Mississippi, and in the Attakapas and Opelousas parishes. They are the tenements of our small planters who own only a few slaves, and they retain the appellation of *Maisons d'Acadiens, or Acadian houses.* Villeré's plantation, situated at the German coast, was not large, and the whole of his slaves, of both sexes and of all ages, did not exceed thirty-two. His friends and brother conspirators, who were among the first gentlemen in the land, did not live with more ostentation. All the sequestrated property being sold, it was found that, after having distributed among the widows and other creditors what they were entitled to, and after paying the costs of the trial and inventories, the royal treasury had nothing or very little to receive. These costs, however, were moderate, for they amounted only to 782 livres, or about $157, for each of the persons convicted.

There were but humble dwellings in Louisiana in 1769, and he who would have judged of their tenants from their outward appearance would have thought that they were occupied by mere peasants, but had he passed their thresholds he would have been amazed at being welcomed with such manners as were habitual in the most polished court of Europe, and entertained by men and women wearing with the utmost ease and grace the elegant and rich costume of the reign of Louis XV. There, the powdered head, the silk and gold flowered coat, the lace and frills, the red heeled shoe, the steel-handled sword, the silver knee buckles, the high and courteous bearing of the gentleman, the hoop petticoat, the brocaded gown, the rich head-dress, the stately bow, the slightly rouged cheeks, the artificially graceful deportment, and the aristocratic features of the lady, formed a strange contrast with the roughness of surrounding objects. It struck one with as much astonishment as if diamonds had been found capriciously set by some unknown hand in one of the wild trees of the forest, or it reminded the imagination of those fairy tales in which a princess is found asleep in a solitude, where none but beasts of prey were expected to roam.

"One of the first acts of O'Reilly's administration," says Judge Martin, in his history of Louisiana, "was an order for a census of the inhabitants of New Orleans. It was executed with great accuracy. It appeared that the aggregate population amounted to three thousand one hundred and ninety persons, of every age, sex and color. The number of free persons was nineteen hundred and two; thirty-one of whom were black, and sixty-eight of mixed blood. There were twelve hundred and twenty-five slaves, and sixty domiciliated Indians. The number of houses was four hundred and sixty-eight. The greatest part of them were in the third and fourth streets from the water, and principally in the latter.

"No census was taken in the rest of the province, but, from a reference to the preceding and succeeding years, the following statement is believed to be correct:—

"New Orleans, as before,	3190
From the Balize to the town,	570
Bayou St. John and Gentilly,	307
Tchoupitoulas,	4192
St. Charles,	639
St. John the Baptist,	544
Lafourche,	267
Iberville,	376
Pointe Coupée,	783
Attakapas,	409
Avoyelles,	314
Natchitoches,	811
Rapides,	47
Ouachita,	110
Arkansas,	88
St. Louis (Illinois),	891
	13,538

About half of this population was white.

"The exports of the province, during the last year of its subjection to France," says the same author, "were as follows:

CONCLUDING REMARKS. 353

In Indigo,	$100,000
Deer skins,	80,000
Lumber,	50,000
Naval Stores,	12,000
Rice, peas and beans,	4,000
Tallow,	4,000
	$250,000
An interlope trade with the Spanish colonies took away goods worth	60,000
The colonial treasury gave bills on government in France for	360,000
So that the province afforded means of remittance for	$670,000

"Few merchant vessels came from France; but the Island of Hispaniola carried on a brisk trade with New Orleans, and some vessels came from Martinique. King's vessels brought whatever was necessary for the troops, and goods for the Indian trade."

"The indigo of Louisiana was greatly inferior to that of Hispaniola; the planters being quite unskilful and inattentive in the manufacture of it. That of sugar had been abandoned, but some planters near Near Orleans raised a few canes for the market."

Such was the embryo colony which France had created, and which she had possessed seventy years. Although ceded to Spain in 1762, it was not under the entire control of that power before the 18th August, 1769, when O'Reilly took formal possesion of the country. It had been much curtailed from its original territorial proportions, but still, from the Balize to its contested limits with the Mexican provinces, and to that almost unknown region which extended far beyond St. Louis, towards the sources of the Mississippi, it contained

23

space enough for an immense population; and a better administration than that of France, conducted on far different principles, might have obtained results more favorable than those which had crowned her efforts. It is not a high estimate to suppose that Louisiana, from 1699, the date of its colonization, to 1769, when it was finally delivered over to Spain, must have cost, directly and indirectly, from fifteen to twenty millions of dollars disbursed by Crozat, the India Company, and France, who never got any returns for this very large expenditure. Of all the great powers of Europe, France, with her spirit of enterprise, her brave and intelligent population, and her vast resources, had been the least successful in her attempts at establishing colonies; and, after an infinite waste of courage and perseverance, of hardy labor, of blood and of treasure, she had lost, at last, almost every inch of her once almost boundless possessions on the continent of America. Spain and England had divided the shreds of that gorgeous mantle which adorned her shoulders, but which she had allowed to drop as a heavy incumbrance.

The preceding pages have been written to very little purpose, if they have not made apparent to the reader, the causes which checked the prosperity of Louisiana, and rendered her a worthless possession in the hands of France. Those causes lie on the surface of the history itself which I have sketched, and it requires no depth of research, nor any recondite analysis to discover them and appreciate their nature. To one of them, however, I must, in concluding this work, make a passing allusion, because it is still in existence, and exercises a fatal influence over the destinies of Louisiana to this present day. It is, that those who came to her, never considered that they had found a *home* in her bosom. With the exception perhaps of the Acadians and of the Germans whom

Law had sent to the colony in 1722, those whom she received in her lap were not grateful for the hospitality, and deemed themselves to be miserable exiles. All the military officers and other persons employed by the government had but one object in view, that of availing themselves, to obtain promotion, of their services in that distant country, and of the reputation of perils which they were really exposed to, or were supposed to have encountered; and they also bethought themselves of nothing else than making money, by fair or foul means, according to their different dispositions, in order to return, with increased honors, or with ampler means of enjoyment, to their cherished native country, to the beautiful France, which they could not forget. With regard to that part of the population which was not composed of officials, a good many had been transported to Louisiana by force, and detested a country which they looked upon as a prison. Others, whose coming had been the result of their own volition, had been deceived by wild hopes, by unrealized promises, and by exaggerated representations of what they were to expect in the land to which their emigration had been solicited. They smarted under the anguish of disappointment, and if they labored at all, it was to acquire the means to go back, before closing their career, to their birth-place in Europe, and they had even impregnated their offspring with these notions. Unfortunately, Louisiana was a mere place of transient and temporary sojourn, nothing better than a hostelry, a caravansary, but *no home* for any one. How could it be loved, improved and beautified? There were none of those associations, not a link of that mystic chain connecting the present with the past and the future, which produce an attachment to locality. The waters of patriotism had not yet gushed from their spring, to fertilize the land. There were Frenchmen in Louisiana, but no Louisianians.

CONCLUDING REMARKS.

Now a change had come in her progressive destinies, and she found herself a portion of the Spanish monarchy. But neither under the flag of France, nor under that of Spain was it, that Louisiana could have had the faintest conception of her future prosperity, and of the development of those immense resources, which, to unfold themselves, required the touch of a mighty magician, whose incantations a quick ear might perhaps, even at that time, have heard from afar. It was not, when a poor colony, and when given away like a farm by a friend to another, royal though they were, it was not when miserably clad with the tattered livery of her colonial bondage, that she could foresee her glorious dismemberment into sovereignties, the least of which occupies so proud a position in the eye of the world. This miracle was to be the consequence of the apparition of a banner, which was not in existence at the time, which was to be the labarum of the advent of liberty, the harbinger of the regeneration of nations, and which was to form so important an era in the history of the rights of mankind.

APPENDIX.

APPENDIX.

Extract from the Despatch written on the 12th of October, 1750, by Livaudais, the Harbor Master and Chief Pilot.

MY LORD:

I have the honor to inform your excellency of the change which was produced at the mouth of the river (Mississippi), by the Equinox of last September. When the king's vessel, Rhinoceros, arrived in July, the bed of the Pass ran south south-east, and north north-west. This has been but too frequent for these twenty-five years, during which I have been employed here in piloting vessels in and out. I rarely took them out by the same way in which I took them in; and these changes generally happen in October, when this river has not much of a current. At that time, the tides ascend thirty-three miles. Now, it will be necessary for vessels wishing to come in, to cast anchor to the east north-east, and west south-west of the houses of the Balize Post.

Regulations of Police.

We, Pierre Rigaut, Marquis of Vaudreuil, Governor of the Province of Louisiana, and Honoré Michel de la Rouvillière, the King's Counselor, Commissary-General of the Marine Department, and Intendant in this Province, decree in the name of the King:

ART. 1.

From the day of the publication of these present regulations, all persons, whatever may be their social condition, and under any pretext whatever, even with permissions from our predecessors, which we annul, are prohibited from distributing any intoxicating beverage, whatever may be its nature, and from allowing it to be used for drinking at their respective houses, or even to be carried away in large or small measures; and any person, contravening this provision of our ordinance, shall be sentenced to be imprisoned for one month, to pay ten crowns in favor of the poor, and to have all the liquors found at his house confiscated on behalf of the king's treasury.

Art. 2.

There shall be established six taverns in the town of New Orleans, under commissions to be issued to that effect.

Art. 3.

The keepers of these six taverns are permitted to supply, with wine or spirits, no other persons than travellers, sick people, the inhabitants, and sea-faring men; and this they must do with the requisite moderation. We forbid them to furnish these articles to a soldier, under the severest penalties, and to Indians and Negroes, under the penalty of paying a fine of ten crowns, of being sentenced to the pillory, and of forfeiting, by confiscation, all the wines and liquors found in the house and shop of the offender; and should there be a repetition of said offence, said offender shall be sentenced to the galleys for life.

Art. 4.

We also forbid tavern-keepers, under the penalty of losing their privileges as such, to retail refreshments, on Sundays and other holidays, during divine worship.

Art. 5.

We also decree that said taverns shall be closed, under arbitrary penalties, at nine in the evening of every day, and, after that time, that no one be entertained in said taverns.

Art. 6.

Said tavern-keepers shall pay for their privilege, each, the sum of two hundred livres to the ecclesiastical treasury of this parish, which needs very much such relief, and also the additional sum of one hundred livres, for the maintenance of the poor of this town, who are in a great state of destitution.

Art. 7.

There shall also be granted the privilege of keeping two liquor shops (canteens), the one to the Major in command of New Orleans, and the other to the officer commanding the Swiss company. One of these shops shall be appropriated to the French soldiers, and the other to the Swiss

—so that the military shall drink at the places only designated for them; and the inhabitants, travellers, and seafaring-men, shall no more be received in these liquor shops, than the soldiers shall be received in the other taverns, which they must not even approach. The soldiers, however, must not be forced into going to drink at any one of these two liquor shops; but they must do so of their own free will; and the keepers of said shops, should they give anything to drink to the inhabitants, travellers, seafaring-men, Indians, and Negroes, shall undergo the same penalties inflicted on the other tavern-keepers, in the 3d article of this ordinance.

Art. 8.

Whereas we have been informed that certain individuals, instead of improving their lands by cultivation, have come to the town of New Orleans, or have removed to certain localities in the rural districts of this province, in order to establish therein some drunken hedge pot-houses, by which means, they do not only tempt the fidelity of the slaves, but also induce them to rob their masters by giving them intoxicating liquors in exchange for the produce of their pilferings, we request all the honest planters to watch the deportment of these individuals in the country, in order to make us acquainted with the disorders of which they are the authors, so that we may punish them with all the rigor prescribed by the ordinances.

Art. 9.

In order to check the disorders originating in the town of New Orleans, from the increased multiplicity of taverns which have been established therein without permission, we decree, that eight days from and after the date of the present publication, all the inhabitants of the German Parish, and of other parishes, who have abandoned their lands to come and settle here, shall return to their former places of residence, under the penalty of being treated as vagrants and perturbers of the public peace, and, therefore, driven away from the country as people of an infamous character.

Art. 10.

All free Negroes and Negresses, living either in the purlieus of this town or in its vicinity, who may become guilty of harboring slaves, in order to seduce them and excite them to plunder their masters, and lead a scandalous life, shall lose their freedom and become the slaves of the king. We beg his Majesty to make them part of his domain, by paying per head, for every one of them, five hundred livres, to be applied to the restoration of the church of this parish, which stands in extreme need of such repairs.

Art. 11.

Any Frenchman who shall be so infamous as to become guilty of the offence described in the preceding article, shall be whipped by the public executioner, and, without mercy, be sentenced to end his life on the king's galleys, &c.

* * * * * * * *

Art. 17.

Any individual who shall buy from a slave any object whatever, without a specific written permission from the master of said slave, shall be sentenced, for the first offence, to the pillory, and, for the next, shall be condemned to serve on the king's galleys for life.

* * * * * * * *

Art. 19.

It having always been the intention of his Majesty that every individual, on his plantation or elsewhere, should punish his Negroes with moderation, as a kind father would correct his children; and most of the inhabitants of this colony having misunderstood the king's wishes on this subject, and overlooking in their slaves such faults as are too important not to be repressed, we cannot recommend too much to the owners of slaves, to be more energetic in checking their disorders, and to chastise them without passion on all proper occasions. We give them notice that, if we discover any undue laxity in the exercise of the authority herein mentioned, we shall cause the slaves whom they treat with too much lenity, to be seized and punished with exemplary severity.

Art. 20.

We forbid all the inhabitants or citizens of this colony to permit on their plantations, or at their places of residence, or elsewhere, any assembly of Negroes or Negresses, either under the pretext of dancing, or for any other cause, that is to say, excepting the Negroes whom they may own themselves. We also forbid them to allow their slaves to go out of their plantations or premises for similar purposes, because his Majesty has prohibited all assemblies of the kind.

APPENDIX. 363

Art. 21.

We also forbid the town and country Negroes to assemble in the town of New Orleans, or in its vicinity, or elsewhere, under any pretext whatever, under the penalty, for said Negroes, of being imprisoned and whipped, and, besides, under the penalty, for the masters, of a fine of ten livres, for every Negro who may thus have assembled with said master's consent.

Art. 22.

Should any inhabitant or citizen of the province permit on his plantation or premises an assembly of negroes other than his own, under any pretext whatever, he shall, for the first offence, pay one hundred crowns to the treasury of the church, and shall, for the next offence of the kind, be sentenced to work for life on the King's galleys.

Art. 23.

Any negro which shall be met in the streets or public roads, carrying a cane, a rod, or a stick, shall be chastised by the first white man who shall meet him, with the very same instrument of which he, said negro, shall be the bearer; and should said negro be daring enough to defend himself or run away, it shall be the duty of the white man to denounce the fact, in order that the black man be punished according to the exigencies of the case.

Art. 24.

Any negro or other slave, proceeding either on foot or on horseback, in the streets of New Orleans, or on the public roads, during the day, and particularly during the night, shall be stopped by any white person meeting said negro or other slave, in order to inquire for his written pass; and should said slave endeavor to escape, we exhort the citizen, cognizant of the fact, to endeavor to know who that slave may be, and to denounce him, so as to have him punished according to his desert.

Art 25.

Whereas negroes break down all the horses of the colony by using them immoderately, and by stealing them, not only out of parks, but also out of their stables; and whereas this is infinitely injurious to the agricultural labors of the colony and to the interests of individuals, we permit said negroes to be shot at when they are thus met on horseback, and when they refuse to stop on their being hailed.

APPENDIX.

Art. 26.

Being informed that the negroes of the town are so licentious as to come out, at night, of the houses of their masters, which they leave abandoned and open, and thereby exposed to all sorts of casualties, in order to assemble with those of the country, who come prowling through the town, to commit every kind of malfeasances, and to be drinking at the taverns, to the amount of what they can obtain for what objects they have stolen from the public and from their masters; we exhort and even order all the citizens carefully to watch these nocturnal excesses, to which our police shall be actively alive; and if, through our combined efforts we can discover the authors of such iniquities, the severe justice which shall be administered to them, shall intimidate all others who may be disposed to produce such scandalous disorders. The inhabitants of the country may powerfully contribute to put an end to this state of things, by retaining their negroes on their respective plantations.

*　*　*　*　*　*　*　*

Art. 28.

Any negro or other slave, either in town or in the country, who shall fail in the respect and submission which he owes to white people—that is to say, who may be so insolent as to elbow them on the high roads and public ways, and who, finally, forgetting that he is a slave, shall offend them in any way whatsoever, shall be punished with fifty lashes, and shall be branded with the flower de Luce on his back (sur la fesse), in order to make known, in case of need, the nature of his crime.

Art. 29.

All the negroes and other slaves who go to church, shall attend the first mass said in the morning. In the country they shall be led to church by the overseer of each gang, who shall take them back immediately after divine worship is over; and should there be servants in the habit of following their masters to any other mass than the first one in the morning, said servants shall stop at the door of the church, and wait there for their masters, under the penalty of being chastised.

Art. 30.

We have just explained the respect and obligations due by the blacks to the whites, and particularly to their masters. But it is proper to inform the public that this does not apply indifferently to everybody. A private person, a soldier, or any other individual, has not the right to

APPENDIX. 365

ill-treat a negro who is guilty of no offence towards him. In certain cases, the person offended may arrest him, and ask that he may be dealt with according to the dictates of justice, because the negro is subject only to the police regulations of the country and to the tribunal of his own master. Consequently, and in compliance with the orders of his Majesty, we forbid that any one should take the liberty to ill-treat slaves; and for any violation of this prohibition, the person so offending shall undergo an arbitrary punishment, according to the circumstances of the case.

Decree of the Superior Council of the Province, referred to in Page 193 of Vol. II.

Louis, by the grace of God, King of France and of Navarre, to all who shall see these presents, greeting : We make it known that the Superior Council of the Province of Louisiana, having taken into consideration the humble representations made, this day, to that Court, by the planters, merchants, mechanics and others ; and whereas the relief of a people, to whom the Council is as a father, the support of the laws, of which it is the depository and interpreter, and the improvement of agriculture and commerce, of which it is the patron, are the motives of the representations of said planters, merchants and others ; said Council has proceeded to adjudicate, as follows, on these important matters :

What momentous objects are these for the Council ! Can it, after having duly weighed them, give attention to any other subject, except so far as it may contribute to favor these ? Let it, for a few moments, suspend its arduous labors, to attend to those subjects, which are now represented as most worthy of its attention and ministry : and thou, dear country, whose prosperity is the object of our most ardent wishes ; thou, that art to us what Sparta, Athens, and Rome were to their zealous citizens, suffer us to pay a legitimate debt by consecrating to thee this weak tribute of our love. It will be dictated by our hearts, whose inspirations an obedient hand is ready to record.

Seven millions of royal paper constituted all the currency of this colony and the fortune of its citizens ; the total withdrawing of this capital, the payment of which his Majesty suspended by an edict of October 1759, has reduced the province of Louisiana to the most deplorable situation. We shall not undertake to enter into a detail of the calamities, of the ruined fortunes, of the downfall of families, which were the fatal consequences of that catastrophe. The Council, every time it assembles to take cognizance of the affairs of the unhappy victims of that event, has before its eyes a more striking picture of our misfortunes than it is possible for us to paint. Recovered from the depression into which they had been plunged, the citizens of Louisiana had begun at last to breathe ; they had considered the conclusion of the war as the end of their misfortunes, and entertained hopes that the return of peace would be the moment destined for their relief. Agriculture (said the planter), that surest and most positive wealth for a nation, that prolific source from which flow all the blessings which we enjoy, will now be revived, and will repair, a hundred fold, during the peace, the losses which we underwent during the war; commerce, without which the fruits of the earth have neither worth nor value, will be vivified and protected, said the merchant. Sweet illusions and flattering projects, what is now become of you? The planter, the merchant, all ranks and classes in the colony, undergo, in the most profound peace, misfortunes and calamities which they never felt during a long and bloody war.

The first stroke by which the colony was afflicted, was the information it received of the cession made of it by his Majesty to Spain. Nobody, doubtless, will be surprised at the profound grief which this news excited in all hearts. The French love their monarch above all things, and a happy prejudice makes all men naturally incline to the government under which they are born. Let us cast a veil over this event; the pen drops from the hand of a Frenchman when he attempts to analyse it. What at present seriously occupies, and should engross the whole attention of the court, is the contemplation of those facts which are the forerunners of that slavery with which a new administration threatens the colonists of Louisiana. At one time we behold an exclusive company, which, to the prejudice of the nation, is empowered to carry on all the commerce of the remaining possessions of the French in North America ; we next see the appearance of an edict, which confines within the narrowest bounds the liberty necessary to commerce, and forbids the French to have any connexion with their own nation ; it is replete with prohibitions and restraints ; the merchants of Louisiana every where meet with obstacles to be surmounted, difficulties to be overcome, and (if it be allowable to make use of such an expression) enemies of their country to be overthrown. In Europe, a period of six months will sometimes elapse before persons that fit out vessels know whether they shall obtain passports; we have no better success at St. Domingo, when expeditions to this river (Mississippi) are in question. The Prince of Monbazon, Commander General of the island, begins to refuse them. In Louisiana, in the very centre of the colony, where a person of the meanest

APPENDIX. 367

understanding sees, at the very first glance, how much it stands in need of encouragement and patronage, we do not meet with more favor.

The government, about twelve months ago, forbade the importation of Negroes, on the pretext that the competition would have proved injurious to a merchant of the English colonies, who was to furnish them. How terrible and how destructive a course of action is this! It is depriving the colony of the materials best calculated to develop its resources; it is cutting up by the roots a branch of commerce, which is of more consequence to Louisiana than all the rest put together. To promote systems of this sort is tantamount to the desire to convert into a vast forest, establishments which have cost infinite pains and trouble. The vigilance of the court will easily discover the cause of these contrarieties; the efforts of its zeal will destroy it; and its affection for the colony will save it from destruction. Constraint keeps the affairs of the province in a state of languor and weakness; liberty, on the contrary, animates all things; no one is at present ignorant that the granting of exclusive privileges may be justly considered as a sort of vampire, which imperceptibly sucks and consumes the people, drains the currency, and crushes agriculture and commerce; it is an oppressive method, which, for the happiness of mankind, has been long since banished from the French colonies.

To what fatality is it owing that Louisiana alone sees sparks of this devouring fire again struck out? These are no panic terrors; and of this the court will be convinced, after perusing the decree, with an extract of which we have here the honor of presenting them. We shall not scruple to affirm, that the carrying of the plan which it contains into execution, would ruin the colony, by giving agriculture and commerce the most dangerous wounds. The inhabitants of Louisiana already despair of the preservation of their country, if the privileges and exemptions which it has hitherto enjoyed are not continued; if the execution of the fatal decree, which has alarmed all hearts and filled them with consternation, is not prevented; if an ordinance, published in the name of his Catholic Majesty, on the 6th of September 1766, of which a copy is here subjoined, is not annulled as illegal in all its points, and as contrary to the increase of agriculture and commerce; if finally, the mild laws, under which the inhabitants have lived till now, were suffered to be violated. We should never forget the sublime discourse, which an illustrious magistrate addresses to the legislators of the earth: "Are you," says he, "desirous of abrogating any law, touch it but with a trembling hand. Approach it with so much solemnity, use so many precautions, that the people may naturally conclude that the laws are sacred, since so many formalities are required in the abrogation of them."

How mortifying is it for Frenchmen, to suffer all the rigors to which their commerce is subjected, whilst a foreign nation, their ambitious rival, openly carries on the trade of the colony, to the prejudice of the nation to which it belongs, which contributed to its establishment, and which is at the expense of it! We do not fear that it will be objected, that the French alone are not able to supply the continent with all the commodities which it wants. A loan of seven millions, which the inhabitants of Louisiana made to the king, from the year 1758 to 1763, will be an eternal monument of the extent of the French commerce, and of the attachment of the colonists to their sovereign's service.

It is just at the time when a new mine has been discovered; when the culture of cotton, improved by experience, promises the planter the recompense of his toils, and furnishes persons engaged in fitting out vessels, with cargoes to load them; when the manufacture of Indigo may vie with that of St. Domingo; when the fur trade has been carried to the highest degree of perfection, which it has as yet attained; it is in these happy circumstances that certain enemies to their country, and broachers of a false system, have imposed upon persons in office, to induce them to sacrifice the inhabitants of New Orleans. Let the court no longer defer the relief of a people which is dear to it; let it make known to those invested with royal authority the exhausted state to which this province would be reduced, if it were not soon to be freed from the prohibitions, which would plunge it into irremediable ruin. What would be thought of a physician, who being possessed of a panacea, or universal remedy, should wait for a plague in order to reveal it? It is by the trade to the leeward islands that the inhabitants of Louisiana find means, every year, to dispose of four score or a hundred cargoes of lumber. Should this branch of trade be taken away, the colony would be deprived of an annual income of five hundred thousand livres at least—a sum, which the work of the negroes and the application of the master produces alone, without any other disbursement. According to the observation of a celebrated author, it would be better to lose a hundred thousand men in a great kingdom by an error in politics, than to be guilty of one which should stop the progress of agriculture and commerce. It is well known that those who present plans to obtain exclusive privileges, are never without plausible reasons to make them appear economic and advantageous, as well to the king as to the public; but the experience of all ages and all countries evidently demonstrates, that those who seek exclusions have their private interest solely in view; that they have less zeal than others for the prosperity of the state, and have less of the spirit of patriotism.

The execution of the decree relative to the commerce of Louisiana would reduce the inhabitants to the sad alternative of either losing their harvests for want of vessels to export them, or of exchanging their commodities in a fraudulent manner with a foreign nation, exposing themselves to undergo the rigor of the law, which ordains that those who carry on a contraband trade shall lose both their lives and liberties. What a life is this! what a struggle! It is but too true, as has been already observed, that the report of the new ordinance alone has caused a considerable diminution, not only in the articles of luxury, but likewise in landed estates. A house which was heretofore worth twenty thousand livres would hardly sell for five thousand. Some will, perhaps, assert that the scarcity of money contributes also to this diminution. But how much greater will be the scarcity of specie, when the colony shall either be delivered up to an exclusive company, or to the ambition of five or six individuals, who form but one body? It will then resemble a member grown to a monstrous bulk, at the expense of the substance of the rest, which would become withered and palsied. The body would thereby find itself threatened with a total destruction. It was only by openly favoring the introduction of negroes, that this colony was raised to the flourishing state which it appeared to have attained in 1759.

Perhaps it will be said, to dispel these alarms, that the gold and silver which has been made to abound in the place by a new administration, may indemnify for the losses of agriculture and commerce. But, judging of the future by the experience of the past and of the present, that resource will be found to be very weak, as nobody can pretend not to know that, among the various treasures which the earth contains in its bosom, gold and silver are neither the chief riches nor the most desirable. These metals have reduced their natural possessors to a deplorable state, and the masters of those slaves have not thereby become more powerful. They appear, from that moment, to have lost all spirit of industry, all disposition to work, like a laborer who should find a treasure in the midst of his field, and thereupon forsake his plough for ever. Besides, how many acts of severity have been committed against peaceable citizens by a stranger, who, though invested with a respectable character, has observed none of the formalities, nor performed any of the duties prescribed by the act of cession, which provides for their peace and tranquillity. We shall mention an old ship captain, who was confined by his orders, and whose vessel was detained in port during eight or ten months, for not having been able to read in the decrees of Providence, that the vessel in which he had despatched certain packets, intrusted to his care, would be cast away. A similar tyranny was exercised by the person invested with this illegal and unjust authority, against two captains belonging to Martinico, who had been guilty of no other crime, than that of not having guessed that the Council of Louisiana had issued an edict forbidding the introduction of the creolized negroes of the Leeward Islands. What ill usage has an old citizen suffered, on account of a packet which had been put into the hands of the captain of one of his ships, who, having met with contrary winds, was unable to deliver it at Havana!

How shall we describe the barbarity with which the Acadians were treated? These people, the sport of fortune, had determined, under the impulse of a patriotic spirit, to forsake all that they might possess on the English territories, in order to go and live under the happy laws of their ancient master. They arrived in this colony at a great expense, and scarce had they cleared out a place sufficient for a poor thatched hut to stand upon, when, in consequence of some representations which they happened to make to Mr. Ulloa, he threatened to drive them out of the colony, and have them sold as slaves, in order to pay for the rations which the king had given them; at the same time directing the Germans to refuse them a retreat. It remains to be determined whether this conduct does not border upon barbarism; but we think we can presume to conclude, without exaggeration, that it is diametrically contrary to the political system which favors the encouragement of population, in all its branches and by every means. Those who complain (and who is there so far broke to the yoke as to bear, without murmuring, inhumanities so horrid?)—yes—we dare declare it, those who complain are threatened with imprisonment, banished to the Balize, and sent to the mines. Now, though Mr. Ulloa may have been invested with some authority, his prince never commanded him to exert it in a tyrannical manner, nor to exercise it before having made known his titles and powers. Such oppressions are not dictated by the hearts of kings; they agree but ill with that humanity which constitutes their character, and directs their actions.

Were we to enter into a detail of all the mortifications which the French of New Orleans have undergone, we should hardly make an end of the recital. It were to be wished, for the honor of the nation, that as many of them as have transpired might be obliterated by the precious effects of the protection of the superior council, which is now applied for; and it is foretold that the inhabitants of Louisiana will, in order that their tribulations be complete, be reduced, in process of time, to live barely on *tortillas*, although the most frugal sort of food would not be a matter of complaint on their part. In the meantime, the preservation of their lives, their obligations to their creditors, their sense of honor, which flows from the sacred source of patriotism and of duty, finally, the circumstance of the attack made on their property and means of subsistence by

APPENDIX. 371

that very decree, induce them to offer their possessions and their blood, to preserve for ever the dear and inviolable title of French citizen. All that has hitherto been said leads them naturally to demands or requests, to which the zeal of the court for the public good, and its steadiness in supporting the laws of which his most Christian majesty has made them the depositories, assure them that it will give the most favorable reception. But before they proceed to state their requests, they must acknowledge the kindness with which they were treated by Mr. Aubry. The wishes of the public have always corresponded with the choice of the prince in assigning him the chief command over the province of Louisiana; his virtues have caused the titles of honest man and equitable governor to be adjudged him; he never made use of his power but to do good, and all unjust deeds have to him ever appeared impossible. They are not afraid of being reproached that gratitude has made them exaggerate in any particular. To neglect bestowing deserved praises is to keep back a lawful debt, and they conclude, finally, by intreating the court:

1. To obtain that the privileges and exemptions which the colony has enjoyed, since the cession made by the company to his most Christian majesty, should be maintained, without any innovations being suffered to interrupt their course, and disturb the security of the citizens.

2. That passports and permissions be granted from the governors and commissioners of his most Christian majesty, to such captains of vessels as shall set sail from this colony to any ports of France or America whatever.

3. That any ship sailing from any port of France or America whatever, shall have free entrance into the river, whether it sail directly for the colony, or only put in accidentally, according to the custom which has hitherto prevailed.

4. That freedom of trade with all the nations under the government of his most Christian majesty be granted to all the citizens, in conformity to the king's orders to the late Mr. D'Abbadie, registered in the archives of this city, and likewise in conformity to the letter of his Grace the Duke of Choiseul, addressed to the same Mr. D'Abbadie, and dated the 9th of February, 1766.

5. That Mr. Ulloa be declared to have, in many points, infringed and usurped the authority hitherto possessed by the government and council of the colony, because all the laws, ordinances, and customs direct, that said authority shall not be exercised by any officer until he shall have complied with all the formalities prescribed; and this condition Mr. Ulloa has not observed. He should, therefore, be declared to have infringed and usurped the authority of the government:—1. For having

APPENDIX.

caused the Spanish flag to be set up in several parts of the colony, without having previously caused to be registered in the archives of the superior council, the titles and powers which he may have had, and of which the assembled citizens might have been informed. 2. For having, of his own accord, and by his own private authority, insisted upon captains being detained with their ships in the port, without any cause, and for having ordered subjects of France to be confined on board of a Spanish frigate. 3. For having caused councils, in which decrees were issued concerning the inhabitants of Louisiana, to be held in the house of Mr. Destréhan. They request that, on account of these grievances, and many others publicly known, and likewise for the tranquillity of all the citizens who apply for the protection of the council, they be freed, for the future, from the fear of a tyrannical authority, and exempted from observing the conditions enjoined in the said decree, by means of the dismission of Mr. Ulloa, who should be ordered to embark on board of the first vessel which shall set sail, in order to depart, whenever he thinks proper, out of the dependencies of this province.

6. That orders be given to all the Spanish officers who are in this city, or scattered throughout the posts appertaining to the colony, to quit them, in order to depart likewise, whenever they shall think proper, out of the dependencies of the province ; and, finally, that the court be pleased to order that its decree, when rendered, be read, published, and set up in all the usual places of the town, and collated copies sent to all the posts of the said colony.

The foregoing representations being signed by five hundred and thirty-six persons—planters, merchants, tradesmen, and men of note ; considering, likewise, the copy of the decree, published by orders of his Catholic Majesty, neither signed nor dated, and another copy of an ordinance published in this city, by order of Mr. Ulloa, of the 6th of September, 1766 ; the interlocutory decree issued yesterday, upon the requisition of the king's attorney-general, ordering and directing that, before the decision of the court, the said representations be put in the hands of Messrs. Huchet de Kernion, and Piot de Launay, titular councilors, to be by them examined, and afterwards communicated to the king's council, in order that what the law directs may be enacted concerning them—all these particulars being taken into consideration, the king's attorney stood up and said :

"Gentlemen,

"The first and most interesting point to be examined is the step taken by all the planters and merchants in concert, who, being threatened with slavery, and laboring under grievances which have been enumerated, address your tribunal, and require justice for violations of the solemn act of cession of this colony.

"Is yours a competent tribunal? are these complaints just?

"I shall now proceed to demonstrate the extent of the royal authority vested in the superior council. The parliaments and superior councils are the depositories of the laws, under the protection of which the people live happy; they are created and organized to be, from the very nature of their official tenure, the sworn patrons of virtuous citizens, and they are established for the purpose of executing the ordinances, edicts, and declarations of kings, after they are registered. Such has been the will and pleasure of Louis, the well-beloved, our liege lord and king, in whose name all your decrees, to the present day, have been issued and carried into execution. The act of cession, the only title of which his Catholic Majesty's commissary can avail himself, to make his demands *auctoritate et proprietate*, was addressed to the late Mr. D'Abbadie, with orders to cause it to be registered in the superior council of the colony, to the end that the different classes of the said colony may be informed of its contents, and may be enabled to have recourse to it upon occasion; that instrument being calculated for no other purpose.

"Mr. Ulloa's letter, dated from Havana, July 10, 1765, which expresses his dispositions to do the inhabitants all the services they can desire, was addressed to you, gentlemen, with a request to make it known to the said inhabitants that, in thus acting, he would only discharge his duty and gratify his inclinations. The said letter was, by your decree, after full deliberation, published, set up and registered, as a pledge of happiness and tranquillity to the inhabitants. Another letter of the month of October last, written to Mr. Aubry, proves that justice still continues to be administered in the colony in the name of Louis the well-beloved. It results from the solemn act of cession and its accessories, that the planters, merchants and other inhabitants have the most solid basis to stand upon, when they present you with their most humble remonstrances; and that you, gentlemen, are fully authorized to pronounce thereupon. Let us now proceed to a scrupulous examination of the act of cession, and of the letter written by Ulloa to the Superior Council. I think it likewise incumbent on me to cite, word for word, an extract of the King's letter, which was published, set up and registered.

"This very solemn act of cession, which gives the title of property to his Catholic Majesty, secures for the inhabitants of the colony the preservation of ancient and known privileges; and the royal word of our Sovereign Lord, the King, promises, and gives us ground to hope for, others, which the calamities of war have prevented him from making his subjects enjoy. The ancient privileges having been suppressed by the authority of his Catholic Majesty's commissioner, property becomes precarious. The act of cession, which was the mere result of good will and friendship, was made with reserves which confirm the liberties and privileges of the inhabitants, and promises them a life of tranquillity, under the protection and shelter of their canon and civil laws. As property accruing from a cession by free gift, cannot be claimed and obtained, except on the condition of complying, during the whole possession of said property, with the reserves contained in said act of cession, our sovereign lord, the king, hopes, and promises himself that, *in consequence of the friendship and affection shown to him by his Catholic Majesty, he (said C. M.), will be pleased to give such orders to his governor, and to all other officers employed in his service in said colony, as may be conducive to the advantage and tranquillity of the inhabitants, and that they shall be ruled, and their fortunes and estates managed according to the laws, forms, and customs of said colony.* Can Mr. Ulloa's titles give authority to ordinances and orders which violate the respect due to the solemn act of cession? The ancient privileges, the tranquillity of the subjects of France, the laws, forms, and customs of the colony, are rendered sacred by a royal promise, by a registering ordered by the superior council, and by a publication solemnly decreed and universally known. The sole aim of the letter of our sovereign lord, the king, was to grant to the different classes of the colony a recourse to the act of cession. Therefore, nothing can be better grounded or more legal than the right of remonstrating, which the inhabitants and citizens of the colony have acquired by royal authority.

"Let us proceed to an examination of the letter of Mr. Ulloa, written to the superior council of New Orleans, dated the 10th of July, 1765. I shall here cite, word for word, the article relative to the superior council and the inhabitants:

"*I flatter myself, beforehand, that it will afford me favorable opportunities to render you all the services that you and the inhabitants of your town may desire—of which I beg you to give them the assurance from me, and to let them know that, in acting thus, I only discharge my duty and gratify my inclinations.*

"Mr. Ulloa proved thereby the orders which he had received from his Catholic majesty, conformably to the solemn act of cession, and manifested a sentiment which is indispensable in any governor who is desirous of rendering good services to his king in the colonies.

"Without population there can be no commerce; and without commerce, no population. In proportion to the extent of both is the solidity of thrones; both are fed by liberty and competition, which are the nursing mothers of the State, of which the spirit of monopoly is the

APPENDIX. 375

tyrant and step-mother. Without liberty there are but few virtues. Despotism breeds pusillanimity and deepens the abyss of vices. Man is considered as sinning before God, only because he retains his free will. Where is the liberty of our planters, of our merchants, and of all our other inhabitants? Protection and benevolence have given way to despotism : a single authority would absorb and annihilate everything. All ranks, without distinction, can no longer, without running the risk of being taxed with guilt, do anything else but tremble, bow their necks to the yoke, and lick the dust. The superior council, the bulwark of the tranquillity of virtuous citizens, has supported itself only by the combined force of the probity and disinterestedness of its members, and of the confidence of the people in that tribunal. Without taking possession of the colony, without registering, as was necessary, in the superior council, his titles and patents, according to the laws, forms, and customs of the colony, and without presentation of the act of cession, Mr. Ulloa has caused a president, three councillors, and a secretary, nominated for the purpose, to take cognizance of facts, which belonged to the jurisdiction of the superior council, and in which French citizens were concerned. Often did discontents and disgusts seem to force you to resign your places, but you have always considered it as a duty of your station of councillors to the most Christian king, to alleviate and calm the murmurs of the oppressed citizens. The love of your country, and the sense of the justice due to every citizen who applies for it, have nourished your zeal ; it has always been rendered with the same exactness, although you never thought proper to make representations on the infractions of the act of cession. You have always feared to give encouragement to a mass of discontented people, threatened with the most dreadful calamities; you have preferred public tranquillity. But now the whole body of the planters, merchants, and other inhabitants of Louisiana apply to you for justice.

" Let us now proceed to an accurate and scrupulous examination of the grievances, complaints, and imputations contained in the representations of the planters, merchants, and other inhabitants. What sad and dismal pictures do the said representations bring before your eyes ! The scourges of the last war, a suspension to this day of the payment of seven millions of the king's paper money, issued to supply the calls of the service, and received with confidence by the inhabitants of the colony, had obstructed the ease and facility of the circulation ; but the activity and industry of the planter, and of the French merchant, had almost got the better of all difficulties. The most remote corners of the possessions of the savages had been discovered, the fur trade had been carried to its highest perfection, and the new culture of cotton, joined to

APPENDIX.

that of indigo and tobacco, secured cargoes to those who were engaged in fitting out ships. The commissioner of his Catholic majesty had promised ten years of free trade, that period being sufficient for every subject of France, attached to his sovereign lord and king. But the tobacco of this colony being prohibited in Spain, where those of Havana are the only ones allowed, the timber (a considerable branch of the income of the inhabitants), being useless to Spain, which is furnished in this article by its possessions, and the indigo being inferior to that of Guatimala, which supplies more than is requisite to the manufactures of Spain, the returns of the commodities of the inhabitants of this colony to the Peninsula became a ruinous trade, and the said inhabitants were delivered up to the most dreadful misery. His Catholic Majesty's commissioner had publicly declared his conviction of the impossibility of this country's trading with Spain: all patronage, favor, encouragement, were formally promised to the inhabitants; the title of protector was decreed to Mr. Ulloa; the hope and activity necessary to the success of the planter were nourished by the faith and confidence reposed in these assurances of the Spanish governor.

"But by the effect of what undermining and imperceptible fatality have we seen a house worth twenty thousand livres sold for six thousand, and plantations, all on a sudden, lose one half or two thirds of their intrinsic value? Fortunes waste away, and specie is more scarce than ever; confidence is lost, and discouragement becomes general; the planter's cries of distress are heard on every side; the precious name of subject of France is in an eclipse, and the fatal decree concerning the commerce of Louisiana gives to the colony the last fatal stroke, which must lead to its total annihilation. The Spanish flag is set up at the Balize, at the Illinois, and other places; no title, no letters patent were presented to the superior council; time flies apace; the delays fixed for the liberty of emigration will soon expire, force will tyrannize, we shall be reduced to live in slavery and loaded with chains, or precipitately to forsake establishments handed down from the grandfather to the grandson. All the planters, merchants, and other inhabitants of Louisiana call upon you to restore to them their sovereign lord, the king, Louis the well-beloved; they tender to you their treasures and their blood, Frenchmen to live and Frenchmen to die."

Let us proceed to sum up the charges, grievances and imputations:

"Mr. Ulloa has caused councilors named by himself, to take cognizance of facts concerning French subjects, which appertained only to the jurisdiction of the Superior Council. The sentences of that new tribunal have been signified to, and put in execution against, Mess. Cadis and Leblanc. Mr. Ulloa has supported the negroes, dissatisfied with their masters. He has presented to the Superior Council none of his titles, powers and provisions, as Commissioner of his Catholic Majesty; he has not exhibited his copy of the act of cession, in order to have it registered; he has, without the said indispensable formalities, set up the Spanish flag at the Balize, at the Illinois, and other places; he has, without legal authority, vexed, punished, and oppressed subjects of France; he has even confined some of them in the frigate of his Catholic Majesty; has, by his authority alone, usurped the fourth part of the common of the inhabitants of the town, has appropriated it to himself, and has caused it to be fenced in, that his horses might graze there.

"Having maturely weighed all this, I require in behalf of the King,

"That the sentences pronounced by the councilors nominated for the purpose, and put in execution against Mess. Cadis and Leblanc, subjects of France, be declared encroachments upon the authority of our Sovereign Lord, the King, and destructive of the respect due to his supreme justice, seated in his Superior Council, in as much as they violate the laws, forms, and customs of the colony, confirmed and guaranteed by the solemn act of cession.

"That Mr. Ulloa be declared to have violated our laws, forms, and customs, and the orders of his Catholic Majesty, in relation to the act of cession, as it appears by his letter, dated from Havana, on the 10th of July, 1765.

"That he be declared usurper of illegal authority, by causing subjects of France to be punished and oppressed, without having previously complied with the laws, forms, and customs, in having his powers, titles, and provisions registered by the Superior Council, with the copy of the act of cession.

"That Mr. Ulloa, Commissioner of his Catholic Majesty, be enjoined to leave the colony in the frigate in which he came, without delay, to avoid accidents or new clamors, and to go and give an account of his conduct to his Catholic Majesty; and, with regard to the different posts established by the said Mr. Ulloa, that he be desired to leave in writing such orders as he shall think necessary; that he be declared responsible for all the events which he might have foreseen; and that Mess. Aubry and Foucault be requested, and even summoned, in the name of our Sovereign Lord, the King, to continue to govern and administer the colony as heretofore.

"That no ship sailing from this colony shall be dispatched without passports signed by Mr. Foucault, as intendant commissary of his most Christian Majesty.

"That the taking possession of the colony can neither be proposed nor attempted by any means, without new orders from his most Christian Majesty.

"That Mess. Loyola, Gayarre and Navarro be declared guaranties of their signature on the bonds which they have issued, if they do not produce the orders of his Catholic Majecty, empowering them to issue said bonds and papers; and that a sufficient time be granted them to settle their accounts.

"That the planters, merchants and other inhabitants be empowered to elect deputies to carry their petitions and supplications to our Sovereign Lord, the King.

"That it be resolved and determined that the Superior Council shall make representations to our Sovereign Lord, the King; that its decree, when ready to be issued, be read, set up, published and registered.

"That collated copies thereof be sent to his grace the Duke of Praslin, with a letter of the Superior Council, and likewise to all the posts of the colony, to be there read, set up, published and registered."

The report, being heard, of Mess. Huchet de Kernion and Riot de Launay, councilors and commissioners appointed for this purpose, the whole being duly weighed, and the subject deliberated upon, the Attorney-General having been heard and having retired:

The Council, composed of thirteen members, of which six were named *ad hoc*, having each of them given his opinion in writing, pronouncing upon the said representations, has declared and declares the sentences rendered by the councilors nominated by Mr. Ulloa, and carried into execution against Mess. Cadis and Leblanc, subjects of France, to be encroachments upon the authority of our Sovereign Lord, the King, and destructive of the respect due to his supreme justice, vested in his Superior Council; has declared and declares him an usurper of illegal authority, in causing subjects of France to be punished and oppressed, without having previously complied with the laws and forms, having neither produced his powers, titles and provisions, nor caused them to be registered, and that, to the prejudice of the privileges insured to them by the said act of cession : and to prevent any violence of the populace, and avoid any dangerous tumult, the Council, with its usual prudence, finds itself obliged to enjoin, as in fact it enjoins, Mr. Ulloa to quit the colony, allowing him only the space of three days, either in the frigate of his Catholic Majesty in which he came, or in whatever vessel he shall think proper, and go and give an account of his conduct to his Catholic Majesty. It has likewise ordained and it ordains that, with regard to the posts established by him at the upper part of the river, he shall leave such orders as he judges expedient, making him at the same time responsible for all the events which he might have foreseen. It has requested and requests, Mess. Aubry and Foucault, and even summoned them in the name of our Sovereign Lord, the King, to continue to command and govern the colony as they did heretofore. At the same time, it expressly forbids all those who fit out vessels, and all captains of ships, to despatch any vessel with any other passport than that of Mr. Foucault, who is to do the office of intendant commissary; it has also ordered and orders, that the taking possession for his Catholic Majesty can neither be proposed nor attempted by any means, without new orders from his most Christian Majesty; that, in consequence, Mr. Ulloa shall embark in the space of three days in whatever ship he shall think proper.

With regard to what relates to Mess. Loyola, Gayarre and Navarro, the Council has decreed that they may stay in the colony and discharge their respective functions, until they have received new orders from his Catholic Majesty, and shall remain sureties of their signatures for the bonds they have issued, except they produce the orders of his Catholic Majesty. It has likewise authorised and authorises the planters and merchants to choose whatever persons they think proper, to take up their petition to our Sovereign Lord, the King, and has decreed that the Superior Council shall in like manner make representations to our Sovereign Lord, the King; it orders that the present decree shall be printed, read, set up, published, and registered in all places and posts of this colony, and that a copy of it shall be sent to his grace the Duke of Praslin, Minister of the Marine Department.

We order all our bailiffs and sergeants to perform all the acts and ceremonies requisite for carrying the present decree into execution; we, at the same time, empower them to do so. We also enjoin the substitute of the King's Attorney-General to superintend its execution, and to apprize the court of it in due time.

Given at the Council Chamber, on the 29th of October, 1768.

By the Council,

GARIC,
Principal Secretary.

I protest against the decree of the Council, which dismisses Don Antonio de Ulloa from this colony; their most Christian and Catholic Majesties will be offended at the treatment inflicted on a person of his character, and notwithstanding the small force which I have at my disposal, I would, with all my might, oppose his departure, were I not apprehensive of endangering his life, as well as the lives of all the Spaniards in this country.

Deliberated at the Council Chamber, this 29th of October, 1768.

(Signed) AUBRY.

APPENDIX.

Collated with the original, left among the minutes of the Council, by me, the first secretary, whose name is hereunto affixed, at New Orleans, on the 2d of November, 1768.

GARIC,
Principal Secretary.

END OF VOL. II.

Printed in Dunstable, United Kingdom